NIGHT
AS
FRONTIER

NIGHT
AS
FRONTIER

Colonizing the World
After Dark

MURRAY MELBIN

THE FREE PRESS
A Division of Macmillan, Inc.
NEW YORK

Collier Macmillan Publishers
LONDON

The Free Press
A Division of Macmillan, Inc.
866 Third Avenue, New York, N. Y. 10022

Collier Macmillan Canada, Inc.

Printed in the United States of America

printing number

1 2 3 4 5 6 7 8 9 10

Library of Congress Cataloging-in-Publication Data

Melbin, Murray.
    Night as frontier.

    Bibliography: p.
    Includes index.
    1. Night people   2. Night—Social aspects.
3. Night work—Social aspects.   I. Title.
HM291.M3995   1987   305.9   86-26816
ISBN 0-02-920940-4

CONTENTS

ACKNOWLEDGMENTS

I am grateful for the intelligent and tough-minded challenges, new knowledge, suggestions, and kind encouragement from my friends and colleagues and from the scholars with whom I corresponded. They helped me with the book I sought to write and then improved it in ways I would not have imagined. I hope the essay expresses my appreciation of their comments. Mohammed Tayyabkhan, Sam Kaplan, Eviatar Zerubavel, Carmen Sirianni, Janice Harayda, Jerry Machalek, and Joyce Seltzer (my editor at The Free Press) gave me critiques of the entire manuscript. Phoebe Kazdin Schnitzer, Julia C. Spring, Joseph Helfgot, Frank Sweetser, Dzidra Jirgensons Knecht, Howard Robboy, Michael Young, and Charles Perrow commented on portions of the essay. Stanley Milgram, Gary Marx, Gerhard Dohrn van Rossum, Leon Sheleff, Richard L. Meier, and Zick Rubin contributed ideas. Scholars in other fields who helped me included Lillian Bulwa and Francine Stieglitz (French, Latin, and Spanish terms), Herbert Scarf (computerized problem-solving), Richard J. Wurtman, James M. Tanner, Gloria Callard, and George M. Vaughan (biology). Ann Getman, William O. Clarke, Shelley Leavitt, Lee Parmenter, Alan Rubenstein, Marilyn Arsem, Bonnie Creinin, Sally Laird, and Tom Lun-Nap Chung carried out the field studies or did library research. My colleagues Paul Hollander and Anthony Harris served as recipients in the key test.

Paul Flaim, Earl Mellor, and Edward Sekscenski at the Bureau of Labor Statistics provided data and counsel. Richard P. Wakefield and Elliot Liebow advised and encouraged me while administering grant MH-22763 from the Center for the Study of Metropolitan Problems (now Center for Work and Health) of the National Institute of Mental Health, which supported the research. Finally, I thank the American Association for the Advancement of Science, whose award of the Social Psychological prize in 1978 further stimulated and inspired me to carry this program through.

1

A Changing Timetable

Time is a container, and we are filling it in a new way. We are putting more wakefulness into each twenty-four hours.

Before we came on the scene, at the time our planet was born, the sun's rays washed against half its surface and left the other side in shadow. We call the shadow night. We sometimes ascribe to it an atmosphere of emptiness or danger or romance . . . night is tender, troubled, restless, sighing, hidden, thick, soft, naked, magnetic, empty-vaulted, the dark of the soul, deep, a lonesome forest, a deserted garden. But night's nature is the absence of light, signaled by sundown and reprieved by the dawn. Its other qualities follow from that. Night is physically the same as any other time, except that it is dark.

As the earth spins, the shadow moves around, and since a cycle of light and darkness was present when life began it gave its pulse as an inheritance to living things. One-celled creatures have twenty-four-hour cycles.[1] Complex animals and plants have internal daily rhythms that are paced by light. We inherited the tempo too. Our body's physiology is attuned to sunlight's comings and goings, and we have established separate phases of labor, leisure, and rest in our daily round.[2] Family life, work, mental alertness, sexual interest, and the conduct of business all fill a timetable synchronized with the turns of the globe. Most of our schedules still follow the regular appearance and departure of sunlight. Even locales that are nocturnally wakeful are surrounded by quiet precincts. Little traffic passes at night in the residential neighborhoods of the biggest cities. There is no one outside except someone walking a dog now and then. A church bell may interrupt the calm by pealing, but there are few answering noises from the houses around. Most of us still believe that practical matters wait until morning, and as night arrives so does a mood that a recess has come.

Long in the past, however, we began to use fire to illuminate the evening. We began staying up after dusk, chatting in the fading warmth of dying embers. Here and there we continued to work after sundown. We began dabbling cleverly to keep fires going, to make them enduring, brighter, more portable. From those early events until the present we have advanced in our power to summon light.

For tens of thousands of years our use of the dark hours increased slowly. During that era we dispersed more noticeably across the land. Tribes dealt with one another territorially. They rearranged habitats and political borders across the surface of the planet. They ranged ever farther from their original home. Our history is a tale of land use and migration, of invading and controlling regions, and of expressing distinctive cultures in the layouts of dwellings, cities, and nations. While that geographic surge went on, if people stayed up longer after dark it was for pleasure or to make a journey. Again and again revelers and travelers drew the attention of villains who would prey on them, and this in turn prompted the recruitment of sentries and police. In little increments the population was growing more wakeful and also more varied in its endeavors. In little increments, too, it was improving its lighting devices. Then, at the beginning of the nineteenth century, the invention of gas lighting enabled the pace to accelerate. People stepped up the scope and amount of their after-dark activity. Nighttime enterprise grew so remarkably thereafter that near the end of the century the writer-politician Ignatius Donnelly published a clairvoyant novel in which he wrote that "night and day are all one . . . and the business parts of the city swarm as much at midnight as at high noon."[3]

We are good at inventing ways to enlarge our realm. Repeatedly we find methods of spreading farther. If an element is forbidding we devise a means to master it. Reaching the continental shores, we developed shipbuilding and navigational skills in order to cross oceans. Shivering at arctic weather, we designed fur clothing and snug shelters in order to edge northward. And, having first occupied much of the usable space in the world, we are now filling its usable times. Although being wakeful at night flouted our natural rhythms, we developed artificial lighting that let us be active after dark. Both the sea and the night must have been feared by human beings. We are a terrestrial and a diurnal species. We have no personal equipment to breathe under water or to see in the dark. Both were strange realms. Both were mastered by our resourcefulness and endeavor. It is a stunning record of enterprising expansions.

An era is now under way in which we are replacing our cyclic community with activities that never stop. Though nighttime affairs are a modest portion of contemporary life, they are increasing more than most of us imagine. Society has broken from the boundaries of daytime. Organizations no longer sleep and instead pay attention to events that happen everywhere. News networks, embassies, field units of international corporations, brokerage houses, and military bases stay in touch with their headquarters night and day. Various staffs monitor the weather, crime, political developments, trends in commodity markets, troop movements, natural disasters, and other news. Large numbers of people are involved, and the action takes place in big cities and smaller towns.

There is widespread factory shift work, transportation, police coverage, and use of the telephone at all hours. Airports, gasoline stations, hotels, restaurants, and broadcasters operate incessantly. Data-processing departments of insurance companies and banks are astir all night. So are platoons of maintenance personnel. Emergency services such as oil burner repair, locksmiths, bail bondsmen, and drug, poison, suicide, and gambling hot lines are constantly available. Meanwhile isolated individuals bend over books and papers on desks in their homes, watch television after midnight, or walk in the streets and listen to the night breathe.

This extension across all hours of the day resembles our spreading across the face of the earth. Look at both trends from enough perspective in distance and time and they appear alike. Hover far above the planet and watch it as it spins throughout the eras. With the planet's surface in daylight, little human settlements can be seen to grow larger as the years go by and small extensions appear at their outskirts. Watch the surface when it is in night and at first some pinpoints of light flicker for a while and then go out. After ages pass those lights become stronger, they stay on longer, and other glimmerings appear nearby. Day and night, over thousands of years, reveal to us widening networks of human settlements and illumination being prolonged after dark. The surface is not uniformly occupied. The hours are not uniformly lit. But both are advancing in order. Observing from a distance and long enough, we can recognize a parallel between what we accomplished over the terrain and over the hours.

Both forms of expansion are frontiers. A closer look will discover more similarity between them and will confirm that both types of advance are urged by the same forces, carried out by the same types of people, and expressed in the same modes of social life.

A frontier is a new source of supply for resources that people want for subsistence or for more profit. It is also a safety valve for people who feel confined. They disperse in response to pressures at home and to appealing opportunities elsewhere. Always there is a combination of dissatisfaction with current circumstances pushing them and the hope of fulfillment pulling them. We resort to the strategy whenever we come up against scarcity in our environment, and those conditions in the past caused us to expand across the face of the earth.

Now, venturing into the night, we have the same motives as our predecessors who migrated geographically. The daytime is too crowded. Its carrying capacity is being strained, and still it does not yield all that the community wants. Production takes time, consumption takes time, and contemporary societies want more of both. The chance to exploit facilities that are left idle also arouses our initiative to use more of the night. Using the same space more of the time is a way to multiply its capacity. Some people dislike the commotion of the day and crave the serenity of night. Others look to it to better themselves economically. It is no accident that personal motives for relief and opportunity are similar to the causes of expansion for the community as a whole. Those are the age-old forces behind all migrations.

To interpret wholesale human wakefulness in this way rests on recognizing that night is essentially a span of time, and that we occupy time as we occupy space. Time is less tangible, but the two are inseparable. Together they form the physical container of existence.[4] As we fill one with an activity we also fill the other. Nothing can occupy space for no time.

We think about space and time in similar ways. We attend a lecture that occupies an hour.[5] Our work expands to fill the time available for its completion.[6] When we make an appointment to meet, it is not enough to agree on the place. We must also propose a certain time, or else we may miss each other and later will ask "When did you come?" "When did you leave?" We rent space-time containers for our cars on downtown streets when we put coins in the parking meters. The coins start clocks ticking, and the spaces are filled legally until the minutes on the meters run out. A lease for an apartment is a contract for space-time. Along with noting "206B, three-room flat," the lease refers to a calendar and gives dates when the monthly payments will be due. Space-time units are bought and sold now in the business of time-shared real estate. A condominium in a resort area will be purchased for certain weeks of the year. Each owner has deed and title to the place for that portion of the calendar, can buy insurance for it, can occupy the place for those weeks, or rent it, sell it, or hand it down to heirs.[7] Property values reflect both the location and the time of year, and prices are higher for the weeks that include Christmas and New Year's Day just as they are higher for prime land. The way we use parking meters, rent apartments, plan itineraries, buy resort condominiums, and schedule appointments shows that we fill time along with space.

If we have much to accomplish we are reminded that time has limited room. In using time and needing more of it we try to fill it more thoroughly, eliminate slack periods, stuff more into it, and speed up the pace. We try to squeeze in another appointment. Hours become dense to the point of crowding. Finally we can no more cram another activity in our day than cram another coat in the closet.

It would be easier to realize that time is a container if we were not acquainted with the clever but misleading idea that time is money. People talk of investing, consuming, making, losing, spending, and saving time. This budgeting outlook treats time as transportable wealth. It implies that one can distribute time itself, and give time to this and that.[8] Benjamin Franklin and others declared that time is money and that a person who is idle is losing it. One writer discussed it as being carried like loose change. "None of us would think of throwing away the nickels and quarters and dimes that accumulate in our pockets. But almost all of us do throw away the small change time—five minutes here, a quarter hour there— that accumulates in any ordinary day."[9]

We do not invest time in daily activities. Instead, time is part of the receptacle in which we invest activities. We cannot pass time from hand to hand like money, but we can transfer activities from time to time. The hours cannot be moved around; activities are often rescheduled. Instead of time budgets, we live by activity budgets. It is not a fiscal matter but an ecological one. Time is valuable but it is not a bank account. Our daily time is automatically replenished without effort, we only wish that would happen to our funds after paying the bills. We can overdraw a bank account, but we cannot overdraw time. We may borrow money, but we cannot borrow from another time period; that time will remain there. Nor can we deposit the hours in which we do "nothing" and save them for future need. The container idea is superior to the budgeting idea, because it portrays our dealings with time just as well while also allowing us to chart arrangements of activities. Many of us chart them in a way that confirms the affinity of time with space. We map affairs over the hours, drafting a plan, penciling in commitments, sometimes erasing and entering them elsewhere. The appointment book, not the checkbook, is the ledger of time.

Calendars and clocks have the markers and units with which we chart events in the temporal order of life.[10] There is a vast clockwork in nature, a regularity of durations, sequences, tempos, and cycles of events.[11] Our sense of a region's ecology is improved by recognizing the nighttime activity of raccoons, owls, and rats as well as by knowing the spatial dispersion of these animals. The same area of a forest or meadow or coral reef is used incessantly by creatures taking their busy turns.[12] We label them by the timing of their wakeful life and use the words diurnal and nocturnal to refer to the interval in which they are active, just as, across the land, we refer to an island people, people of the savannah, or urban folk.

In Molière's play, the would-be gentleman was impressed to discover that for years he had been speaking prose. He would have been struck also to learn how much he is a temporal being, how pervasively we all live within time. Growth and development, digestion of food, resting, parenting, teamwork, hours assigned to jobs, school holidays, cinema showing times, legal ages for permission to drive and to marry, terms of elected political office, and organized prayer are distributed according to time of day, of week, of year, of the life cycle, and of history. We make daily commitments and carry them out according to an agenda that includes rush hour, lunchtime, and bedtime. Coordination and punctuality are watchwords of the day. We follow schedules for railroads, airlines, and stores, and for household routines in preparing meals and doing chores. The schedules of those events are part of the structure of our niche.

Filling the dark hours with more activity means that some people's daily timetable will be revised. If two people are awake, even if they are at opposite ends of a continent, they can talk to each other. If they are awake at different times, they cannot chat together even if they live in the same building. People who are active at night are more remote from us, as out of touch as if they were on a distant outpost.

As we colonize the night it yields much of what we seek from it. It gives us respite. It puts many services at hand. Consider the public aspect of incessant activity that makes food and fuel and other goods and personal counseling available at any hour. We note the locations of all-night restaurants and gasoline stations and grocery stores. They settle in our consciousness as broad security against unforeseen wants. In larger cities the public interest is wide enough to prompt newspapers to publish guides of where to go and what to do after midnight. To some extent different people avail themselves of those opportunities night after night, but folk from all over town trek to the always-open oases. When twenty-four-hour retailing moves into the neighborhood, it launches a little period of adventurous curiosity. We go shopping to test whether we can actually buy milk or flashlight batteries at one o'clock in the morning. After midnight it seems unusual to be waiting in line for the cashier at a small neighborhood food store. Otherwise we shop in vast, nearly deserted supermarkets whose piped-in music has been turned off, and maneuver around pallets stacked high with cartons of goods that are waiting in the aisles to be transferred to the shelves. By giving access to helping agents such as hot lines, medical care, police, and equipment repair, the incessant community also offers peace of mind against possibilities of urgent need. From greengrocers in New York to kebab houses in London to telephone hot lines in Moscow, the never ending availability of goods and services is an unprecedented convenience of the twentieth century. Just as a we-deliver-anywhere company performs a role in space, the always-open service offers continual access as an appropriate role in time.

Yet there never was an ecological balance sheet showing benefits without costs. Establishing a frontier is not a matter of entering an empty realm; it fills an area differently. The region may seem to be almost empty, but pioneers displace other forms of life when they colonize it. The western land frontier of America was already occupied by native tribes, buffaloes, and wild grasses when the Europeans moved in. Now with people and their pursuits overflowing from daytime into dark, the sleep that fills nighttime will be compressed or displaced as the interval is invaded.

Activities in time are objects in a fixed container. As we fill it densely, we cannot stretch time. We cannot do with it as we did with space by digging into the ground or building up into the sky. There is no alternative but to have one revision in a schedule jostle another activity, and the latter in turn may do the same where it has been displaced.

Establish a new environment, especially as momentous as dispelling darkness, and biological and social forms that were adapted to the former milieu no longer fit as well. It affects the body's rhythms, the organization's schedule, the clockwork of family life, and the public timetable. All procedures that are guided by the sun become candidates for change. People who switch between day and night undergo upsets in physiological functions that naturally conform to the cues of light and dark. Someone who makes a habit of staying up late moves out of phase from other people, and out of touch. Friends may drift apart. Since an organization has a hierarchy of authority, who is in charge while top managers sleep? Power is transferred downward, and deputies must make decisions that in the daytime would be made by their superiors. Shift workers usher incessance into their households. Someone is moving around the house in unusual hours, and upon waking from sleep the night worker chews on a roast in order to join the family for its evening meal. Outside, people are bustling about when others want quiet, so interest groups form to argue over whose rights will prevail.

We cannot loosen ourselves from an ancient rhythm without shaking arrangements that were suited to it. Even sleep, the great citadel of our natural rhythms, shows signs of being undermined. A change in the temporal order jolts the social system. It harks back to a well-known comment that the integration of scheduled activities is so vital that if the clocks in a city were to go wrong for one hour the town would tumble into chaos.[13] Like a work of kinetic art, the timing of everyday life has a certain form and character because each piece supports the other in a particular way, and none will stay in place or deliver its regular force if some of them are nudged.

While advancing into the night our destiny is to be carried along by the momentum we stir up and to accommodate to conditions we introduce. Pioneers who dispersed geographically imposed themselves on their milieu and also were affected by their new environments. Now we do more than merely expand in time. We redesign our community to be ever wakeful and, in the course of that, as the proprietors and inhabitants of it, we are also changing.

2

The Colonization
of Night

When and how did we manage to become active at night? It began long ago and was achieved by gaining control of light. When our bold ancestors gingerly nurtured some burning material, it marked the first step toward human-controlled illumination. They could be active in the dark. Staying awake longer and improving methods of lighting went hand in hand. Sometimes a new development in the mechanics of lighting shed its radiance before they sought to use more of the dark. At other times being up at night made them aware that they wanted more light. First they relied on fire and the glow of embers, then they tried burning tallow and oil to make lamps brighter and more dependable. Every surge in the effort to extend the active day prodded them to improve incandescent devices. And with every step in mastering illumination they deducted from the time alloted for sleep.

Yet lighting inventions, indispensable as they were, were not the causes of more wakefulness. Light is an enabler. Enablers are useful rather than forceful. The oceans, for example, were not crossed until shipbuilding, navigation, and food preservation had been mastered, but those arts, while they made it possible, were not the driving powers behind sailing the seas. The specialized covered wagons called prairie schooners—with curved bottoms that prevented baggage from shifting around—gave pioneers an effective way to haul their possessions across uneven terrain, but they did not set off the mass migration beyond the Mississippi Valley. In the same way, since prehistoric times there is a two-sided account of nighttime behavior. One is the continual give and take between activity and illuminating devices, and the other tells the reasons why people stayed up later.

A half-million years ago people used fire domestically and left remains of wood ash, singed animal bones, and charcoal as archeological evidence.[1] By 7000 B.C. they had developed reliable firemaking techniques. Fires produced light as well as heat, and people gathered around them for sociable assemblies that lasted hours after darkness fell.

Ever since then there has been some activity over the twenty-four-hour cycle. Soldiers tended fires in military encampments, sentinels stood guard at city gates, seamen took their turns at watches on ships. Innkeepers served travelers at all hours. In Asia Minor by late March it became so hot during the day that pilgrims waited till night to trudge the miles to the annual Easter festivals.[2] People used fire in cultural practices as well. There were prayer vigils in temples, curing rites that began at sundown and ended at sunrise, and midnight betrothal ceremonies.

The ever burning flame acquired religious significance. The legend of a lamp that burned for eight days in the Second Temple of Jerusalem is celebrated in Chanukah, the Jewish Feast of Lights, and conveys the meaning of inextinguishable faith. Divali, the festival of lights in India, and similar celebrations by Thais and Tibetans, show involvement with light as a special force and symbol. So do the candles in Christian devotions. According to John's gospel, Jesus said "I am the light of the world: he that followeth me shall not walk in darkness, but shall have the light of life." Centuries later the devout Augustine equated light with God.[3]

By the Middle Ages some religious services called for relays of choirs to recite psalms around the clock.[4] The extended schedules symbolized holy commitment that did not weary in the night. The Benedictines, emphasizing orderliness in monastic life, established precise schedules for sleep, work, and devotions, and likened punctuality to piety. They sounded bells to mark the hours of the day and to summon the brethren to their obligations. By the fifteenth century public clocks in Italian cities were striking all twenty-four hours.[5]

Productive labor also began invading the period traditionally reserved for rest. The records of European guilds in the thirteenth century include references to work after dark.[6] Water wheels were driving the bellows in iron foundries and sustaining higher heat so that iron in the ore was liquefied. Before that iron production had been a batch process. The furnace had to be shut down daily and taken apart so that the partially smelted, porous mass of iron and slag could be removed. Then artisans transformed smelting into at least a semicontinuous process. They fed and coaxed the furnaces day and night. They were not only working later but beginning to revise the way they worked.[7]

Those religious and manufacturing practices are hints that artificial light is not the cause of expansion after dark. People had various reasons for staying up later. Controlled light made it feasible; it gave them access to the nighttime.

Since the end of the Middle Ages every century was marked by distinct growth in wakeful practices and improvements in lighting. Medieval and Renaissance cities had no regular public illumination. Assaults by ruffians and thieves were common after dark, and often a curfew was imposed at night. In sixteenth-century Nuremberg people had to be off the streets by two hours past sundown. Wealth and social class were accorded special privileges. Rich folk could stay in their clubs past that hour, though they too had to be off the streets before midnight. Wayfarers took to paying others to precede them through the streets carrying lighted torches. In the seventeenth century such an escort-for-hire was called a link boy in London and a falot (lantern companion) in Paris.[8] Parisian police in the eighteenth century sought to deter crime by hanging lamps along the city streets. A considerable part of the police budget was used for buying tallow, and hundreds of lamplighters were employed to set the lanterns burning once the sun went down.[9] Londoners introduced a series of Lighting Acts for similar reasons. "Its due execution," say the district records, "would greatly contribute to the preventing of murders, burglaries, street robberies, fires, misdemeanors and debauchery."[10] The evening social life of urban areas came to depend on public lighting. Dwellers in the other great cities of Europe also began to hang lanterns outside buildings after dark.

Everywhere the lanterns were faulty. They lacked steadiness and burned out unexpectedly. They had to be checked and maintained often and were impractical for lighting large areas. Scientists sought to intensify the meager rays sent out by the lamps. They introduced better wicks, finer fuels, and more radiant incandescent materials. Then two inventors capped the efforts to produce artificial illumination. William Murdock and Thomas Edison each developed a reliable method of delivering energy to the lighting device, Murdock for gaslight and Edison, later, for the electric lamp. Their solutions had immediate, widespread effects. Murdock was a clever and likable engineer employed by Matthew Boulton and James Watt, the manufacturers of steam engines. He experimented in his own household by burning coal gas that he sent through pipes from a central source to fan-tailed burners. The inflammable property of the air distilled from coal was already known, but Murdock was the first to use the knowledge in a practical way.[11] He improved the methods for making, purifying, and storing coal gas, and in 1803 Boulton and Watt allowed him to illuminate the interior of their main foundry in Birmingham, England. He sent coal gas from a central pumping station through pipes to burner jets mounted in several locations. When other mill operators nearby saw how feasible it was, they quickly adopted the method.

At first not everyone understood the use of gas for lighting purposes. People can meet the future face to face and still not see it. When Murdock testified before Parliament about his scheme, one member asked, "Do you mean to tell us that it will be possible to have a light without a wick?" "Yes, I do indeed," said Murdock, "Ah, my friend," the legislator retorted, "you are trying to prove too much."[12] The innovation dodged around such skeptical authorities, however, and others soon used the method to distribute gas to all buildings and street lamps in an area. Pall Mall in London became one of the first avenues to be illuminated in this fashion.

While gas lamps were being installed widely, other inventors were experimenting with electric lighting. In 1860 in England Joseph Swan demonstrated a primitive electric light, but it would not last long. It lit only feebly, because he could not achieve a good vacuum in his glass tube nor provide an adequate source of electricity. Thomas Edison perfected the design and produced a successful lamp in 1879. Edison went on to develop a practical generator that supplied electric power steadily to keep the filament glowing. Now it was possible to distribute electricity from a central source and place the lamps wherever they were wanted. In tandem Murdock and Edison had solved the puzzle of consistent delivery of the energy needed for illumination.

Present-day lighting is the descendant of our ancient success in using fire. The light switch is the latest model of an apparatus that also took the forms of the rubbed stick and the struck flintstone. The introduction of gas lighting stands out in this chronicle because its method of distribution gave us the first convenient and reliable means to banish darkness wherever and whenever we chose.

The use of the dark hours escalated. Twenty-four-hour activity had been a fraction of all human endeavor until the nineteenth century, but then it started to spread vigorously. Whole factories and cities could be lit at night. Artificial illumination permitted multiple-shift mill operations on a broad scale. Gas lighting was developed in the context of the Industrial Revolution, and the invention itself cast a spell over the Revolution's engineering and laboring forms. Even if prolonged processes were known beforehand, their use had been restricted by daylight ending. Now the continual mode of production became possible. Industrial methods for reworking metal ingots or making clay products could be carried on. Earlier they had been interrupted by darkness. Gas lighting made people believe the day was longer. All daytime activities could be extended. If day was the time for work, then work could be extended. So manufacturing mills began to call for two shifts—each twelve hours long—in order to run continuously. Artificial lighting also assisted the nighttime entertainment industry. Just as the gas lamp served the gin mills of London in Charles Dickens's time, the electric light helped public night life bloom on Broadway in New York in the 1890s.[13]

Night's riches is time itself. This form of natural wealth lured entrepreneurs to exploit the region for the profit opportunities it offered, and much of the dark's organized activity was evoked because of access to more time. It is not a material, but it is a natural resource nevertheless, with attributes like that of space. In its basic form it has a uniform quality, for every hour is like every other. It is valuable, finite, and often scarce, and yet time's supply is reliable, for it comes steadily night after night. It is easy to employ, neither hard to reach nor requiring further preparation before putting it to use. In use it is also versatile, for filling it multiplies the capacity of people and equipment, lowers costs, and accelerates accomplishments. It is like an additive to the engine of production. As entrepreneurs were earlier drawn to newly accessible wealth in the land, they were now attracted to the promise of fortunes in the night.

A land frontier is turned to for what can be extracted from it, nighttime for what can be produced in it. The underlying motive is the same, an incentive to exploit the region for economic gain. The great surge into the night began in manufacturing plants. Recognizing the idle capacity in their factories, entrepreneurs inaugurated the industrial expansion once gas lighting was developed and recruited large numbers of people to be active then. By running available equipment in those hours, the total volume of materials handled was multiplied, as were the goods produced. They already wanted to use the invested capital, but it remained dormant after midnight until the shop floor could be lit. In the present day, nonmanufacturing equipment may be underused too, and when an airline found its passenger craft being flown at night to carry freight in their bellies, it offered a night coach service with low passenger fares to fill the seats in the cabins.[14]

Among the ways of achieving profits by using the night, one of the most popular is by reducing costs. The more expensive the machines and equipment, the stronger the stimulus to operate them more in order to amortize their expense. An investment might be so steep that it will be profitable only if the equipment is kept in use all the time. The longwall mechanical miner, an especially effective coal mining machine, costs so much that the companies purchasing it say the machinery must be run around the clock.[15] The same outlook guided the use of large computers when they were first introduced. Executives felt they could not afford to leave several million dollars' worth of equipment idle at night.[16] Incessant operation is commonplace in rapidly changing technical fields, where managers use costly equipment continually in order to make the investment worthwhile before the machine becomes obsolete.

In processing raw materials, shutdowns are often costly interruptions. The safe cooling of industrial furnaces takes days to accomplish, then several more days are required to reheat them to their proper temperature again without cracking the walls. That is one of the reasons aluminum smelters are kept going for years. Glassworks kilns are operated day and night for long periods and are closed for repairs and maintenance only biennially. Engineers want continuous processing of chemicals, because otherwise the output may be left in an unacceptable form (unstable, dangerous, or soon unusable) if the required sequence of steps cannot be completed. A different form of this cost of interruptions led shipping companies to put pressure on the captains of their ocean-going vessels to keep them moving. Turnaround time in the harbor is an expense. So tankers and other cargo ships, which operate incessantly in the course of their voyages, are also kept active when they are in port. The crew does not get off duty, and unloading and loading go on continually.[17]

With the same goal in mind, managements withdraw shift work commitments if they discover it would cost a good deal to run the enterprise during off-hours and that it would be more profitable for the firm to be idle some of the time. When the costs of projects after dark are calculated, they often disclose a point at which expenses offset the profits.[18] That is why, although the hours of using factories per day have increased, plant use remains below the designed-for maximums.[19] Such cutoff points are not limited to manufacturing. The contract between Local One of the Stagehands' Union and the League of New York Theaters and Producers calls for extra payments if a performance runs later than 10:30 P.M. Accordingly, the shows are often scheduled to end by that hour. For many decades space and labor were abundant, and being so they were cheap. Even after World War II bonuses paid for shift work in manufacturing in the United States remained small relative to regular wages and did not keep pace with the rise in wages in general. That weighed favorably in a firm's decision to operate two or three shifts. The labor cost was low enough to make the net returns worthwhile. More recently labor costs and the pay premiums given to employees for night work have risen.

Another utility of the time resource is that it accelerates accomplishment. Speed is stressed to avoid losses of profit or costs that rise with delay. To accomplish something sooner, to beat the competition, to be first, to gain or maintain an advantage are all forms of the speed motive that induces nighttime efforts. It is expressed in transferring drafts and bank checks at night in order to clear them quickly and gain the credit rather than pay borrowing fees. It spawned a little industry of overnight package delivery companies. Customers readily pay for express mail, fast filling of orders, photo finishing, printing, laboratory test reports, prompt repairs, quick turnaround times, and swifter service in general.

We live in an era that insists upon rapid response no matter what the hour. A sudden military move or missile attack makes immediate defensive action critical. A turnabout in the stock market can ravage an investment position quickly. There may be very little time to cope on the brink of calamity, and swift reactions are mandatory for survival. A wide variety of organizations, government agencies, and news and business headquarters maintain staffs around the clock at monitoring posts to be able to respond sooner to urgent matters. If an oil drilling rig in Indonesia bursts into flames, firefighting teams in Dallas will mobilize in the middle of the night. Direct links exist between aircraft controllers in Japan, the Soviet Union, and the United States in order to inform one another quickly about the presence of an aircraft moving along an unusual or questionable route. A vital issue does not wait while people sleep on it.

In emphasizing speed, modern society created its own condition of limiting capacity: the deadline. The demand or promise to deliver at a certain time intensifies striving before the moment of reckoning. More and more, meeting that deadline means staying awake. People who do not achieve what they seek by the end of a regular work day take project papers home for a session at night. College students "burn the midnight oil" when obliged to hand in a written assignment or take an exam the next day. The United States Congress holds flurries of all-night sessions when grappling with decisions on issues that cannot wait, or when a recess is approaching. Staffers of a government agency, such as the Bureau of the Budget, keep lights burning till dawn while preparing a proposal due on a certain date before a fiscal year. An architectural firm's employees stay in the office drafting plans or a grant application to meet a promised delivery date. Management representatives and union officials actually stop the clock on the wall in the bargaining room during difficult negotiations and continue efforts to reach an agreement before a scheduled strike begins. So do state legislatures working on proposals and budgets within fixed calendar limits.

Businesses that cannot meet their customers' calls for goods or services by running at top capacity during the daylight hours introduce second and third shifts. In Hong Kong an around-the-clock custom-made clothing industry is based on the three-day visits of charter tours. The visitors will depart on the third day, and so they are fitted upon their arrival at the hotels, sometimes even before they go to their rooms. Then sewing goes on through the night in order to complete the garments on time. There is no allowable delay, for failure to deliver before the tourists leave means the sale is lost. Whatever is done during the dark hours brings a project further along by morning. Whenever the daytime schedule is filled and more production is wanted, the prospects for continuing after dark begin to mount.

Frontiers are also created for what they can absorb. This cause is a push, a form of overload or density pressure. An existing settlement can become so crowded and congested that its capacity is burdened to the point where some elements—whether people or activities or physical facilities—are squeezed out. For a while, as the locale's capacity is nearly filled, people try to live more densely. They redouble efforts to exploit existing arrangements. But here success itself diminishes the remaining capacity and increases the strain. Many kinds of shortages are experienced as crowding. It may be felt directly as population pressures or through scarcity and overloaded facilities drawn on by the population. Then persons and their projects begin to disperse.

Traffic congestion at first modestly pushes some of the flow into adjacent hours. In order to ease rush hour jams, London, Moscow, Strasbourg, São Paolo, and other cities tried to stagger the opening and closing times of business firms.[20] The push may continue until it fills all day. Rome was obliged to relieve its daytime crowding in the first century A.D. by restricting chariot traffic to the nighttime.[21] On the principle that less urgent services should not add to the city's congestion, Cairo recently banned its garbage collectors from daytime use of the streets and sent them on their rounds in the night.[22] Major metropolitan airports have become so busy that their runways are clogged in the daytime. Since they do not have the room to be enlarged, their growing use elbows some operations into the dark. Cargo work is usually rescheduled first.

The problem of burdened capacity takes different guises, and time is often substituted for space to ease matters. To be sure, people may first think of building additional facilities or installing more equipment to cope with the load. Besides the difficulty of inserting new units into a crowded area, construction is costly and may be impossible to complete soon enough. At a textile firm, newly installed looms worked so well that they outran the supply of yarn. Since there was no space to put additional yarn-producing equipment, one of the company's mills began to run its carding and spinning machinery day and night in order to maintain the needed supply.[23] The decision to expand in space or spread over the hours is often so nearly equivalent that the choice is made according to cost or how fast overload can be relieved.

Demand for a product may grow so suddenly that the only way to reduce the backlog fast enough is by working more hours. And some backlogs are steady rather than sudden. News and other communications often arrive faster than they can be digested in busy organizations, yet to be up to date current information must be assimilated. Data-processing departments in banks, insurance companies, brokerage offices, and mail-order stores keep going around the clock to cope with the massive inflows as bills are recorded, orders typed, inventories updated, payments made, and accounts tallied.

Other facilities become cramped, not only profit-making ones. When a tornado wrecked a high school in North Carolina, a full second shift was introduced in the evening at another high school to serve the displaced students, who could not be fitted into the regular classes. As the number of legal cases crowd courtroom dockets, municipalities decide to hold night sessions.[24] New York City's night court, for example, begins in the evening and continues until the docket is cleared, which may be after midnight. Though the night court sessions were introduced to ease the load on the calendars of cases awaiting action, they have two more functions. They save the city the expense of housing arrested individuals in jail overnight, and they serve the constitutional privilege of *habeas corpus*. By providing a speedy hearing for citizens involved in misdemeanors and minor felonies, night court fulfills the civil ideal of reducing the length of unlawful detention.

The physical plants of electric power companies, telephone services, airports, and mass transit systems are large and expensive. They were usually built to accommodate peak levels of use, only to be followed by growth in demand that began to exceed their capacity. Electricity use is so high during peak periods—as early on a summer evening when people come home from work and turn on

air conditioners and ovens—that even large power utilities become
burdened and brownouts occur. Usage fluctuates widely over the
day. Existing plants are brought to full operation for relatively brief
intervals and are nearly idle during the balance of the twenty-four-
hour cycle. In the past managers responded by building an additional plant as the call for the utility continued to rise. Energy was
cheap, capital plentiful, and interest rates low. Now, to postpone
paying for more expensive equipment and still ease the strain, the
utilities have begun to redistribute their daily load through differ-
ential pricing. The time-of-use rates are highest during peak demand periods, somewhat lower in the "shoulder hours," and far
lower during the night.[25]

The introduction of time-of-day pricing affected the Kohler
company, Wisconsin Power and Light's biggest user. A maker of
sinks and bathtubs, its furnaces draw power to heat up to 2,700
degrees. Kohler responded to the peak-load rates by moving a considerable amount of work to the night shift and reassigning 230
employees to those hours.[26] In the same way, to draw people from
overload toward unused capacity, airlines charge lower fares for
night flights and telephone companies offer bargain rates for long
distance calls from late evening onward.

As space becomes scarce, people will disperse in time even in
households. In Hong Kong persons who work at night rent their
beds to other people for sleeping while they are at their jobs.[27] In
some of New York City's crowded apartments family members work
out of phase with each other and take turns using the same beds.
Shift sleep is a partner of shift work.

Millions of shift workers are diverted from the more crowded
evening and weekend hours at movie houses, taverns, sports stadiums, and beaches to the daytime periods for their recreation. Because there are so many of us, it may seem as if the entire population is pressing onto the highways and down into the subways in
the same half hour, queueing up in supermarket lines all together,
and surging onto beaches in the same period. But it would be de-
cidedly more packed if the other 20 percent who now spread out
from the peak-use times were to meet in the same daily schedule.

Two ideas contribute to understanding why nighttime wakefulness grows. One is that the container of existence is composed of
time as well as space. The other is the set of causes of frontiers—
responses to economic opportunities and quests for relief. The riches

of the night are additional hours, and that natural resource beckons to people who see chances for improving their fortunes. Resources become scarce and facilities overloaded. We are often filling to capacity and then probing and pushing out. Land expansion relieved shortcomings that were felt in the existing settlements. The nighttime expansion relieves the congestion of the day. Those are the first incentives for frontiers, established for what can be put into them and for what can be taken from them.

As a colony is successful, its own presence becomes a source of further growth. New ventures respond to and build on what is established. It begins with very few auxiliary services on hand; some utilities do not appear until enough development has been attained.[28] After more facilities are in place, they enhance the opportunities and lure more people into staying awake longer. Over the long term, the result from initial causes may seem modest compared to the broad-based outcomes and the size of the wakeful population that assembles for secondary reasons.

Squads of additional enterprises are drawn to those hours in response to the new activity. Nighttimers want amenities and pull in complementary businesses. Incessant organizations call for other helping units. They want maintenance and repair services and special products, and they hire other firms to mend equipment, deliver materials, cart away goods, feed their employees, remove trash, and guard the premises.

As merchants notice untapped markets in the people up and about, they begin to offer late-hour shopping. After night work was introduced in the mills of New England, horse-drawn night lunch wagons began to appear on the streets.[29] Eating places now stay open near stadiums, cinemas, factories, and college dormitories. Breakfast parlors open earlier near wholesale food and flower markets. Grocers, fast food restaurants, and other retailers lengthen their hours once they discover the size of the wakeful group. We can see the growth pattern in the history of one food retailer in the United States who in 1946 christened its chain of small town convenience stores "Seven–11" to proclaim that it stayed open sixteen hours a day. By 1978, 82 percent of the 6,599 Seven-11 stores operated twenty-four hours daily, and another 9 percent stayed open beyond the 7 A.M. to 11 P.M. margins. This reflected growth in the numbers of retail clientele at night as well as in persons employed.

Service enterprises fill in a foundation of elaborate support.

Gasoline stations and motels attend customers along turnpikes and near turnpike exits. Taxicabs line up at office building entrances at change-of-shift times. Rent-a-car agencies wait to serve passengers arriving at air and railroad terminals. Pharmacies stay open longer near hospitals. The concentration of an activity in an area raises awareness about its possibilities, and an ever widening scope of projects extend into the dark.[30] Colleges, discovering how many shift workers are available, offer them evening and night courses. New York's John Jay College of Criminal Justice scheduled classes both day and night because many of its students were members of the police department and worked on shifts.

In the early stage of expansion many organizations and individuals are daunted by the inconvenience and the isolation of the night. The increased hours of one large organization may draw taxicabs to its portals and attract a small coffee shop into staying open late, but company managers who would have to provide services for many employees hold back from multiple shifting because of the costs of feeding, protecting, and transporting them. Whatever the enticements at first, there may not be enough of an infrastructure to dispel their reluctance. Ample shops and services must be present to persuade some institutions to extend their hours. Yet here and there the advance goes on, and in these fragmented beginnings are the seeds of further colonizing.

The organizations that introduce nighttime operations are diverse, but the secondary enterprises they enlist are the same. The steel mill and the bank, the hospital and the police station, inasmuch as they want services and utilities, call for the same electricity, telephone, restaurant, maintenance, and transportation facilities. Merchants reacting to the presence of those populations open the same types of retail stores regardless of the night workers' occupations. Progressively responding to what the nocturnal phase misses and requires, further development fills in clerical, municipal, service, and communications-related arrangements. In this way a large corps of cooks, waiters, drivers, desk clerks, porters, projectionists, store clerks, technicians, teachers, mechanics, cashiers, and salespeople are recruited to employment in the off-hours.

As the colony matures it acquires safety, familiarity, and services that make it more hospitable. Enterprises bred by nighttime activity are now more numerous. They make the remote hours less forbidding, and it becomes easier to live out of step with the main rhythm. The setting begins to attract a more diverse group, including people who were uninterested earlier. If a grocery remains open to tap the patronage of night workers, some daytimers will buy goods at one o'clock in the morning for the adventure of it, and a few of them will make it a custom. Hesitant people learn of the decreased risks and increased comforts. Managers who were deterred because the supportive utilities were missing, who were loath to assume the added costs, now assess nighttime possibilities more favorably and judge that it is suitable to lengthen their firms' hours. The population's composition changes as the night begins to recruit more widely and the flow toward wakefulness swells.

By now some factories and industrial plants, transportation systems, hospitals, and newspapers have been running day and night for more than a hundred years. On the other hand, although they are relative newcomers, even gambling casinos operate continually. Today they are among the most thriving overnight scenes. More than half the total work force of Las Vegas is on the job at night; while crowds in other parts of Atlantic City are sparse, the gaming halls are packed.[31]

Twenty-four-hour radio broadcasting in the United States illustrates this later stage of expansion, for its growth was stimulated by the perception of the Federal Communications Commission (FCC), in the early 1960s, that there were many people up at night who were not receiving broadcasting services. Seeing a role for radio then, the FCC encouraged FM broadcasting by resisting licensing new AM channels if an FM channel was available that could bring the same service to an area. That rule was based on FM's technical qualities. At night AM signals generate a great deal of skywave interference, while FM intrudes much less and also transmits music better. By rejecting AM applications for a while and favoring FM because of its lesser interference, the FCC spawned many more radio stations and enabled more after-dark broadcasting. As the agency declared, it was done because "some needs, such as nighttime primary service to large portions of the country, were not being met."[32]

The spreading hours of radio and television broadcasting reflect recent increases in wakefulness in the United States, for broadcasters authorize surveys to learn about the market that can be reached in order to plan programs and set advertising rates. Those research estimates of the number of potential listeners and viewers influence broadcasting activity. Therefore the hours that the stations are active can be interpreted as an index of the number of people awake then.

The trends in daily broadcasting hours in Boston spanning the first half-century of commercial transmission for both radio and television reveals a steady advance toward twenty-four-hour programming in each medium (see Table 2–1). In recent years the gain in twenty-four-hour stations occurred at a faster rate than new stations were introduced. Boston received its first twenty-four-hour television broadcast in March 1972; by 1979 two stations were beaming programs around the clock regularly, and since 1980 cable television by subscription has provided several additional twenty-four-hour networks. As well as reflecting the growth, the broadcasting patterns fostered more night activity, for viewers at home postponed their sleep in order to watch the Late Late Show. Television broadcasts persuaded a diverse population to stay awake longer.

The United States currently represents a large portion of the worldwide pattern. It is a populous land and well developed in the kinds of industry, services, recreation, and communications that involve staying up at night. An estimate of its wakefulness could be multiplied to reflect such activity around the globe. Worldwide, if the people who are up and about in even the quietest hour of night were a nation, it would surpass in size all but a handful of the largest countries.

People are pulled into wakefulness at night by daytime events far away. They need not be physically close. Activity picks up on the other side of the planet when local affairs quiet down after dark. A global instant-access network ensued from long distance communication technology. As a means of quickly crossing many time zones and uniting the world's daytimes with nighttimes, it increases the likelihood of being aroused from sleep. The New York Stock Exchange, recognizing the international nature of its activity and the distribution of trading centers abroad, has more than once considered a move to around-the-clock operations. Several of its investment house members are already active that way. Trading on the Sydney–Melbourne, Tokyo, Singapore, Hong Kong, Milan, London, New York, and San Francisco–Los Angeles stock and foreign currency exchanges, which are listed in this order because of

TABLE 2-1
Radio and Television Stations and Their Hours of Broadcasting in Boston

	April 1929	April 1934	April 1939	April 1944	April 1949	April 1954	April 1959	April 1964	April 1969	April 1974	April 1979
The Span of Commercial Broadcasting											
Radio											
Number of stations	7	7	8	7	8	14	15	20	26	27	30
Number of 24-hour stations	0	0	0	0	0	1	3	8	12	15	22
Percent of 24-hour stations						7%	20%	40%	46%	57%	73%
Television											
Number of stations					2	4	4	4	5	7	9
Number of 24-hour stations					0	0	0	0	0	1	2
Percent of 24-hour stations										14%	22%

SOURCE: Listings in Boston newspapers—*Globe, Herald, Record,* and *Traveler*—and the broadcasters themselves. If the content of a broadcaster's AM and FM radio programming or VHF and UHF television programming differs, that broadcaster is counted as two stations.

the hours they are open, forms a continuous time bridge around the world.

Nighttime pursuits have increased in most countries. The number of people on shift work worldwide has more than doubled since World War II. By the 1970s those portions of the labor forces ranged from 10 to 25 percent of the economically active populations.[33] In Great Britain, for several decades after World War II, the growth of the manual labor force on manufacturing shifts was about 1 percent yearly. The percentage of all employed workers in the United Kingdom that were on shifts rose to over 14 percent in the 1970s.[34] The English are also staying up later when they are not at work. More of them are outside their homes as midnight nears, attending classes, meetings, and sports events, and seeing one another socially.[35] In 1978 the British Broadcasting Corporation began around-the-clock radio service for the first time in its fifty-six-year history. In 1986 channel four of British television announced plans to extend its programming into the hours after midnight because, a spokesman said, "All our analyses show the audience is there."[36]

Other nations in Europe, Asia, South America, and Australia are also the sites of around-the-clock activity. The Soviet Union's first twenty-four-hour emergency psychological counseling service was introduced in 1982.[37] The Japanese are attempting to replan Tokyo on a twenty-four-hour basis. Singapore, with its ever busy harbor and traveling night markets, has been tagged as a model for distributing activities around the clock.[38] Not every great city is busy after dark. In Peking, for example, no teahouses or shops, no restaurants or bars, are open at night, and even street lighting is lacking except for a few major boulevards. After 8 P.M. the streets are practically deserted.[39] Still, although Peking's public areas are dim by evening, the city's foreign-run hotels already have nightclub life, and the Great Wall Hotel offers around-the-clock room service.

Nor is incessance found only in population-dense places. The number of inhabitants is not a reliable sign of the expansion. The city seems more awake because the concentration of activities make them more noticeable. Some undertakings need the critical density of a metropolis to be tried at all, so nighttime endeavors are more common in large cities. But always-open restaurants, food stores, turnpike toll booths, and auto service stations gleam along the highways between towns. In the railroads and telephone and power utility grids, many continuously operating sites are far from urban centers. There is a network of incessance distributed in large and small municipalities and in the areas in between. Where factories, mills, and refineries are located in smaller towns, an entire district may be caught up in the timetable. In such places the nighttime operation of a plant is often proportionately greater than the percentage of the population involved in incessance in a metropolis. Even in sleepy communities there is likely to be a continually staffed police department and telephone service, a late-hours dining place, perhaps an all-night garage, and some truckers delivering foodstuffs to the local stores. Guards in remote areas continually patrol national parks and missile launching sites. Conservation officers maintain surveillance in forests and nature preserves after dark as well as by day. They do so on several continents to protect deer against out-of-season hunters and to safeguard alligators, rhinoceroses, and elephants against poachers.

How many people are up and about at night? According to a tally for the United States during a week in May 1980, just after midnight there were 29 million people active.[40] That does not include persons getting ready to go to sleep. Their numbers can be sorted into three main categories: people at work, people who are otherwise outside the home as clientele of public places and travelers, and people inside the home. The categories are explained more fully in the "Time Census" (Appendix A). Many of us know someone who works at hours other than the day shift or who otherwise stays up late, but few of us realize the scale of the populace awake in the night. The greatest fluctuation takes place outside the home in public places. In the workplace at night, from the beginning of nighttime to its end, there is also a large downswing and then a rise hour after hour. During the sleepiest hours of night, 3 to 5 A.M., the active legion still numbers well over ten million throughout the nation. Perhaps it is the heart of incessance. The core of nonstop community life is found in those quiet hours that link one day to the next. The sum of activity in that interval, at work and in public and in dwellings, reflects our replacement of the sun as ruler of the daily round.

The wakeful filling of night has an orderly form with predictable stages. An incessant community passes through that regular sequence in the course of its development, and it looks different in its maturity from what it was at the start. We can anticipate the likely course of colonizing the night upon noting the signs of ex-

tending the active day. Differences between beginning and later
stages are clues to the status of development wherever it is found.
If a community or society displays little public activity after dark
and yet is industrialized, it means the secondary expansion has not
yet swelled. In any year, activity at night differs among the countries around the world because they are in different stages of the
expansion. As the separate undertakings in a region come together,
adjustments among them begin to produce a coherence that was
absent when people first carved open the night. Because it is the
outcome of those plural causes, wakefulness after dark is both grand
and motley.

3

Frontier Comparisons

Nighttime activity, since it stems from the same forces that promoted geographic expansion in the past, should look like a land outpost, behave like one, and follow the same course of development. Frontiers have traits in common. They unfold in typical ways and show certain qualities of social life. Each characteristic of a new land colony would predict its counterpart after dark. Will we find serenity, hardships, splendid vistas, lawlessness, and helpful hospitality at night? Compare a spatial frontier with the nighttime, and the two should be similar. Sometimes the match is so obvious that pointing out the trait will be enough to persuade us. In other instances, if the comparison raises doubts we may conduct experiments to confirm or refute the idea. There are numerous tests to apply and much information to scan; the pattern is so broad that the hypothesis can be checked in many ways.

One of the best sets of available materials describing a land frontier deals with the United States West.[1] The records and scholarly writings about it are abundant, well organized, and accessible. Pioneers documented their own experiences, travelers recounted their tours, and historians portrayed and interpreted notable features of that expansion. The migration west of the Mississippi River took place during the middle decades of the nineteenth century, from 1830 to 1880. That fifty-year span encompasses such undertakings as the fur trade of the 1830s in the northwest territories, the California gold rush of 1848–52, and the building of the railroads in the 1850s and 1860s. Understandably, there are variations over the decades and diverse terrains. It will be more pertinent to single out the main social patterns of a half-century than to clutter them with particular details.

The frontier line in the U.S. West was drawn by the Census Bureau through an area containing not less than two nor more than six inhabitants per square mile. On one side of the line lay the settled region and on the other side the wilderness. In the closing decade of the nineteenth century the Bureau of the Census announced that the land frontier in America had come to an end, because it was no longer possible to draw a continuous line across the map of the West to define the edge of farthest settlement. From the east came more and more enterprising people. At some points on the other side they had linked up with Spanish colonies on the Pacific Coast. The settlement of this major land frontier was being completed just as the nation began using electric lights and increasing its hours of wakefulness. The Census Bureau's announcement seemed to mark the changeover from space to time as the realm of most vigorous expansion in the United States, as if the flow across the continent swerved into the nighttime rather than spilling into the sea.

Night, for the purposes of this comparison, is the interval from midnight to 7:30 A.M. Of course darkness begins earlier in many places. But though there is little difference in darkness between evening and night, there is in the way people use those periods. Just as major land frontiers of the past are well-settled regions now, our evening is no longer a raw offshoot beyond the perimeter of ordinary society. Evening's routines have been established and linked so thoroughly to daytime life that we may forget they represent a human achievement rather than natural evolution.

The remaining interval, the one-third of the daily cycle in which most of the people in a community are asleep, is the portion that deserves recognition as a frontier. In modern times it is becoming more wakeful. Though the pattern is evident everywhere, the contemporary city at night offers the most concentrated set of information about its growth. Urban life readily supplies much evidence for the denser filling of time.

Stages of advance. After a few bold explorers returned to tell of the huge continent to the West, it was not simply settled in one event. Colonizing the new region followed a sequence of being discovered and rediscovered by generations of different people.[2]

They ventured into the outskirts in a series of waves. The hunter and fur trader pushed into Indian country, followed by the cattle raiser and later by the pioneer farmer.[3] In each stage the participants created a distinctive life-style. Hunters and trappers did not dwell like the miners who followed and they in turn lived differently from the pioneer farmers who came later.[4] Living conditions were generally crude, but the farmers who settled in one place realized far more comfort than the earlier trappers who kept on the move.

The first reports from the frontier that were sent back to the East encouraged further expansion. Entrepreneurs discerned untapped markets in the settlements, and opportunities to sell household goods, snake oil, whisky, and newfangled gadgets. Peddlers and tavernkeepers and craftsmen were drawn to migrate. Proselytizing ministers began their tours. The Western population began to call for protection, repair, and cultural services, and the settlements diversified in character as they appointed sheriffs, opened general stores, and imported schoolteachers.

Similarly, each stage of expansion after dark fills the night more densely than before and uses those hours in a different way. First come isolated wanderers on the streets, then groups of shift workers engage in production. When that population becomes established it presses for additional utilities and services. Once the colony has a foothold it assumes a relevance that it did not have before. It is no longer sheer wilderness but a thin arm of civilization that reaches back and touches the core of society. Reports about it convey a revised sense of the region, redefining it for others and propagating more development. Then retailers arrive, and consumers. Patrons of restaurants and bars, gamblers clustering at gaming tables, people dancing at vacation resorts, and audiences of radio listeners and television viewers fill in the scene.

The rates of advance are uneven on both types of frontiers. Their development and their population sizes fluctuate. In the West, periods of economic depression, dry seasons, and other hardships drove many to abandon their homesteads and move back east. Some onetime dense and lively settlements were abandoned to become dust bowls and ghost towns when valuable resources such as water, metals in the lode, and fertile elements in the soil were depleted.

In the nighttime, adversities such as crime drive pedestrians and small businesses away. So does the scarcity of needed resources.

During the oil embargo of 1973–74, the shortage of fuel prompted retreat from nighttime activity; restaurants, automobile service stations, and other businesses cut back their hours of serving the public.

Organized sponsorship. Popular myths credit independent frontiersmen with exploring the West, and yet a sizable portion of the ventures were formally sponsored.[5] Commercial, governmental, and religious organizations promoted new settlements. Spanish, French, and American explorers petitioned monarchs and governments to authorize and subsidize their trips westward.[6] During the nineteenth century the government sent trained agents out on research expeditions. The Lewis and Clark trek across the continent and John Wesley Powell's journey down the Colorado River are among the best known. They were commissioned in order to locate the land's abundant resources, chart feasible routes, gain scientific knowledge, and provide useful information for the administration of the new territory. Powell's explorations of the Colorado River in 1869–70 was funded by grants from the Illinois State Natural History Society, Illinois Industrial University, the Chicago Academy of Sciences, and the federal government.[7] Meanwhile churches sent their missionaries out to spread the gospel.[8]

The powerful pulls to the West were vast resources of furs and hides, mineral deposits, timberlands, and fertile pastures, as well as space and freedom. Fur traders and timber and mining companies underwrote the region's colonization for the sake of exploiting its wealth. They offered trappers, prospectors, and woodsmen the stakes they needed to get started. The commercial object of these industries and later of the cattle business was the transfer of goods to distant markets.[9] Individuals could not do it alone. In the wave of expansion that followed, numerous companies lent their funds and administrative support for the purposes of establishing banks, stockyards, shipping depots, stagecoach services, and the trans-Mississippi railroads. Steamers on the Missouri added traffic by carrying men and supplies to trading posts and bringing back furs and hides.[10] One scholar concluded that "The economic history of even the pre-agricultural frontiers, once a pageant of individual adventure, is coming to rest on the cold facts of investment capital."[11]

Likewise, business firms have been leading sponsors of nighttime activity. With gaslight on hand, factories began by exploiting their idle equipment in the early phase of modern expansion. Utility companies later reacted to levels of demand that strained their existing capacities by redistributing services through fees that favored after-dark use. Governments joined in by fostering shift work to improve the economy and to cope with unemployment. Whereas capitalist enterprises led the way, socialist countries were not impervious to the allure of nighttime contributions to financial health. States with centrally planned economies, defining large numbers of unemployed persons as "idle labor" and prizing more development, used shift work to provide jobs as well as to increase national productivity. Poland, for example, rebuilt its economy after World War II through more plant use via shift work. Since many of its factories had been destroyed and it did not have recourse to ample investment funds, it turned to using its available plants more hours per day.[12] A decade later the U.S. federal government promoted widespread broadcasting services at night.

Sparse and homogeneous population. Initially the persons who tried to sustain themselves beyond the fringes of settled society were few and from a distinct group. The demographic composition of the Western frontier was at first mostly young men. Many of them were unmarried. The West had a surplus of bachelors, and Eastern states had proportionately more women and aged persons.[13] In the nighttime too, there are fewer people up and about, and most of them are young adult males.[14] Women and older persons feel more physical danger then and are likely to stay inside their homes. Figures 3–1 and 3–2 are ecologically equivalent charts of the populations in space and in time.

Young people are more numerous on the outer fringes because they are less enmeshed in various social obligations. They can respond readily to new opportunities and more easily adapt to them. In the West, even the men who were married typically left their families behind when they came to spy out the land. Young husbands went forth to establish a holding and then, having made a new home, sent for their wives and children.[15] Matching that pattern, a census taken of people on Boston streets disclosed that whereas persons of all ages were outside during the day, no one over fifty-nine was seen between midnight and 5 A.M., and from 2 A.M. to 5 A.M. there was almost no one over forty-one years old. The sharp changes in number and composition of persons outside after

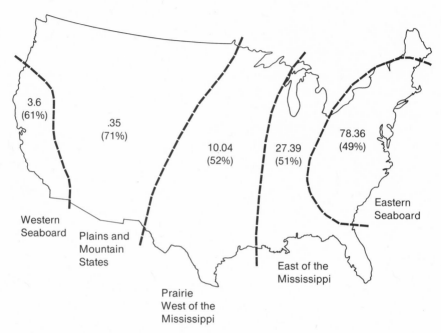

FIGURE 3–1
Persons Per Square Mile (and Percent Males Per Square Mile) During the 1870–1880 Decade
Source: U.S. Bureau of the Census, 1975: Vol. 1, ser. A195-209.

midnight stands in the same relation to the rest of the day as the region west of the Mississippi stood to the East a century ago.[16]

If the pioneer group that moves beyond the outskirts gains hold, it will change the environment to be more hospitable to others. With that change, people who are quite different from pioneers will feel more comfortable in the milieu, and more of them will begin to migrate.

Escape and opportunity. If there is tumult or harassment in a region, people try to leave it. The West held out chances for various kinds of freedoms to be enjoyed. The landscape offered tranquility and relief from feelings of being hemmed in. It was viewed as a haven from crowding, oppressiveness, and persecution. Some of the first persons to go there were drawn by the serenity of the wilds. Fur traders were said to be psychological types who pre-

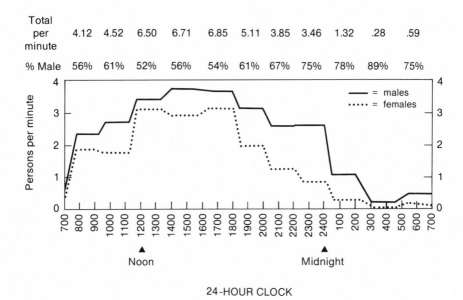

FIGURE 3-2
Females and Males Passing (Per Minute) on the Streets of Boston, 1974

ferred forest solitudes to the company of their fellow men.[17] It was appealing to leave deceit and vexing duties and impositions of the government behind.[18] Kit Carson was said to enjoy communing with the silence, the solitude, and the grandeur of the wilderness.[19]

Just as the New World was a haven for outcasts from Europe, the Western frontier accepted some of those who were harried in America's Eastern settlements.[20] Mormons and Hutterites, for example, both made their ways westward to avoid abuse from others because of their religious and cultural practices. Driven from their homes by threats and violence, they abandoned their lands and property and sought refuge beyond the reach of their persecutors. The West served also to buffer strains between generations. Frederick Jackson Turner's portrait of the West notes that each frontier furnished new opportunity, a gate of escape, and that the West was a sanctuary from the rule of the established classes, from the subordination of youth to age.[21]

Far more people migrated westward to improve their economic lot. Many of them were disadvantaged. They came from regions

where they had been squeezed by density and competition, impelled by a need for subsistence and looking for opportunities to
make a living. Western lands drew marginal farmers from the hill
towns of New England and from the spent farms of New York and
Pennsylvania. Insolvent ones became tenant farmers beholden to
absentee landlords. Members of minority groups came. Thousands
of Negroes went to work as cowboys.[22] Others were lured by hopes
for greater gains. They viewed the West as a horn of plenty and
counted on chances to make a fortune. Whenever competition becomes severe enough to make life uncertain or leaves people dis-
satisfied about the size of their share, some of them disperse to seek
opportunities elsewhere.

The search for opportunity arose beyond national borders.
Great pressures had built up abroad. Population increases and food
shortages in Europe generated pushes to emigrate. About one million persons left Ireland after the second potato crop failure at the
end of the 1840s, and most of them came to America.[23] Although
hordes from the waves of immigration settled along the Eastern
shore, many foreigners, including skilled farmers, set out for lands
across the Mississippi. From the far side of the Pacific Ocean
hundreds of thousands poured in to labor in the gold mines and on
the railroads in the next few decades. More than half the miners in
Idaho and more than one-fifth of the miners in Montana in 1870
were Chinese.[24] By giving asylum to people everywhere who sought
to escape persecution, by absorbing migrants who were seeking
work, and by taking some of the influx of immigrants from the
overpopulated areas of Europe and the Orient, the American West
served as a safety valve for the world.[25]

Others with higher ambitions aspired to social advancement and
wealth. They were not so much pushed by failure to make a living
as pulled by promise of greater reward. Experienced, successful
farmers from Eastern rural regions took their savings and moved
farther west to work the land.[26] Small entrepreneurs opened saloons
or general stores, built hoisting works and stamping mills near the
mines, or invested in ranches and herds.

Like the colonization of the West, conquest of the darkness opens
a new zone capable of meeting people's needs for escape and opportunity. It offers privacy and fewer social constraints. Persons who
are disparaged or oppressed retreat to its tolerant atmosphere. Even
before this century the darkness was a refuge. Masters on planta-

tions in the South tried to impose a formal religion on their slaves, but the slaves preferred their African ways. Where these were prohibited, they resorted to nighttime songfests and prayer meetings. If they were to be in bed by a certain hour and foremen came around to make sure of it, they complied and then arose later and went out. One man recounted that they "used to have a prayin' ground down in the hollow and sometimes we come out to the field, between eleven and twelve at night . . . and we wants to ask the good Lawd to have mercy. . . . Some gits so joyous they starts to holler loud and we has to stop they mouth."[27] Slaves could not escape to the West, so they escaped to the night.

Night's hush and solitude attract people looking for a haven from stress. They draw away from daytime commotion, unpleasant encounters, and torment inflicted by powerful persons or groups. Some night owls are urban hermits. Some who are troubled or stigmatized, such as the very ugly or obese, retreat to the dark to avoid humiliation and challenge. They stay up later, come out when most people are gone, and are more secure as they hobnob with nighttime news dealers, porters, and elevator men. In the daytime some of them would be censured for not following socially approved behavior. Street people and homosexuals find more peace in the dark because surveillance declines.

The night is also a region of opportunity for improving one's economic circumstances. In Hungary just after World War II the peasants were dismayed at the centralized controls, requisitions, and taxes in kind. In a strategy that came to be called the "Moonlight collective" they tilled the land at night to hide their produce from authorities. In current times the deprived, the hopeful, and the ambitious all take jobs after dark. For some it barely allows sustenance. For others it is a port of entry to the work force, since beginners start their jobs on night shifts and move to the daytime as they earn seniority or promotions. For families needing more income, one of the parents will do shift work so that both can take turns caring for their children.

Unlike land frontiers, night is much closer to the settled center. One can reckon its distance in hours of waiting rather than in miles. The ease with which people could reach the West affected their decision to move there. Now, with opportunities for work on shifts, a jobless person need not incur the expense of packing up and relocating to find employment. Instead of having to equip a covered wagon and travel for weeks across the prairie, one can wait till midnight and arrive at the frontier.

Isolated settlements. The first outposts beyond a society's margins are detached. Land frontier settlements were small and apart from one another. There was little communication across districts and each carried on self-sufficiently. People in the East did not think of the relevance of borderland activities for their own affairs, and the pioneers were indifferent to outside society.[28]

As night advances, the population switches from coordinated actions to less connected ones. Pacing of activities becomes less orderly.[29] Enclaves of wakeful pursuits are separated from one another. They are smaller in scale than daytime events, and there is less communication between them. The outpost does have ties to the daytime, for the persons employed are members of households, and enterprises and agencies transfer materials and information between phases of the day. But most daytimers give little thought to those active in the dark and do not think of them as part of the main community.

A wider range of tolerated behavior. Frontiers allow more individualism because the constituted authority and rules implied by familiar settings are absent. People who move to the fringe break from ordinary society in their dress and conduct and display more varied and unusual manners. They are not rebellious. Since a frontier demands more attention to survival, their novel behavior may come from neglect rather than an aim to flout social customs. To cope in the uncommon milieu they bend the frameworks of formality and develop unconventional methods of adapting that carry over into interpersonal behavior.

Travelers who met Westerners portrayed them as direct, unpretentious, and energetic. Their image fared worse when viewed from a distance. Easterners thought that Westerners were unsavory and commented disdainfully on their boorish ways. They were described as crude, degraded, eccentric, and of an inferior social class.[30] Early in the nineteenth century the president of Yale College said: "The class of pioneers cannot live in regular society. They are too idle, too talkative, too passionate, too prodigal, and too shiftless to acquire either property or character."[31] Although the tales of their adventures were often exaggerated, frontiersmen eased the tensions of efforts to survive with bouts of uninhibited drinking and revelry.

Many pioneer wives lived on their homesteads for extended periods without ordinary social contacts, especially when their husbands left on journeys for days or weeks. These women often became withdrawn and untalkative, so shy and uneasy with strangers that they would run away when one approached. From the evidence at hand they were normal, happy women in the cities when they were growing up, but they were affected by the remote environment.[32] Out west, others were used to this demeanor on the part of lonely, isolated women and accepted it. In the Eastern cities the same conduct would have been taken as odd.

Both the conduct and the character of nighttimers have been disparaged for a long time, and night has a popular image as a haunt of freaks and lost souls. William Hogarth made an etching 250 years ago titled *Night* that shows lurching drunks and vagrants on a London street.[33] That outlook still persists and was illustrated in the newspaper comic strip Orphan Annie, in which a flower seller discusses the people passing by after dark with disapproval:

> Now it's evening—notice the difference, Annie? . . . The bluffers who pose and strut. . . . The shoddy and disreputable . . . now it's after midnight, and you see another change. . . . Derelicts—prowlers— Shadows that are in fact the shadows of what once were human beings.[34]

At night people dress more casually. They tolerate more varied public behavior than found in the subdued daytime. One can find people who, having lived normal lives, are exposed to unusual circumstances that draw them into unconventional conduct. Jazz musicians, for example, work late in the evening and then associate with few daytime types in their recreation after midnight.[35] The young players model themselves after the older professionals in a subculture that tolerates and even expects different behavior. The same pattern can be observed in a hospital. "Left without interference by supervisors, the nightworkers could stretch out and rest their feet on the desks of those who ruled the hospital in the daytime. [They] lived and worked unencumbered by the rules and restrictions . . . even staff members who normally follow the rules carefully in the daytime are likely to be a bit more lax at night."[36]

It is a time for more extremes of mischief and play. Workers in a main post office used to lug one another around on the wheeled pallets that were ordinarily used for moving mail pouches. Production workers and drivers of cranes in a factory hurled various articles at each other as the cranes trundled by on a monorail hanging from the roof of the plant.[37] In another factory, after midnight workers and foremen would race one another in the forklift trucks normally used to transport materials in production.[38] The temptation for such antics appears in public as well. At three o'clock on several mornings on a main shopping street in Boston, a man in white facial makeup was observed racing along and propelling another person in a wheelchair down the middle of the empty avenue.

Fewer status distinctions. Every society develops expressions of power and status in its social order, but when people travel beyond its confines they relax its rules of deferential conduct. Western settlers and visitors alike left behind the trappings of social grades and became just plain folk to one another. They showed no special respect to someone of higher rank, and those holding such rank often made it a point of pride to be treated like everyone else.

Groups of people who usually stay in their separate haunts meet after midnight in public places and exchange pleasantries. In Rio de Janeiro, the frequenters of nightclubs on their way home greet the vendors setting up stalls in the little farmers' markets. In Madrid the popular middle-of-the-night custom of eating fritters and melted chocolate at the *churrerias* selling them brings together discotheque clientele on their way to bed and laborers on their way to work. Crêperies in Florence and cafeterias in New York are similarly democratic in those hours. Compared to daytime, at two in the morning the cafeteria regulars are more likely to see men in dinner jackets and women in gowns sitting at the tables next to them. On the job at night, out of their own desire for companionship, the shift foremen seek the company of whoever is available. Workers and supervisors alike relax and dispense with the proprieties that distinguish them in daytime.

Novel hardships. The remoteness of the frontier and lack of knowledge about it allowed people in the settled centers to create myths about it. Both the United States West and the night have been made out to be regions of romantic adventure, but pioneers in both realms found mostly physical adversity and obstacles to ordinary social opportunities. Throughout the ages people everywhere have had to toil to survive. Frontiers are no different in this respect. But each new frontier also presents its vanguard with an unusual environment and delivers unique challenges. The farmers who settled Western lands found them unlike the land they left behind. The region that now comprises Nebraska, Kansas, Oklahoma, and Texas was so bereft of trees that at one time it was labeled on maps as the Great American Desert. It took a long time to realize that the arid plains west of the Missouri River were habitable at all, and almost no one thought that some day many people would want to migrate and settle there.[39]

When the pioneers arrived in Kansas, Iowa, and the Dakotas and found themselves on an open, dusty range, they did not know how to make do on the treeless terrain. The prairie had never been tilled before. It had been tamped down by millions of buffalo hooves for thousands of years, and the sod was reinforced by networks of roots into such a stubborn compactness that an ordinary plow could not turn it. One had to chop a hole in the earth with an axe in order to plant corn.[40] There came into existence an occupation called a sodbuster, a man who could be hired by the day and who used a team of eight oxen to pull an oversized iron plow to tear open the ground. Familiar farming methods would not work. Cultivation called for adding new procedures to agriculture's state of the art, including techniques of dry farming, reservoirs, and irrigation systems.[41] During the decades it took to develop these methods, the settlers endured confusion and severe hardship.

They had natural and economic misfortunes too. Nature sent sandstorms, tornados, locusts, glare, vermin, and extremes of temperature. Scorching summer droughts damaged the crops and dessicated the livestock. In the winter the cold entered through gaps in cabin walls and froze the buckets of water and loaves of bread. Persons of all ages were beset by diseases, which, in the sketchy diagnoses of the day, were called mountain fever, lung fever, and dropsy on the brain.

For all the spellbinding vistas and scenic beauty of the West, despite all the promises and compelling dreams of hope, the pioneers' life was arduous—hemmed in by isolation and drudgery, filled with rigors imposed by the new environment, and enveloped in loneliness and disillusionment. Disheartened, husbands and wives

quarreled over whether to remain or retreat. The hardships drove
many settlers back from the Western fringes. Their words of fare-
well were "In God we trusted, in Kansas we busted."[42] One-third
of all domestic settlements established under the Homestead Act
were abandoned.[43] Yet Eastern pushes and Western pulls continued
to exert force. Hope is the poor man's consolation. People continued
to go to the frontier in search of subsistence. Gainful employment,
wherever it was, drew them to it. Great numbers of settlers were
steadfast in accepting the discomforts and privations and grew re-
sourceful while they hung on. They converted the West from scattered outposts to an extension of the full society.

As denizens of the nighttime, shift workers are like the pioneers
on the land. They too venture forth with more willingness than
aptitude, finding themselves in a new environment and having to
undertake a way of life different from what they know and for
which they are unprepared. For them the novel rigors are having
to be awake at the natural time for sleep and having to rotate their
hours on the job. The fluctuating phases of work disrupt the body's
physiological rhythms. These physiological impositions are distinct
from any faced previously and were hardly present in human experience before 1800. The effects have been popularized recently
as jet lag, because they bother travelers in rapid transit across time
zones around the world, but long before the airplane, ever since
the introduction of night work, those disorders were being felt.
When physiological functions are in cadence, people perform best.
When the functions are out of step, their ability sags. Neither biological nor cultural heritage prepares shift workers for such upsets.
The oft-reshuffled schedules also make chaos out of family routines,
deprive spouses of one another's company in bed, and give workers
little chance to see their friends or participate in organized social
activities. Yet they hang on, despite the assaults on body and on
family and community ties, because it is their means of livelihood.

Decentralization of authority. Whatever top-level group
may decide the policies and rules for a community or an organization, outside its purview subordinates make decisions that would
otherwise be the responsibility of higher-ups or subject to their approval. As the land frontier moved farther from the national center
of policy-making, it was ever more thinly administered. Interpretation of the law and judicial decisions were carried out by persons

who rarely consulted their seniors and who were scarcely supervised. Settlers formed associations and made their own laws. Events took place remote from the courts and authorities, and the frontiersmen not only enforced their own law but also chose which laws they would obey.[44]

At night, too, the top administrators of ongoing organizations and cities go to sleep, and a decentralization of power follows. Lesser officials make decisions that in the daytime are left to upper-echelon personnel. Foremen on their own at night deal with many matters that in other hours call for notifying superiors. The way an organization or city is run at night changes with the remoteness of that top command. It represents the styles of those in charge, who may be more or less humane, arbitrary, wise, or foolish than their superiors. Supervisors usually impose less control. They leave workers alone and are indulgent about minor rule violations. Even among police, decisions by officers at night will be based on a softened professional role. A truck driver observed that "the troopers will let you get away with a little bit more at night."[45]

Lawlessness and peril. Both the land frontier and the nighttime have reputations as regions of danger and outlawry. The Western frontier seemed typically a place of risky journeys and unruly towns. Inhabitants lived with the fear of attack from either Indians or bandits. Horse stealing was widespread. The stagecoach was held up again and again. Soon stagecoaches were accompanied by armed guards called shotgun messengers.[46] Pioneers setting out across the countryside joined one another for mutual defense. The covered wagons that crossed the plains usually traveled together, were accompanied by armed convoys, and drew up into an impromptu barricade with guards each time they encamped. Former hunters and trappers found a new occupation by becoming guides to safe passage through the wilderness. On certain routes the U.S. government sent a military escort along, and occasionally from the destination a force of cavalry would ride forth to meet the caravans.[47]

Some settlements were renowned for concentrations of gamblers, gougers, and bandits, of dance-hall girls and honky-tonks and bawdy houses. Practically everyone in the cow towns and mining camps carried guns. Fighting words, the ring of revolvers, and groans of pain were common sounds out there. Francis Parkman said of one town in Kansas, "Whiskey . . . circulated more freely in Westport than is altogether safe in a place where every man carries a loaded pistol in his pocket."[48] The number of law enforcement agents seemed altogether inadequate when matched against the frequent reports of brawls and shootouts. Given so few marshals on hand, the citizens banded together for self-protection and practiced constant watchfulness. They formed anti–horse thief societies and vigilante groups to impose law and order.[49]

Actual mayhem, however, was selective and concentrated in certain places and times. Quiet and sober men were rarely involved. Most settlers were lawful and peaceful, mob law was rare, and murders were so infrequent that when one did occur the community was shocked and outraged.[50] In the cow towns the tumult was seasonal, occurring when the cowboys finally reached Abilene, Ellsworth, and Dodge City after a long cattle drive.[51] Such towns as Tombstone, Virginia City, Dodge City, and Deadwood, and the states of Texas and California, had more than their share of gunfights and assaults. In these and the mining towns of Aurora and Bodie on the Nevada–California border, the one form of crime that did occur at a higher rate than in the East was homicide. Otherwise, larceny, bank robbery, burglary, theft, racial violence, and juvenile crime were less frequent out west.[52]

Why, then, did the land frontier have the reputation of a Wild West? Possibly because the outlaws were drifters. The same fugitive from justice contributed exploits over large areas.[53] Another reason was boredom. Stories of thievery and hangings persisted and spread because there was little to do or read about in pioneer homes. The tedium of daily life was relieved by having neighbors tell and retell hair-raising yarns while warming themselves around the stove in the general store.

Nighttime has a popular image as a period of anarchy and risk, crime-ridden and outside of social control.[54] Bringing in black market goods is accomplished under cover of darkness. For marijuana and cocaine smuggling operations, crude airstrips in rural areas of the U.S. South that are scarcely used in the daytime become busy with small planes landing and taking off after midnight.[55] Of all the twenty-four hours, homicides occur most often near midnight.[56] Carrying arms is more common then. People are more on edge about burglars and intruders and, with a siege mentality descending on them, they bolt themselves in their homes and lock the doors and windows.

Nighttime muggers may have an outlook similar to that of Western desperados. Both would believe there is less exposure in their milieu, lowering the risk and improving chances to carry out nefarious deeds. The desperado relied on dry-gulching and the mugger uses the dark to set an ambush. Escape is easy because both could move from the scene of the crime into unpopulated areas and elude pursuers. There was a lack of policemen in the West, and now at night police coverage is sparse.[57]

To guard against mugging or rape, escort services are provided for women going from their places of work to the parking lot or subway station, and on college campuses for women returning to their dorms after dark. An increase in muggings at night arouses the community. Citizens mobilize to demand more police protection. They distribute handbills and organize watchful patrols. In several nations, thousands of women join in an annual protest march called "Take Back the Night" to show their distress over rapes and violence and to urge public safety measures.

In several cities an alliance of young people calling themselves the Guardian Angels began patrolling the subways in paramilitary fashion between midnight and morning to prevent crime or harassment of passengers.[58] Many riders welcomed them because the subway police had been too few and too ineffective, but the Angels made others uneasy; in their readiness to make citizens' arrests they reminded people of vigilantes who sometimes took too much of the law into their own hands.

Lawlessness and violence at night, however, are concentrated in certain hours in certain locales. Residents of a city, aware of this, make distinctions between the safe and risky neighborhoods after dark. Just as peaceful Western towns turned disorderly during an influx of strangers such as the cattle drovers or new miners, so a placid section of Boston's daytime business district becomes a combat zone in the presence of pleasure-seeking young men at night. During the daytime many people shop at department stores nearby or otherwise patronize the stores and eating places there. After dark, prostitution is common, bars and lounges feature nude dancers, and scuffles and muggings take place. The zone then quiets down after 2:30 A.M. For most of its hours, in most places, the night is tranquil.

Helpfulness and sociability. The land frontier had a reputation for friendliness and generosity toward both neighbors and strangers. Pioneers were kind to one another. New arrivals would be given supplies and food to tide them over. Pioneer women who were working around the house during the day considerately fed passing travelers and donated water and provisions for the route.[59] Members of the community cooperated to build their houses, raise barns, and help people who were sick or in need. Neighbors shared their equipment and tools. They plowed the widow's land. They would not pass someone on foot if they could offer a ride.[60] Strangers benefited from such good will, and travelers returning from the outlands declared they were treated more kindly than they had been in the cities.[61] A tourist writing during the nineteenth century noted: "Even the rough western men, the hardy sons of the Indian frontier, accustomed from boyhood to fighting for existence, were hospitable and generous to a degree hard to find in more civilized life."[62]

Frontier people cooperated with one another because they realized how they depended on one another in the challenging environment. Although there was plenty to be done, often they had nothing to do. They were not closely synchronized in daily tasks, as people were in the Eastern cities, nor did they emphasize a punctual schedule. They could afford the time to be sociable and alleviate their lonely lives.

Nighttime, too, is a period evoking helpfulness and friendliness toward strangers. A journeyman engineer who worked nights in a railroad steam shed in England one hundred years ago recognized the outpost character of those hours:

> [S]upper commenced, and cooking, eating, and yarn-spinning became the order of the night. This latter was a rather important feature of our proceedings; for as we glanced into the surrounding darkness, and remembered that we had still to work on . . . a campfire-like feeling would fall upon our circle, and a good yarn would have for us that added charm which it has for a company of prairie-hunters. . . . Seeing a strange figure moving about in the light of the large grate containing the "live" coals used for getting up steam, you go out, and find some hungry, footsore, wayworn tramp, who apologizes for his presence, and hopes the "hands" will let him lie down by the fire. But the hands *won't.* "Lie down by the fire be blowed!" they say; "come on into the shed, and have a bit of something to eat, and then we'll find you a better place than that to lie down in"; and so saying they take him in, and having seated him by the stove, assail him with invitations to "Have

a bit of supper with me, mate." . . . To share his "bagging" with some houseless wanderer is an ordinary occurrence with a man on the night shift.[63]

These days, when people meet in an all-night diner or grocery they are cheerier, more outgoing, and more affable with strangers, and show more willingness to become personal with one another than is noticeable in the daytime. Night work shifts are also scenes of fraternity. The employees are more congenial. They share tools more readily and help each other on difficult tasks. People everywhere are less rushed at night, more relaxed, and glad for each other's company.

Policies to exploit and regulate. One of the last things to happen in the development of a frontier is that ways of using or protecting its basic resources is finally proposed as a policy. Although westward expansion began with official encouragement of exploiting economic opportunities, a long time passed before there was full recognition that the land frontier resources were finite or that places left in their natural states held benefits for society. The catch phrase Manifest Destiny was not applied to colonizing the continent until 1845, centuries after the effort had been under way. Horace Greeley introduced the slogan "Go West, Young Man, go forth into the Country" because he looked upon such migration as a means of relief from the poverty and unemployment caused by the Panic of 1837. By 1854 he was urging, "Make the Public Lands free in quarter sections to Actual Settlers . . . and the earth's landless millions will no longer be orphans and mendicants." In 1862, with the passage of the Homestead Act, the government introduced a program for using the Western territory to help relieve the conditions of tenant farmers and hard-pressed city laborers. A member of Congress declared, in support of the act, "I sustain this measure . . . because its benign operation will postpone for centuries, if it will not forever, all serious conflict between capital and labor in the older free states." The advocates of expansion also recognized it as a way to draw off great numbers of people from the cities and forestall crowding there.[64] Policy-makers finally saw the use of Western space as a means of solving social problems.[65]

Similarly, in the first 150 years after coal-gas illumination was used to convert mills in England to around-the-clock operations, there was no national consciousness there or in the United States about colonizing the nighttime. People went ahead, expanding their activities into the dark hours without declaring that a twenty-four-hour community was being forged. Then policy-makers began to view the chance to exploit unused capacity after dark as a means of increasing jobs and improving the economies of nations.[66] Multiple-shift work would reduce unemployment and improve the welfare of people by giving them a chance to earn a living. One economist made the case for overpopulated, underindustrialized countries by saying that if a nation is well endowed with people but short on money, it makes sense to use its capital intensively and to apply its labor extensively by running manufacturing plants for many hours a day and employing workers on several shifts. The result would be newly employed workers having money to spend, thus creating more demand for goods. Some of that demand would be for the very merchandise that their countrymen are producing or for goods that use those products. Also, more hiring would be generated in the utility and service sectors—transportation, restaurants, and recreation facilities—that minister to the work force.[67] Others agree that governments, responding to pressures of population growth, will have recourse to night work in order to use available equipment to increase job opportunities.[68] These suggestions for using cheap time echo the attitudes of nineteenth-century proponents of using cheap land to solve the problem of those who were out of work.

After World War II Poland acted with such benefits in mind. It produced more jobs despite the nation's limited capital, and almost half the percentage of total gain in its industrial employment during 1951 to 1956 came from after-dark use of available capacity. The Soviet Union and Hungary also adopted that strategy.[69] Mexico and Peru encouraged multiple shifting for the same reasons. It is a policy with appeal in advanced industrial countries too; given the existing capital stock, it was recently advocated in the United Kingdom to engender more employment.[70]

Experts in urban planning also recommend dispersing activities across the hours as a means of reducing congestion.[71] One wrote: "Scarce land and expensive human time can also be conserved by encouraging round-the-clock operation. . . . By such means people can live densely without stepping on each other's toes."[72] A sociologist from the Soviet Union asserted, "Time . . . is a particular form of national wealth. Therefore it is imperative to plan the most efficient use of it for all members of a society."[73]

Zoning rules that control development in space have their equivalents in time. Curfews, licenses, and regulations of the hours of business after dark help resolve clashes over the use of the night. When the night is almost filled, we are finally prompted to discuss the prospect of conserving some of its hours, as we have tried to keep some land undeveloped and wilderness areas reserved.

Interest group conflicts. When a frontier pushes out from the main settlement, it detaches itself from the existing order and, out of reach, operates largely on its own. It is concerned with securing a foothold. Its problems are mostly with the strangeness of the environment, and its dealings with the core of society are slight. As it succeeds, its interaction with the settled center increases. Conditions emerge from their widening contacts that begin to alter their relationship. A frontier that is mature enough to have its own momentum and strength will exert influence on the main community. Outpost and core begin to find that some of their interests are incompatible. They do not share priorities about what to do and how to do it. Conflicts usually crystallize around issues of personal rights or threats to economic opportunities.

West and East became more interdependent as the land frontier matured, and the expanded dealings made the pioneers aware of their distinctive concerns. Turner wrote that the West felt a keen sense of difference from the East.

> The interior of the colonies was disrespectful of the coast, and the coast looked down upon the upland folk. [The West finally] became self-conscious and even rebellious against the rule of the East . . . it resented the conception that it . . . was the dependency of one or another of the Eastern sections. . . . It took the attitude of a section itself.[74]

Westerners became sensitive about the condescension with which they were viewed by Easterners. More provoking, even, was their realization that the East undercut some of their economic interests. Resentful over being neglected and exploited, they finally organized to improve their lot. That gave rise to such pressure groups and farm bloc organizations as the Greenback Party, the National Grange, and the Populists. The Granger movement, for example, grew with the Westerners' problems about transportation in their region. There were no significant river or canal systems out there, and the settlers were at the mercy of the railroads. The rates in Western territories were far higher than those in the East, and the movement was spurred in the 1870s by the recognition of the disparity.[75] The West continued to show solidarity in pursuing economic and political goals throughout the twentieth century.

The night also isolates a group from the main society, and it too notices that it follows a different life-style and has distinct priorities. Its people recognize that they share common concerns. They develop antagonism toward daytimers as the latter ignore or deprecate them or pass ordinances to curb their activities. Gradually becoming unified as a self-conscious minority bent on their rights, they form politically oriented social movements. Two groups whose public activities were customarily linked with the nighttime, homosexuals and prostitutes, took such a course. The former established such nationwide organizations as the Gay Liberation Front to publicize their cause and to work for their rights. Prostitutes (called nightwalkers in New York and in Massachusetts law) also formed a union. Appropriately they adopted the name of a creature in the United States West noted for howling at night, the coyote. COYOTES (Call Off Your Old Tired Ethics) seek legislation to decriminalize prostitution and protest courtroom discrimination against women who earn their livelihood that way.[76] Other nighttime alliances have grown out of disputes with daytimers who wish to sleep undisturbed and try to ban night airplane flights. The people employed after dark at the airports band together to resist this threat to their jobs.

The several comparisons just concluded reveal that life in the night hours resembles conditions beyond the outskirts of settled land areas. They testify to a frontier society after dark. The general traits of the land frontier have been described, not local features. In the same way there are local differences in nighttime pursuits, although the essentials apply to all parts of the globe.

Some terms and ideas have stuck together so long that they appear to be inseparable. The words frontier and settlement seem to refer to space alone because we are accustomed to using them that way. We need language to express our ideas, and yet its terms can shackle our thought. Insights usually outrun vocabularies. We have to remind ourselves that words need not rule. Often when we broaden our understanding we enlarge the meaning of an appropriate term. The seventeenth-century Dutch scientist Christiaan Huygens gave us a fine example of this. He was studying light, and light rays, he observed, rippled and flowed. So Huygens announced that "this movement . . . spreads . . . by spherical surfaces and waves: for I call them waves at their resemblance to those which are seen to be formed in water when a stone is thrown into it, and which present a successive spreading of circles."[77] Huygens was living in Paris at the time, and he wrote in French. In that sentence he appointed *onde*, the French word for "wave," to mean this other kind of undulation too. Maybe readers of the day murmured to themselves that it is odd to talk of light as a wave. Perhaps those who understood the idea assumed that he had found a suitable metaphor to help them comprehend the nature of light. But today we cover light waves, sound waves, shock waves, and water waves in a single theory of undulating motion, and we assume that all of them are real.

In the same way, the night's frontier is neither metaphor nor analogy. It is a word enlisted in the service of thought, just as Huygens did with "wave." "Frontier" may put on different empirical guises, but it is one idea. It is an edge of expansion and development. To colonize time is to annex a band of hours and fill it with active people. To recognize this is to obtain a coherent explanation for its varied features: the kinds of people up and about after dark; what brings them there; why they are more helpful and friendly than daytimers; the beginnings of their political efforts; the reasons for the stir after midnight in such diverse places as food stores, metal smelting plants, freight carriers, indoor tennis courts, mayors' complaint offices, hospital emergency wards, and data-processing departments; and the slow realization that public policy might be applied to time itself. Bit by bit all of society is migrating there. We are expanding our niche. One hypothesis accounts for the spreading of people in both space and time. It helps us recognize the sequel to our geographic dispersal in the past, and we capture it within the familiar themes of migration and settlement.

Not every characteristic of the U.S. West in the 1800s need have its counterpart in the contemporary night. The idea of frontier is an abstraction. Although point-by-point similarities between one geographic outpost and the after-dark endeavor confirm it, the frontier idea is more encompassing than can be shown by looking at only two of them. Some day, a historian wrote, a study of frontier advance may show the traits common to all of them.[78] Advancement on different frontiers may proceed at different rates. Not all features apply to all stages in which expansion takes place. We have not yet seen the full development of the night. The early conditions of growth will be found where the push of wakefulness beyond midnight is just beginning and the pattern will change as the outpost matures.

The society that we are creating at night reiterates the panorama of our past. At one point in Turner's essay on the West, which he wrote in 1893, he declared: "And now, four centuries from the discovery of America, at the end of a hundred years of life under the constitution, the frontier has gone."[79] But the frontier had not gone. During the era that land settlements were being completed, there began—into the night—a large-scale migration of wakeful activity that continues to spread over the world.

4

Who Is Active at Night?

As a group, nighttimers are not as diverse as the entire population. Certain persons stay up later while others do not. They have their motives for doing so; some conditions encourage them and hinder other people. On one hand it seems to be an individual matter. Each person establishes a place in society, each looks for a suitable station in life, and being a nighttime regular connotes having found a part of it there. Since most people grow up within the daytime schedule and follow it, being active so late implies a departure from the norm as well as a choice of the unusual. Persons who leave the main settlement and move to its margins are guided by a combination of leaving a situation they feel is somehow undesirable and responding to prospects in another.

The new region has to be seen as offering fair chances, for without such opportunities people remain immobile even as dissatisfactions grow. A crowded neighborhood may give rise to an urge to leave, but it will become increasingly dense and its inhabitants will make remarkable adjustments to the congestion if there is no promising region to go to beyond its bounds. Each person makes the decision to leave individually. Each sums up a personal psychological balance sheet in reckoning costs and benefits. Some will rate the attractions of night above its obstacles, while others who also see some advantage will be deterred by the risks they sense in those hours and by the costs of missing opportunities offered by daytime.

On the other hand, from the perspective of the whole community the night group appears to have been carried there on an ecological tide. The persons active then have been sorted according to social and environmental conditions. Broad forces promote the migration for certain segments of the population.[1] The results can be seen in the workplace. In looking for jobs, people are caught up in a general competition. At any time the contest involves the relative numbers of jobs available and people wanting them. There is a finite number of openings for work, and all seekers become rivals affecting one another. Every success deducts from the pool of chances. Persons looking for jobs distribute themselves according to available opportunities. In an overcrowded field, some will try elsewhere.[2] The daytime offers the most opportunities; most of the population prefers daytime jobs, and they are chosen first.[3] The people who lose out in the competition migrate for employment, and some of them find it at night. Knowing that there are more males and more young persons on the streets, we may assume that many of them are going to or coming from their jobs. Those are also the characteristics of shift workers.

Many occupational careers start with assignments at night. Employment on evening and night shifts is a passage along which young people will advance toward the main social timetable. The cub reporter's first salaried position on a daily newspaper begins on the 7 P.M. to 2 A.M. shift. In the post office and in the printing industry newcomers must accept after-dark schedules.[4] These openings allow them a foothold in the labor force, and they wait their turn to fill a day shift opening. The medical interne accepts a thirty-six-hour span of duty in the hospital. Beginning law associates stay at the office late and even overnight to complete research reports. Aside from being more vigorous, more of the young group are unmarried. Being without the ties and commitments that accumulate with age, it is easier for them to adapt to opportunities at any hour. Moving up in rank also means moving to more desirable working hours, as when hospital internes who perform overnight duty switch to days upon becoming resident physicians. In other cases, years may pass before one can make the move, but as daytime slots become available, seniority, if nothing else, ultimately delivers the chance.

Evening and night work is composed of higher proportions of blue-collar and service jobs than white-collar and professional occupations.[5] Therefore more people whose social circumstances lead mainly to blue-collar and service vocations will be recruited to the night. Differences in education, training, and social contacts, and discriminatory hiring practices put minority groups and immigrants in that category. Blue-collar and service occupations employ relatively more blacks than whites.[6] Recent immigrants are handicapped in the labor market because they lack education and language skills. Some industrial companies manage to sustain their operations after dark only by hiring foreign-born workers.[7] The London Transport system had difficulty providing its scheduled services at all hours when its supply of immigrant labor for the less attractive shift jobs dwindled.[8] In the economically strong countries of Europe, "guest workers" from other countries work more at night.

Blue-collar occupations also employ more males, and to that extent more men than women work after dark. In some nations certain after-hours jobs were effectively reserved for males because of laws prohibiting women from working then. The statutes were imposed mainly for the protection of females, on the assumption that they are physically less able to labor after dark, and for the sake of preserving women's roles in family life.[9] In England permission for women to work at night requires authorization from the Secretary of State for Employment or an exemption order from the Health and Safety Executive. Reflecting the increasing emphasis on equal opportunities between the sexes, officials are rapidly granting exemptions as asked.[10] The United States no longer bars females from working at night, but fear is a filter keeping their numbers lower. Discouraged by crime and risks to their personal safety, fewer seek after-dark jobs. Just as those who dreaded the Blackfoot Indians did not step into Montana, older persons as well as women are less likely to step out at night.[11]

Psychological and economic needs, however, stifle those trepidations. Women with young children turn to shift work as a way of gaining independence without abandoning their responsibilities as parents. Economic pressures on single-parent families reverse the customary pattern for the sexes, especially within occupations filled by minority groups. As porters and office housekeepers, males usually work daytimes and females work evenings and nights.[12] A woman who cleans offices at night says, "If we weren't poor, we wouldn't be out here at night. . . . It's just a matter of need, that's all."[13]

The United States Current Population Survey,[14] which monitors employed persons' working hours for their principal jobs, generally confirms these predictions. (See Table 4–1.) Higher percentages of younger people work evenings and nights. More of the youngest group (16–34) work evenings, and fewest of the oldest group (over fifty-four) work from midnight to 8 A.M.[15] As for sex of workers by shifts, more males work on night shift and more females work evenings. The percentage of females in the evening is so large because they outnumber males in part-time work as their principal job. More than 2.5 million women work part time on the evening shift, while 1.66 million men work part time then.

Blacks work after dark in greater proportions than other workers, especially on the midnight shift, when 4.1 percent of them are

TABLE 4–1:

Percentages of Workers by Hours of Day in the United States in 1980 by Age, Race and Ethnicity, and Sex (Full-Time and Part-Time Combined)

	Day	Evening	Night	Other[a]	Number (Thousands)[b]
1. Age					
16–34	77.2%	16.1%	3.1%	3.6%	39,656
35–54	85.6	7.2	3.1	4.1	27,711
Over 54	86.3	7.4	2.4	3.9	10,330
2. Race/ethnic					
White	81.6	11.5	2.9	4.0	68,702
Black	79.6	13.5	4.1	2.8	7,586
Hispanic	82.4	11.1	2.8	3.7	3,968
3. Sex[c]					
Male	80.2	11.3	3.6	4.9	43,457
Female	82.8	12.3	2.3	2.6	34,238

[a]The "Other" category represents odd work schedules, including split shifts and work spans longer than 1.5 shifts.
[b]Differences in overall totals among age, sex, and racial and ethnic categories result partly from rounding and partly because the data are taken from different tables in the Survey.
[c]If only full-time workers are counted, the distributions by sex are:

	Day	Evening	Night	Other	Thousands
Male	82.9%	8.3%	3.6%	5.2%	39,154
Female	87.7	6.9	2.5	2.9	24,760

SOURCE: From the Current Publication Survey carried out by the U.S. Bureau of Labor Statistics, May 1980. A portion of the people on any given shift are rotating personnel. Individuals are substituted in the rotations from one week to another but that does not alter the distributions by types of people.

on duty, as against 2.9 percent of the whites. But the only available evidence to test the idea that more immigrants labor on shifts did not support it for Hispanics, although it may be borne out for other immigrant groups. Hispanics show work schedules much like those of whites. Perhaps that is because they are not fully distributed throughout the United States. The five Southwestern states of California, Arizona, New Mexico, Colorado, and Texas have the largest Spanish-speaking populations in the United States, and in those states some relevant blue-collar jobs are not shift work. In California, for example, about 250,000 Chicano and Mexican itinerant workers are employed as fruit and vegetable pickers; it is mainly daytime labor and represents 6.3 percent of the Hispanic work force, large enough to influence the findings.[16]

One does not have to be young, poor, a minority group member, or a recent immigrant to feel economic pressures. In a recession there are fewer jobs available for everyone, competition is more intense, and more persons from all social groups turn to the night when the chances for day work are slimmer. During the 1981 recession in the United States a white pilot who flew planes for a nighttime air cargo company said: "If I worked for one of the big airlines I'd be unemployed right now. This way, at [company] I'm a chief pilot."[17]

Others who take shift work do so for extra earnings. Firms often pay a premium to compensate for the inconveniences of working after dark and sometimes give an extra bonus to workers who accept a rotating schedule. At an aluminum plant in Indiana the president of the local union says, "Our people don't squawk about shifts . . . The money's there, and our people are going for the money."[18] A man in a copper tubing factory tells a typical story of only being able to get a night job originally, and now that he makes $24 extra each week with the shift differential, he turns down offers to move him to days because it would pull down his earnings.[19] Nylon spinners in England accept shift work because they are paid more.[20] Taxi drivers who prefer to work at night say they receive bigger tips then from people who are out for a good time. The higher earnings are not always direct wages and may come through a saving on work-related costs. At a Midwestern university, in addition to the shift work differential, custodial workers had the privilege of using the parking lot without paying.[21] For some persons everywhere, the premium for a night schedule is worth more than easy hours, and the wages lure them there even though they can find work in the daytime.

Shift work also makes it easier to have more than one job. In France, workers who had difficulty making ends meet acknowledged that they chose a late shift because it afforded free time, which they used to hold a second job during the day.[22] The overriding reason some workers in the United States gave for wanting to retain their shifts is that the schedule allowed them to have two jobs.[23] Many night factory workers interviewed in another survey reported that they either had a second job or ran their own small businesses.[24]

To jobholding couples who have small children, shift work offers offsetting schedules as a way of dividing child care. One of the two adopts off-hours work and they take turns caring for their children.[25] If the husband works during the day, the wife looks after their offspring and is free to take employment when he comes home to substitute for her. This arrangement may help explain the large number of women working part time in the evenings. (See footnote c in Table 4–1).[26] Every couple must contend with the possibility of overlapping schedules when they work. In one family the wife worked the night shift and her husband was on day shift in his job. When their first child was born the arrangement seemed promising, because they could take turns with their baby. But he had to leave for his shop before she reached home, because her shift ended only a half hour before his starting time. Every morning they would arrive at a point on a busy highway where they would stop their cars on opposite sides. The father, who had brought their baby along from the house, would step across the road through the traffic with the infant in his arms and hand it to its mother. He then continued to work while she took their baby back home.

Staying awake long after midnight may also express a penchant for the quiet and splendid solitude. Writers, artists, and others who could labor at any hour prefer the dark because it is tranquil and freer of interruptions. Here the appeal of working at night is not financial but to escape the commotions of the daytime. Artists in the music industry often avoid daytime recording sessions and work at night because it is quieter. They deal with fewer intrusions and fewer disturbances from the vibrations of trucks passing in the street. The calm at night attracts people involved in creative intellectual tasks, who justify the habit by saying they can concentrate better. Perhaps, as a result of this parting from the ordinary world, working in an arena floating among shadows and odd hours, a sense of release from space and time descends on them and they become bolder and more creative in their efforts. The night's less structured qualities allow more room for fantasies about mysterious worlds. Without the reminders of well-entrenched formats and customs, the isolation and amorphousness allows them to idealize possibilities and contrast them with familiar conditions. They escape for the sake of productivity.

Escape also has high priority among tactics that people of all ages use to deal with social-psychological problems. They want release from the harness of a hectic pace or to be concealed from scrutiny and unpleasant attention. Emotionally difficult entanglements, trying mates, risky exposures and overexposures, and social annoyances dispirit them, and they consider withdrawing. They daydream about running away and starting over again. The emphasis on facing one's problems and trying to work them out is a policy conditioned by the absence of a reasonable escape alternative. Retreat is often preferred if there is a realm to go to.[27] Almost every long-distance road, train, and bus carries someone who has pulled up stakes and is moving with baggage and hopes to a new locale.

Now a temporal safety valve is at hand. One does not have to strive to resolve matters by negotiation or compromise or to endure the wearying daytime life. Night offers an exit from troublesome interpersonal situations, a way to evade certain social groups or daytime's crowds and pace in general. And it is so accessible that its slower tempos and calm are turned to more often than other alternatives.

Most of us have enjoyed the experience of walking at night along a street that is ordinarily jammed during the day. Persons who are astir then regularly report feeling relief from the crush and anonymity of daytime life. Chafing under the obligations of ordinary society, they find their private place at night. The stillness of late hours appeals especially to young people, who come to feel that they possess the streets. Strolling outside, they inhale the clear air and pause at corners where the vistas widen. Each person feels distinct in the surroundings. A newsboy wrote a poem declaring that the rising sun shone for him alone as he coasted on his bicycle de-

livering papers at dawn. A security guard who is also a painter said
he liked to watch the sun come up and then go home and paint.[28]
The serenity, the sparseness, and the easier pace strike a chord. Even
daytimers who happen to be outside as the night draws to an end
are exhilarated in the early morning before the crowds appear.

Some escape from family tensions. Moving away in hours is a
means of distancing oneself from quarrels while still living in the
same place. It is cheaper to move out of phase than to move out of
the house. A man who worked as a printer acknowledged the opportunity this way: "Night workers don't have to punch the family
time clock."[29] One boy who could not meet his parents' expectations
about homework used to stay up so late that he was incapable of
being wakened in time to go to school next morning. Teenagers will
not eat with the family and will keep late hours away with friends
to avoid dominating or questioning parents. They try to dodge disputes and being nagged, although the very tactic of keeping late
hours evokes new pressures and admonitions from their elders. Time
separations insulate spouses from one another just as separate bedrooms do. Husbands work late in the garage or in the basement and
do not go to bed at the same time as their wives. The splintered
schedule relieves both parties. It may be a prelude to divorce, but
it may also be an alternative to it.

Shift work is sometimes said to be the cause of marital strife,
but it is also a haven from such discord. A couple may schedule
their employment so that they see each other rarely and thus min-
imize the chances for friction.[30] Considering the strains of contemporary married life and the wide range of tactics—including eva-
sion—that people use to cope, the connection between shift work
and the quality of a marriage probably has influences going one
way as the other.

The nighttime seems to harbor a different culture, a little Boh-
emia of artists and poets and literati, along with street people,
homeless persons, carousers, pushers, pimps, and prostitutes. That
such men and women are active then tells us the night gives freedom and safety for nonconformists and marginal persons. After-
dark society bespeaks a tolerant milieu. People who have an eccentric manner or an unusual appearance, or who follow disapproved
pursuits, would rather avoid contacts with the daytime majority.
Too frequently those contacts are strained and tinged with harassment. Parting company is a simple way to ease the strain, so they

retreat to times when most others are gone.[31] A woman explained that she had a habit of talking out loud and developed the custom of walking at night. Homosexuals are not naturally nocturnal. They often lead double lives, concealing their disposition during the daytime and waiting until near midnight to join their friends at gay bars. Night offers them more security because observability and the pressures for conformity have eased.

Incessance brings legitimate reasons for being unavailable. One can give a night job as an excuse. The diffused community schedule also has room for other arrangements. The hours can serve almost anyone, and a wider variety of people step into the night from time to time. In this respect the after-dark population is almost like that of the general society. Night has its habituées, but it has many more transients from the humdrum day.

Recreational opportunities multiplied in the early decades of this century, and people flocked to clubs, theaters, restaurants, and saloons. Artificial lighting blazed the way to places of enjoyment. The first performance at midnight in America came at a New York theater in 1911. A New York cabaret named the Midnight Frolic made its appearance in the same decade.[32] A writer whose pen overflowed as much as his heart gave forth about Broadway:

> I stood the other night looking northward from Forty-Second Street, into a narrowing cañon of illumination. . . . The Broadway signs are our folk-art writ in fire on the sky. They are quite as worthy of attention, perhaps, as the songs of the Cumberland mountaineers. . . . When I turn into Broadway by night and am bathed in its Babylonic radiance, I want to shout with joy, it is so gay and beautiful. I melt into the river of pleasure-seekers.[33]

These raptures, like those an explorer might jot down on a mountain crest or at the gate of a valley, were brought on as well by loosening the strictures against after-dark merriment. Big and small amusements drew the populace. Once the province of males only, cabarets became respectable places for both sexes. When the public gave approval for all to attend the follies, it signaled more broadminded codes. In the 1920s New York's Mayor Jimmy Walker spoke for the attitudes when he said it was a sin to go to bed the same day you got up.[34]

Now all kinds of people stay up late for revelry. They drink and flirt and make merry at neighborhood bars, resorts, casinos, assemblies for sports, and at conventions for politicians, academicians, and businessmen. Mardi Gras, folk festivals, jazz concerts, and informal parties are breakouts from the institutionalized timetables that usually bind people's lives. They celebrate release not only by what they do but also by when they do it, by flouting the ordinary schedule of wakefulness.

The large numbers who stay up for temporary relief may mislead us into thinking that the regulars who are there for escape have also come to the scene voluntarily. In a job-oriented society, it is easy to believe that people who need work are forced to the night whereas people who want serenity simply choose to move there. But one person may be as driven by feelings of persecution as another by joblessness and economic need. Escape and opportunity are both powerful motives. Tumult and harassment force people from a region just as intense competition for jobs and subsistence does. Both kinds of migrations take place in space or in time.

The issue of whether we choose to or must be active at night calls attention to a possible role of our bodies in the timing of wakefulness. People have a biologically based disposition to stay up later. Maybe some are sent by their bodies to nights. Human biology is often assumed to set the boundaries and force us to act within its limits; it may be in the physical makeup of some individuals to be "owls."

Many physiological functions show a twenty-four-hour rhythm in their high and low levels. The list of processes with such a cycle is long and includes the rate of breathing, heartbeat, blood pressure, urine excretion, presence of iron and of sugar and of white corpuscles in the blood, body temperature, secretion of various hormones, decision speed in the brain, the rate of cell division, liver function, amino acid levels, DNA synthesis, and RNA synthesis. Their periodicity is called circadian, after the Latin phrase meaning "about a day." Some, like pulse, breathing, and temperature, normally increase their levels from morning onward and reach a peak during early afternoon. They ease off by evening and decline during sleep, until early the following morning when they begin to rise again. Each function has its own cycle, but all of them work in harmony. Some coincide in their timing, others follow one another in fixed sequences, and the synchronization among all is so clear-cut and regular that we refer to it as the body's clock.[35]

Although the disposition for daily fluctuations in the physiological processes is inherent, their actual timing is affected by when we are active and by outside light. We respond to the environmental cues of light and dark. More peaks in our body's rhythms are coupled to the daylight phase. Light stimulates physiological activity, and that is why it is usually easier to get out of bed on a sunny morning than on an overcast one. Although the mechanism is not fully understood, we know that the duration and amount of light are monitored by a group of brain cells.[36] That nerve center takes part in interpreting the length of daylight (the photoperiod) and acts as a pacemaker to synchronize physiological functions coincident with periods of activity and repose.[37]

The rhythms complete their rounds in about a day, but humans have a natural disposition for a slightly longer circadian cycle. People who were studied in caves or in windowless rooms, illuminated at all hours so they could not tell which phase of the light–dark cycle existed outside, allowed to follow their own sleep–wake schedules, spontaneously showed free-running rhythms that averaged close to a twenty-five-hour period.[38] They tended to stay up longer and repeatedly lagged behind the passage of days. The same number of hours that composed twenty-four days on our calendars would be apportioned over twenty-three daily cycles as a result of their routines. Our inbred disposition is therefore being compressed into twenty-four-hours by the natural environment (the photoperiod) and the social environment (explicit schedules of work and appointments). Most people would otherwise stay up longer. A trait like this, which characterizes an entire species, always has a corollary: Among members of the species there is substantial variation. The free-running rhythm is 24.8 to 25 hours on the average, but there are considerable individual differences, which may be genetic or may have resulted from early conditioning. Persons who are on the longer side of the twenty-five-hour average (knowable by measuring their free-running rhythms) have their inborn dispositions squeezed the most and probably feel most uncomfortable by the constraints of the natural day and community schedules fitted to it. Here is a biological basis for people to become "night persons." They would be strongly inclined to stay awake later, and of course as they indulged in their bent they would have trouble awakening next morning. Body temperament could therefore play a part in selecting which persons would be active at night.

That influence, however, is relatively subtle and is usually masked by external influences, as the behavior of other animal species tells us. We think of animals as being more controlled by their biological makeup than humans are, and less able to act against innate or physiological dispositions. If they are diurnal or nocturnal, we would expect them to continue that way. If something threatens their survival in their home range, we would expect them to disperse in space. Yet they also use the tactic of retreating in time.

A century ago the African buffalo was abundant until a severe epidemic of rinderpest in 1890 almost exterminated it in many places. Rinderpest is a high-mortality, contagious viral disease that affects cattle. These normally daytime animals defend themselves against predators by forming close-packed circles, facing outward, with pregnant females and the young huddling in the centers. As the epidemic raged on, there must have been too few buffalo in one place to form secure circles. Whereas they used to feed in herds in the open by day, the survivors retreated to forests and dense swamps and fed only at night. Several years later, after the epidemic abated and their numbers increased, the buffalo resumed their former daytime habits.[39]

A well-known experiment in which overly dense colonies of rats were established in pens supplied a similar pertinent finding. Rats are ordinarily nocturnal, but once a social hierarchy developed in the crowded pens, some harried individuals withdrew from the ordinary times of activity and prowled about to glean food when most of the others were asleep. Subordinate males in the pens developed the habit of arising early—that is, in the daytime—when they could eat and drink in peace.[40]

If animals switch to nocturnal or diurnal schedules for the purposes of escape and subsistence, then their biological tendencies cannot be strong in this respect. Biological leanings are subordinate to social conditions in settling whether or not an animal will be active at night. If it can happen in species we think are governed more by their biology, then it applies to humans as well. Other circumstances must be decisive in affecting who will or will not be a night person.

Nor is the explanation lodged in a certain type of personality. Workers who have after-dark occupational commitments are not the types, in either mood or outlook, that want to be active then. Most of them are not devoted to the night, as they demonstrate on their days off by habitually readjusting their schedules to join in the daytime community. The greater proportions of young people, males, and members of minority groups among shift workers fit the familiar picture of migration in search of economic opportunity to improve one's lot and not of a deep psychic affinity for darkness.

The main cause of being active at night is the nature of social commitments already made and whether people have the autonomy to change them. Most of us are disposed to stay up later but can do so only if our schedules allow it. If we have to work the next morning, we suppress our tendency to be owls and drag ourselves from cozy beds to meet daytime obligations. Those who have to work at night suppress any tendency to be early birds. In both instances circadian rhythms yield to social commitments. Making a decision to stay up late overrides the body's clock and imposes a timetable that it cannot resist.

Many who say they are night people turn out to have the privilege of setting their own schedules. They can choose when to stay awake and when to sleep because their social status gives them autonomy. Professional people, college students, academicians, and self-employed persons such as free-lancers have such control. People who work at home have discretion over when they will work and are more likely to slide into a timetable that includes being up at night. The wealthy who do not work stay up at will. All these groups are usually free of compulsory schedules and can arrange to be awake later and sleep later the next day.

The unemployed are also not constrained to follow regular hours. Jobless persons lose touch with community schedules. In a study of some of them, it was found that if the clocks in their homes stopped, they left them unadjusted.[41] In the city unemployed young men get up late and come out on the street late.[42] People who do not work, but who are at an age when one customarily holds a job, sleep a good deal. Maybe some of them shun public appearances during the main working day in order to avoid the contrast between themselves and others who are employed.

One final process decides who is active at night. The full answer to the question does not end with describing all those who move to the setting, for not everyone stays. One of the effects of migration is on the migrant. Some people find they fit well in the new milieu, and they remain and thrive. Others, though they have more trouble adjusting, manage to adapt and become assimilated after a period of tribulation. They will be changed by the experience itself, developing characteristics suitable to fitting in and holding on. Some fail to adapt and return to the day; their choice did not end with making the move to night. Biological and personality factors may not have swayed the initial moves so much, but they can become more critical in the challenge of adjusting to the nighttime environment. All persons are tested by its demands; only those who reach a passable adaptation stay on.[43] According to the findings of a Norwegian study, which reported that about 20 percent of the people who tried it could not adapt to night jobs, shift workers are a survivor group.[44] Actual experience supports or revokes the move to the night after it is made.

Looking at nighttimers, it is easy to forget that some other types of people may have tried it too. But on every frontier only a portion of the people who venture there find the fit good enough to stay. The milieu drives out those who do not fit well psychologically or biologically. Success or failure to sleep at odd hours, for example, is probably a strong influence in adapting. Its impact is felt quickly. The capacity of the body may be decisive, and those who have great difficulty sleeping in daylight will retreat from night work. Some of the stayers suppress their dislikes and resort to rationalizations about the pleasures of privacy and elbow room. Since one's self-image is conditioned by one's environment, they begin to view themselves as special personalities because of the context of after-dark activity. There will always be a portion of the population that finds advantage in an unusual niche.

5

Adversity and Good Will

To dwellers in the center of society, it is extraordinary that pioneers are so cooperative and generous while facing challenge and danger. That is a hallmark of frontiers which invites an interpretation of pioneers' character. Their conduct is so admirable, and noticeably unlike that in secure settlements, that folklore makes them out to be a special breed, bolder and more humane than their kin in more comfortable surroundings.

In spite of all the risks and rigors in the West, its settlers were noted for their helpfulness and warmth even toward strangers. At first such accounts of openhanded hospitality may seem inconsistent with the reputation of a lawless territory. It appears to confound reason. Why, in the face of hardships and scarcity, do frontier people act generously to others, even to persons they do not know? They do so because lawlessness and friendliness are related. Isolated settlers were drawn together in fellowship as a result of loneliness and shared fears of desperados. In the face of threats from outlaws, Indians, and raw nature, members of frontier communities intensified their cooperation.[1] Their unity was also boosted by clashes with Easterners over transportation rates and by the feeling that Easterners looked down on them and belittled their manners and character. Hard times promote a spirit of solidarity among people who realize that they have challenges in common and that they live as equals in the face of risk and threat.

Maybe that tendency is ingrained, for the same behavior is found throughout the animal kingdom. "[T]here is not a single gregarious animal species," Konrad Lorenz wrote, "whose individuals do not press together when alarmed, that is, whenever there is a suspicion that a predator is close at hand."[2] In reactions to crime, the anxiety that spreads among humans draws them together. They close ranks and cling to one another in the face of danger.[3] In a psychological experiment, when a researcher arranged a condition of outside threat, he found that strangers wanted to associate with one another. Being together in the same boat allowed each person to appraise and adjust his feelings and reduced anxiety for all.[4] People appreciate not being alone if they find themselves in a predicament. Stress becomes more bearable and danger less awesome when they confront it with others. That is how good will emerges in adversity.

The conditions found in the West are reiterated at night. Those who are up and about then encounter social challenge as well as physical danger. Daytimers oppose some after-dark activity because they are not participants and yet live nearby. Their households may go to sleep but be unable to retreat fully from what is happening. Pedestrians chat outside. Young people gather after midnight at twenty-four-hour stores that have become rendezvous for socializing and make a racket or start a brawl. Street lights shine around the edges of window shades and onto the walls of the bedrooms. Vehicles rumble by. Some dwellings are so cross-cut at all hours by trajectories of sound—clattering on the tracks, whine in the air lanes, and drone on the expressway—that there is a constant loud hiss inside even with the windows shut.[5]

Because they cannot insulate themselves from those surroundings, daytimers are galled over losing their sleep. They are riled by the nighttime din of voices and vehicles, by the hissings and clankings of mills. Their bedrooms are invaded by ground-shaking construction work and thundering airplanes, as well as by raucous passersby and the clamor from persons congregating at the always-open shops. Topping their feeling of harassment from actual decibels is their indignation at losing the sleeping privileges they took for granted. Tradition and the norms of comfort are on their side. Sleep is supposed to insulate them from the impositions of others.[6] So they introduce formal prohibitions against the endeavors of nighttimers. They persuade municipal licensing boards to restrict noisy projects at night. They make drilling and dynamiting for subway construction taboo. Zoning ordinances bar trucks from rumbling through residential areas after dark. At airports they try to ban night flights. New laws trim the late hours of saloons, fast-food outlets, and all-night groceries. Apartment leases stipulate that no loud sounds may be made after a certain hour. At work or at play nighttimers learn that a large, drowsy population wants them to keep their noise down.

Of all the curbs imposed, none is more certain to spark disputes as the objection to airplane flights after dark. Residents in neighborhoods surrounding airports bring lawsuits against cities and the airports for the vexation caused by jet planes taking off and zooming overhead. A man living near the Los Angeles airport testified during one litigation: "You'd either be sleeping or watching TV or something at night and you'd swear that the plane was coming right into your house. I couldn't get away from it." On that occasion the court agreed that people near the airport become nervous and irritable because of jet noise interfering with their lives, and the man won his case against the city for suffering mental and emotional distress.[7] In turn the night groups rally to oppose the constraints. In communities where curfews on night flights are sought, aviation organizations and government agencies sue to prevent the bans. They fought the prohibition on night flights at the county airport in Westchester, a suburb north of New York City. There the federal judge struck down the injunction as being unreasonable, arbitrary, and too broad.[8] An administrator of the Federal Aviation Administration explained his bureau's efforts to block another airport's night closing by describing how chances for spatial expansions of airport facilities had become limited and concluding that in such circumstances "it is essential that we squeeze all the capacity out of the present airport system that we can."[9] Usually daytimers fail to halt the flights if the night group makes concessions to lower the level of noise.

Frontier and core wrangled over this issue in Boston. The city's Logan Airport is flanked by residential neighborhoods, and its after-dark activity became a nuisance to people wanting an undisturbed night's sleep. In 1976 dwellers in those neighborhoods, as private citizens and through two organized groups—Fair Share and the Massachusetts Air Pollution and Noise Abatement Committee—made a concerted effort to stop flights between 11 P.M. and 7 A.M.

It led to counterarguments by the business community stressing the economic benefit of continuing the flights. Commercial interests, airline companies, unions, and airport employees holding jobs at night (some of whom lived in those neighborhoods) formed a pro-nighttime alliance. They contended that the curfew would result in the loss of thousands of jobs and millions of dollars in sales, and further would discourage business investment in New England. Joined by the governor, the mayor, and many legislators, the co-alition won a decision from the Massachusetts Port Authority that the nighttime flights should continue. A plan for reducing aircraft noise was included. One month later Eastern Airlines announced it was adding an airbus and expanding its staff at the airport as a direct result of the decision not to impose a night curfew. As one businessman remarked, "The curfew decision was regarded as the shootout at the OK Corral."[10]

Without the benefit of prior design to accomplish the change-over, without explicitly formulating principles of how it will operate, the community that put forth the frontier has to accommodate to a merger with it. No disinterested referee comes to the fore to reconcile the differences between the two groups. Each side musters what power it can exert to its own advantage, or at least to block the other side and force a compromise.

An invasion energizes the group defending its territory, and the contest usually ends up in its favor. Therefore we would expect day-timers to repel the noisy intrusions. Why do the nighttimers win some of the disputes over disturbing the community's sleep? The core has transferred some of its prowess by investing in the offshoot, just as the East did for the West. Daytime contributes sponsorship, funds, and hardy personnel to the night. The undermanned frontier also benefits from the support of daytime parties interested in financial profit. Inasmuch as these constituents weigh in the outcome of clashes over nighttime activity, they testify to the settled center's effectiveness in nurturing the new outpost as much as it confirms the latter's growing strength. The night group's momentum of success also adds power, for only after it has established itself and proved its importance can it mount a serious effort to continue.

Perhaps the most potent rallying force is that the frontier perceives more menace in the confrontations, that it has more to lose. Usually in a territorial conflict, those who invade it want the same things for the same purposes as those who defend it. However, in clashing over nighttime, both parties clearly distinguish between using those hours for work and using them for slumber. The night group fights harder because its jobs and profits are at stake. Feelings about those matters mobilize a group more effectively than does distress over losing sleep.

Aside from those skirmishes, many daytimers pay little attention to the people who are employed regularly late at night. Notwithstanding their resentment over being disturbed, daytimers seem unaware that ordinary persons are active then, or they view night work with distaste and mix pity with condescension when they meet a shift worker. Even inside a twenty-four-hour organization day staffers have little contact with their after-dark counterparts. In Boston in the holiday season, when a commercial computing center planned a Christmas party, its daytime and nighttime crews chose to hold separate celebrations because the workers knew hardly anyone on the other shift. A chaplain on the night shift in Kansas City declared: "They call us 'the forgotten people.' " A courier who transfers payroll checks and canceled checks among several towns after dark said, "Day people don't realize that there are people who work at night. . . . You know that last place we stopped? My sister-in-law works there and she didn't know I was the one delivering there."[11] Houston's City Council passed an ordinance requiring that its dance halls close at 2 A.M., the state law's deadline for serving liquor, in order to ensure that drinking would not continue thereafter. Within two days, besieged by protests from discotheque dancers and club owners, the council members decided to vote for an amendment to allow late dancing on Friday and Saturday nights and nights before major holidays. The mayor acknowledged that the city administration had not known how much dancing went on that late.[12]

Consequently the attitudes of nighttimers toward daytimers resemble those of Westerners toward Easterners a century ago. They see the conflicts of interest and they lament the gaps in understanding. Nighttimers may have different perspectives on many matters, but they are brought together by their realization of a common fate and a common opponent. Georg Simmel observed that, insofar as they have a similar practical interest against a third party, people who ordinarily have little to do with one another appreciate that they belong together.[13] It is a pragmatic reaction too, for joining a group multiplies the resources that can be marshaled against the odds. A group can often do things more effectively than each person acting alone. This new group blossoms with comradeship and cooperation and bristles with resentment and hostility toward the outside party.[14]

Nighttimers also have more diffuse threats to cope with. They are apprehensive about assaults and crimes. Deterrents are slight where public scrutiny is missing and police coverage is sparse. The activity of footpads and muggers is itself a sign of the colonization of night, for predators haunt locales where they expect to find prey. Cities, particularly, are thought to be risky after dark. In the United States the populace views urban settings as hazardous once evening passes and has misgivings about going outside.[15] In London too, a man commented on the changing times: "Years ago you had the pub at the corner. . . . Basically, of a night-time. . . . You could walk about anywhere. No one would touch an elderly person if they came out of the pub drunk and rolled down the street. They'd help her up and she'd have her purse and her money, everything on her next morning. She wouldn't wake up to find someone had gone to her pocket."[16]

Neighborhood residents stop taking lone walks. A church canceled its evening mass because its elderly worshippers were being mugged. Small businesses, newsstands, and drugstores close earlier because of robberies. Fearful drivers will not take their taxicabs out at night for the same reason. Larger firms that are unable to protect their employees from harassment on the streets abandon plans to stay open after dark. A sole pedestrian prepares to flee if a muscular stranger approaches to ask directions. Even streetwalkers begin to shun certain vicinities. A well-publicized assault prompts women to change their traveling habits and to ask permission to leave work earlier. In many places women and older people simply stay indoors. Apartment houses with their sentries at the portals become vertical stockades to which city dwellers retreat at night.

In that kind of milieu, the most fearful do not venture forth. Older persons and females, who are most uneasy and would shrink from others who approach them at night, stay inside their houses after dark. Outside, meanwhile, the rising crime rate leads citizens and businesses to protest, and the municipality introduces more police patrols and extended street lighting. One of the original reasons for illuminating the avenues of London and Paris was to discourage criminals. Adults have long believed that lighting contributes to security.[17] If out at night, aware that they are in a risky environment, they want to congregate and be reassured. They need each other and they seek each other out. They gather in places that remain open for business and bask in more gregariousness. The sense of safety that spreads over people together in a coffee shop or a diner after midnight fosters cheer and camaraderie there.

And on the streets, those who go out are conscious of peril. It governs their behavior in a certain way. They have committed themselves to being abroad. They are more alert to strangers whom they pass on the street. Each tries to judge whether the other is potentially dangerous, and each one's frame of mind shifts from vigilance to expansiveness after deciding that the other is to be trusted. If not foe, then friend. Outdoors, strangers feel a togetherness even if they do not have a personal relationship or know one another. They are conscious of themselves as distinctive, and that forges a common identity and increases their mutual attraction. A young man explained, "At 4 A.M. if someone sees you walking the streets at the same time he does, he must think, 'Gee, this guy must be part of the brethren, because no one else is awake at these times.' "

It is a principle of humanity that empathy and helpfulness are aroused indiscriminately when fate itself seems indiscriminate. When fate appears to be inflicting harm aimlessly or universally, people sense they are vulnerable in common. Accordingly, even in cities that have been portrayed as arenas of aloofness, people act differently after dark and create a public mood of more helping and warmth. They become more willing to cast their lot with each other. Mutual concern is transformed into friendliness among strangers. And so, in the middle of the night, denizens of the dark are drawn toward one another and are more kind and outgoing than people are at other times of day.

This prediction from the frontier hypothesis is more controversial than most. Does not fear lead to avoiding strangers at night? Chances of criminal assault could scare cordiality out of nighttime settings. People could give in to anxieties about being attacked, which would discourage encounters among people who do not know one another. They would avoid strangers in public places.

The issue deserved to be assessed directly, so the prediction was tested. Experiments were carried out in several parts of Boston over all twenty-four hours across all days of the week. The studies were conducted on 166 separate occasions during the summer, fall, and winter seasons. In all, more than 2,500 people were observed and rated on how they behaved towards others in public. The researchers were teams of couples dressed like ordinary people, acting naturally. The situations were common ones, and there was no inkling that the people knew they were being judged on their cooperativeness and sociability. The events passed as ordinary encounters in daily life.

The experiments were carried out on the streets. The streets are favorable sites for such evaluations because preexisting ties among persons there are minimal. Strangers come together. They reflect the heterogeneity of an urban area. They are supposedly indifferent to others' need for help or, in the unsupervised milieu of public places, reserved because they do not know whom to trust. Out on the streets at night, one of the initial elements of frontiers is reiterated, the setting is less structured because people are sparse and some communal activities have ceased. The experiments (described in detail in Appendix B) dealt with ordinary situations that are part of the stream of common social events, not emergencies to which one has to respond under stress. They focused on the willingness of people to give time, attention, and personal warmth to others.

In one test a couple asked directions to a well-known location. In response a few passersby shuddered evasively and darted away. They veered from the speaker as if dodging a panhandler. Some avoided the issue by acting as if they did not realize an appeal had been made. One person assumed a rigid pose and kept walking, brushing against the couple without speaking. One or two turned to the questioner and uttered an insult or an obscene remark. A few tersely told him to ask someone else. These reactions fulfill the stereotype of a chilly and ominous public setting.

But far more people were helpful. Most strangers provided the directions agreeably. A few apologized for not knowing how to get there. Now and then a person who was approached for directions enlarged the encounter. For example, one woman upon hearing the question answered it and added, "My son lives there." That is, after giving directions, the passerby volunteered something to develop personal contact. Several asked, "Are you tourists here?" and showed a willingness to linger and chat. A few people offered the couple a ride to the destination—"I'll be glad to give you a lift, my car is right here." Such unpretentious moments of friendliness and aid bestow a soothing mood upon the brief encounters among persons in contemporary surroundings. Reaching out toward strangers and assisting them in a modest request furnish community good will.

In a second test, a couple approached passersby and asked them to answer some questions in a survey being conducted about people in cities. The queries concerned one's personal feelings, employment, and living situation. By consenting to the brief interview the stranger would be trusting, whereas urban dwellers are said to avoid revealing themselves to strangers. As in the first test, some passersby gave nasty refusals and some refused politely. Many stopped long enough to answer the questions. The interview seemed to gratify some of them and they welcomed the moment of sociability it afforded. This reaction may itself testify to the stereotype of the city as a lonely place where people do not slow their pace to chat or take an interest in others' feelings. The interviewer's respectful attention was occasionally interpreted as kindness. One young woman talked of her unsparing job and of her difficulties in adjusting to isolation in the large community. After the interview, in the midst of the goodbyes, she said: "I hope I'll see you again and we can talk more."

A third experiment focused on what would happen if a person found a key with an address tag lying in the street. To find a key is to come across an implied need for help. It is like noticing a fire in an empty store or a leak in the dike. No one may be nearby, but the sight itself is a signal. A tagged key on the ground would be recognized as an object of value belonging to someone the finder does not know. A person who sees such a key picks it up and walks a while trying to decide what to do. Would the finder care enough about the stranger who lost it to send it back? The first two tests were face-to-face; in this case, on the other hand, one could feel more insulated from social disapproval if neglecting to return the key. However, of more than three hundred tagged keys that were picked up from the streets and taken away, two-thirds were sent back through the mail immediately.

Many were simply dropped into the mailbox, but a number of people took the trouble to wrap them. A few included letters that said, "I'm glad to have a chance to help you." Others penned advice, "I found this key on _____ Avenue. Be more careful" and, in a similar vein, "We found your key near _____ on December 10th.

In the future it would probably be better to lose your key rather than have the 'wrong' person find it with an address." A clergyman wrote on his church's letterhead, "I found this key on _____ street and am returning it to you. Of course, my specialty is celestial keys."

Three people took the trouble to look up the phone number of the name on the tags and telephone the person. They called to reassure him that his key was in safe hands and would be in the mail soon. One caller also admonished him: "If you're going to be careless and lose your key then don't attach your name and address to it!"

The fourth study was a set of observations carried out in several twenty-four-hour supermarkets. The researcher couple posed as customers and positioned themselves near the checkout line to note the exchanges between customers and clerks at the cash register. As a social setting the supermarket typifies the way of life in a massive community. It generates anonymous meetings between people where no objective reason for sociability exists. Strangers pass one another and meet briefly in highly specific dealings in the market place. It is an arena of the impersonal, segmented, rational contacts that stand for human relations in the city.[18] The checkout clerk, serving hundreds of people daily, barely has time to fill one customer's shopping bag before another confronts her with a pile of groceries.[19]

Sociability was rare at the checkout counter. Three-quarters of all such meetings were limited to identifying prices, paying, and bagging the merchandise. A few people smiled. Fewer chatted. These were the two criteria used to judge sociability. To smile would show some warmth; to chat about something other than the transaction itself would expand the scope of the meeting. Occasionally a customer would address the clerk—"That's a nice shirt; where'd you get it?" or "Are you a high school student? Do you go to _____ school?"—or would report general news. Although that is a narrow measurement of sociability, these are initial, modest steps in developing a personal relationship.

Giving help depends on how direct and personal the plea is and the kind of aid being sought. Some appeals are passive and others are frank in their calls for cooperation. Sociability also takes many forms. The four tests do not cover the entire range of helpfulness and warmth. Nevertheless, to give directions when asked, to consent to be interviewed, to return a lost key, and to be sociable when paying for goods at a checkout counter exemplify the so-called little things that people often refer to when they talk about a humane quality of life. The combined effect of these practices would make a noticeable difference in the social atmosphere. For the mood of each hour, like that of a place, is formed by an accumulation of little events that convey a general feeling. "The trust of a city street," Jane Jacobs wrote, "is formed over time from many, many little public sidewalk contacts. . . . Most of it is ostensibly trivial, but the sum is not trivial at all."[20] Those familiar behaviors are the seeds of more elaborate reciprocity among people who share a community, who become friends, who break the ground for further mutual involvement by adding up small pleasant exchanges.

All the variations in conduct happen at all hours. People are aloof or neglectful of others—and show warmth and give aid— around the clock. The findings of the tests, however, reveal clear differences in the proportions of each act according to time of day. They confirm the idea that nighttime is a period of more helpfulness and friendliness. (See Figure 5–1 and pp. 165–67.) Three of the tests show impressive consistency. Nighttime scores are highest. Not only does it show up best in these three cases, but no other time of day is consistently second best. The atmosphere of sociability and cooperation has a rhythm to it that peaks at night.

In these lights the outcome of the key test is striking. The pattern is clear-cut and contrary to the other situations, for in this experiment nighttimers were the least helpful by far. They returned the smallest proportion (50 percent) of the keys they picked up and made the least extra effort beyond dropping unwrapped keys in the mailbox. If nighttimers are so amiable, why did they not respond to the plight of the key losers as well?

Their behavior testifies that the fear of strangers did not have a dampening effect. If fear ruled, it would have been more inhibiting in face-to-face encounters. Apprehensive people would be more guarded, would shun approaches by strangers, and would give less help if it had to take a personal form. They would see less risk in the passive appeal of a lost key tagged "Please return" and be more willing to drop it in a mailbox. But just the opposite happened. After midnight people on the street were more helpful and friendly toward strangers they met in person, while of the keys

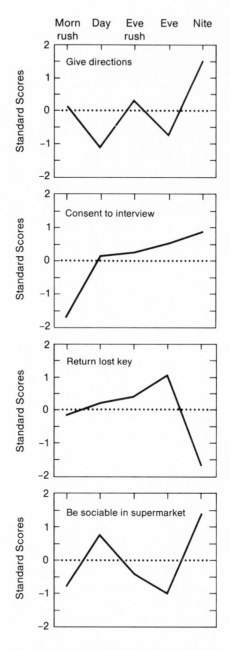

0 = average score of the five time periods.

FIGURE 5–1
Helpfulness and Friendliness over the Twenty-four Hours

picked up they returned the fewest. They clearly distinguished between face-to-face encounters and remote instances and were more obliging in face-to-face situations than in the anonymous one.

The types of people did not make the difference. Conceivably, the public climate at all times of day and night could be a reflection of the kinds of people up and about, since more of certain types are out at certain times. Shift workers, for example, disproportionately young, male, and members of minority groups, make a contribution to the culture of the nighttime that is not limited to their labor. They are abroad both before and after their hours on the job, and they participate and add to the general scene. But such characteristics cannot account for what happened. Because of the sampling procedures, whatever personality types were present at any hour would have been randomly distributed across the tests. A given social type was just as likely to be studied in one experiment as another. If social type did affect behavior, there should be a consistent pattern for the four tests, and it should be so in each time period. The outcomes refute this idea by differing so much among the tests. Indeed, except for the nighttime period, even the three face-to-face tests showed differences within each time of the day as well as among different hours. Given that the random sampling procedures were followed carefully, there is no consistent pattern for the four tests in any time period to support the idea that personal characteristics made a significant difference.

Looser schedules at night can explain some of the helpfulness and friendliness then. In the daytime the pressure of timetables forces people to make their encounters specific and short. An emphasis on meeting obligations punctually hurries them along.[21] They cannot fit in unanticipated meetings and do not linger to talk. The pace becomes easier as dusk falls, and after midnight the tempo slows further. The few who are out then rush less because their schedules are less tightly packed. Having no competing commitments, they feel available to help and to become involved with others, and they are more forthcoming. An experiment demonstrated this by observing people who had to hurry to an appointment when they encountered a person coughing, groaning, and apparently needing help. Only 10 percent of the persons who were late to their appointments stopped to help the crouching and suffering man, whereas 63 percent of those who had ample time stayed to give aid.[22]

That may help to explain why nighttimers are generally more helpful and friendly, but not why they only favor others whom they meet during the night. A more coherent explanation of nighttimers' reactions to the keys, one that also makes the finding compatible with the results of the other tests, is that the nighttimers thought the keys belonged to daytimers. Having found a key and picked it up, they could assume that everyone who passed that way was equally likely to have lost it. There was no visible presence to confirm that its owner was a part of the night. Knowing that they themselves are few, they concluded that the unseen person who lost the key was a daytimer.[23]

People are more friendly and helpful toward others of their own kind. Nighttimers feel comradely toward strangers they meet after dark because they identify with them and are concerned for them. One reason is that they share the risks of danger then. They see that they are equally vulnerable to lawlessness and feel a strong bond with one another. It is a solidarity born of sameness. The second reason is their common opposition to the daytimers, who threaten them as a group. They chafe over being disdained by people who neglect their contribution to community life and who try to restrict their activity. Ban the nighttime airplane flights, and their jobs are threatened. Close the bars and twenty-four-hour stores, and they do not have a place to chat. As night people endure the wranglings over whose claims for the night will take precedence, they band together to struggle for their interests. It is a solidarity of interdependence.[24] Having drawn the conclusion that the anonymous key owner was a daytimer, they were less concerned over that person's need for help. They vented whatever antagonism or unconcern they felt toward daytimers by not returning the keys.

The lesson of this frontier inquiry is that the way people treat each other is not simply an upwelling of a magnanimous spirit or some long-established essence in personal character. It is a creative adaptation to the milieu. It is immediate, situational, and conditional. It pulls some of human nature out of the depths of the individual and locates it at the juncture of dealings among people in their environment. Cordiality and altruism toward strangers arise in conditions of equality in a challenging situation. When everyone is vulnerable either because of random risk (as in street crime) or because of being grouped as a target (as when night activities are opposed), they adopt a "we" feeling. As long as they believe in a randomness to their fate, perceive an equality of vulnerability, and are made similar by an outside threat, they will be more friendly and helpful to one another. These are the conditions that lead nighttimers to act like land pioneers. They feel that danger lurks nearby and they are aware of being opposed by another group. Common interests bind them together. As the environment is mastered, as some individuals acquire personal protection, as risks and vulnerability are no longer equal, people do not identify as much with one another. This is not an explanation of all helping and friendliness, but it fits with what we have noticed everywhere: In a well-established society there is less adversity and less good will than at the precarious edge of human settlement.

6

Incessant Organizations

Because of colonizing the night we give the entire twenty-four hours a new master schedule, with new ways of connecting one day to the next. The natural timetable, in which events are clustered in daylight, is now supplemented by two others. One disperses different activities around the clock; the other stretches a single activity across all the hours. The three forms blend with one another in a more elaborate scheme of social life. Each reflects a different stage in how we use the daily hours. Each new timetable, also, is more novel and less smoothly functioning than the original.

In ancient and agricultural eras we all behaved as if it were a rule to get up at dawn, work in daylight, relax during sundown, and sleep in the dark. As long as light came and went, each segment of the day had its established role and did not contend with any other. Activity ended when the populace went to sleep, and each person could rest knowing that everyone else in the village did the same. All left the fields, the fishing traps, and the shops and suspended the course of human affairs.

The second schedule emerges as affairs reach out from both edges of the daylit boundaries. Wholesale food markets become active earlier in the morning. Theaters stay open later in the evening. Chains of events link up according to the logic of their purpose. Companies specializing in cleaning offices send porters, charwomen, and maintenance men out after business hours. Day and night progressively adapt to each other and enter a fuller partnership. The endeavors themselves are not continuous. They join in appropriate little sequences that displace them into later or earlier times. Some connect haphazardly, as when a late-phased and an early-phased activity reach so far in their own directions that they overlap. They have spread out until they result in overnight connections between one day and the next.

Late-phased events trail the profusion of daylight affairs. Since most people work during the day, their recreation is shunted into evening. As evening arrives the theaters, cinemas, sports arenas, and neighborhood bars begin to thrive. So do the cocktail lounges, cabarets, bordellos, and private drinking clubs. Few of those activities last all night. They take their turns, and as they end other projects begin. Restaurants, dance halls, and public bars shut their doors in the early morning. Private sanitation companies wait for them to close before beginning to collect trash, so that customers will not be disturbed. In San Francisco trash trucks begin collecting at 4 A.M. In Paris street cleaners with wheelbarrows and long-handled shovels are on their rounds by five in the morning.

Early-phased affairs precede the main set of events. Fishermen leave the docks to trawl before sunrise. The boats in Stockholm's interlaced harbor become active about the time its bars and clubs shut down. Elsewhere in those hours, farmers pick crops, bottle milk, and pack eggs. Truckers start their trips to market. Wholesale markets stir as trucks arrive with foodstuffs and flowers so that stores and restaurants will get fresh supplies by breakfast time. Bakers light their ovens, and newspaper delivery vans move out as the market stalls open for business. Tokyo's Tsukiji market is animated by that hour, beginning as the boats return to unload fish and then continuing with arm-waving shouts in the vegetable auction after produce is carted in. In other parts of main towns, since international flights will arrive just after sunrise, customs officials, money changers, luggage handlers, tour guides, bus drivers, and taxi drivers who deal with the passengers make their way to the airport in advance. In city after city, in the half-light of dawn individuals in working clothes carry their lunchboxes and walk purposefully along. Municipal transit systems renew their operations shortly thereafter. By daybreak the personnel of the streets have been replaced and affairs are under way for the community at large.

This timetable shows a tendency to gather rejuvenating tasks in the once-dormant phase. The new order of the day is to rely on nighttime to restore the community's well-being. Many of its projects represent a service connection between one day and the next, functions that overhaul and revive. It is the time to clear the system's arteries, absorb input, replenish stock, update, renovate, and renew.[1] Depots and office buildings are swept and mopped. Down in the subways, crews realign and weld sections of tracks while others clear the track beds of newspapers and candy wrappers. Work squads repair the runways at airports. Road crews work on bridges, tunnels, and intersections.[2] Teams out on the streets cart away garbage and trash. A good-sized portion of the activity is cleaning, repairing, waste removal, and maintenance. In commercial offices the pile-up of orders, invoices, and payments will be recorded by dawn. In supermarkets by late evening cartons of goods are towed into the aisles to be stacked on the shelves before morning. Night serves the day, and by doing so it breaks down the apparent self-sufficiency of the daytime. With this layout over the hours, the community begins to resemble an organism. It becomes more like a living thing that recuperates overnight.

Those distinctively phased, loosely assembled events have achieved a continuity together. They still keep in step with personal tempos, though they take place at odd hours. The people involved still follow cyclical lives. Each endeavor also has a cyclical beat, with daily starts and stops pulsing in the passage of hours. Separate affairs, linking and overlapping, complete the circle of wakefulness.

The third schedule is incessance. Its ventures never stop, they fill the limits of the day. A telephone central exchange, a factory assembly line for goods in great demand, and a metropolitan airport's runways are active all the time.

Such undertakings are usually embedded in formal organizations. The system does not perform all its functions around the clock. By late evening some production lines may shut down, and most administrative offices empty out. But the ongoing project has a timing unlike that of the personnel engaged in it. Each staffer will join in for only a part of the twenty-four-hour period and the organization's schedule will be enacted by people taking turns. This discrepancy between the timetable of the activity and the personal timetables of its staff members is the reason the organization must develop a new form. It introduces special structures and procedures to carry on, and predicaments spring up to reveal that such organizations are still in the throes of working out effective measures. Follow the trail of problems that arise, and they point to adjustments made from earlier designs to later ones. Trace the trail of changes, and they circle about issues of coverage, continuity, and control. Coverage refers to how projects will be staffed with the personnel to carry them out. Continuity entails maintaining a course of action in a habitual, coherent way. Control concerns the supervision of the enterprise and how its decisions will be made.

Personnel replacement is a general rule in organizations. Not only will substitutes be found for those who leave, but employees who stay will occupy a series of positions as they move along their careers.[3] Now, in addition, relays of personnel are introduced by the method called shift work. When some employees leave at the end of their stint, others will come to take over the jobs. A fresh crew streams onto the factory floor as a shift ends and the weary workers leave. A bus driver hands over the ignition key to his replacement, and the bus begins another run. Several times a day, groups of people will replace others and transfer responsibility for the same tasks.

The organization must decide how to assign its personnel. For the sake of coverage, it must allocate teams with the right combination of skills to carry out functions and must substitute them repeatedly. An airplane flight must be staffed with a pilot, copilot, cabin attendants, and sometimes a flight engineer. That crew must be planned for each of the flights offered by the airline. A hospital needs a certain team of nurses, licensed practical nurses, aides, and ward helpers on a ward, for each ward in the hospital. At the end of a shift similar groups must replace them. Such scheduling is a puzzle multiplied, for the types of perplexities that come up in planning vacations now crop up daily. The planner must use available employees and fit them together in the right arrays of various roles on various shifts day after day, so as not to jeopardize coverage.

Shall each individual who stops work be replaced by another? Which functions can be suspended temporarily without any resulting harm? What may be lost if a staff member is not replaced? When incessance is first introduced, the organization gives two contrasting answers to these questions. At lower echelons personnel are replaced in relays, while at upper echelons they are not. Administration is called for at all times in such settings. One might speculate that the president's office would have three different occupants over the course of each twenty-four hours.[4] The idea fits the principle of relays and the format of shift work, but no arrange-

ment is made for it at the executive level. Society's norm for chief-
tainship is that it is the status of a single person. Even under committee rule, a first among equals emerges. Leaders do not expect to
be superseded or replaced while they are incumbents. They expect
lower-level personnel to transfer batons of responsibility while they
themselves retain their power. Since directors, mayors, and superintendents need sleep too, the system repeatedly enters a phase in
which top decision-makers will be absent.

Where replacements are practiced, the next matter to solve is
a smooth and effective changeover. The system will hold its breath
for a moment as some employees leave and their substitutes arrive.
Personnel are supposed to stay on duty until replaced, but actions
speak louder than rules. Some moments are left unattended for one
reason or another. Often the staffing gaps cause only mild inconveniences, such as an empty information booth in an airline terminal. Occasionally when a post is left vacant, a life or the national
security is unprotected.

That is what happened at Buckingham Palace in July 1982. One
night just before dawn, a man broke in. He set off an alarm, but
the officers who were alerted investigated so casually that they did
not find him. He walked along the palace halls and ultimately made
his way to the bedroom of the Queen of England. There, because
the night policeman outside the royal bedroom had gone off duty
and his daytime replacement had not yet arrived, the man was able
to enter the Queen's chamber. When he woke her up, she kept her
wits about her and talked with him, meanwhile managing to set
off a bell in the corridor outside her room. Because of the shift in-
terlude, the signal did not attract anyone.[5] The Queen chatted with
the man for a while, and finally a maidservant entered. A footman
was called, and the intruder was led away. The Queen's own presence of mind and conduct prevented anything worse than temporary uneasiness, yet the situation developed that far because of the
gap at relay time.

Problems in more ordinary situations coincide suggestively with
relay breaks. In a hospital's surgical care unit, over a five-year period the most human errors daily were found to correspond with
the midnight period of nursing personnel changeover. Patients were
left unattended. Some fell out of bed. Others missed receiving their
medications. Nonmedical job responsibilities were also neglected.[6]
We do not know about the full impacts of shift transitions, because

their possible relevance is not considered routinely whenever an accident occurs.[7]

When replacements come on duty, matters may not be the same as when they left the day before, so the changeover must include briefings on recent developments. An assembly line that is run around the clock is rather stable, as are most procedures for machines and materials in industrial settings. Factory workers are usually able to walk away from their equipment before the next shift arrives because a drill press or another mechanical setup will be the same tomorrow as today. In other jobs changes are a matter of course. Does the 94 degrees for the patient in the recovery room represent a rise or a fall in his temperature? How near to delivery is the shipment of insulated cable? What subsystems are yet to be checked before the rocket launch? In the conduct of political affairs, in news coverage, on construction projects, in medical care, and when weather is a significant factor, the enterprise depends on information that is current and shared.

The larger society that goes on generation after generation also transfers knowledge and tries to sustain performance. It exists beyond the participation of any member and must develop methods to ensure continuity while replacements occur. To do that, society resorts to a variety of tactics and programs, beginning with the socialization of children. It continues at transition points in people's lives with ceremonies and festivals such as puberty rites, graduation ceremonies, marriage celebrations, and retirement parties, all to induct people into new roles. Most rituals involve personal instruction, but published manuals also exist—for example, about the steps one should take before reaching the age of sixty to prepare for later retirement. In the incessant organization, the task is more critical. Instead of overlapping replacements as in generations, shift relays are rendered all at once.

Ships at sea have a tradition of making entries in a logbook about the vessel's location, the course held, and wind direction for the officer who takes over the watch. Some industrial companies insist on the logbook method for their supervisors, so that the next team will know the problems it inherits. Hospital staffs carry out transition rituals at the end of each shift. Incoming house officers are briefed by departing physicians about conditions of the patients at evening rounds and morning rounds, and they delay their clinical work until that information is passed. Nurses convene for their own briefing session to help the next shift carry on; they summarize diagnoses and patients' conditions and recount other events that took place in the past few hours. This ritual is so important that being on time to work is defined as reaching the ward before the report begins. While it is under way, nurses suspend other responsibilities, even treatment. They sometimes refuse to help doctors when they are in the process of giving or getting their report, so the continuity-maintaining ritual itself interferes with the continuity of nursing care.[8]

Sharing information as well as tools merges the viewpoints of people doing the same job. It is a tiny version of the common consciousness that links successive generations in society to one another.[9] But evidence that shift-to-shift mind-sharing is flawed is revealed by incidents that happened early in the course of the industrial catastrophe in Bhopal, India, around midnight between the third and fourth of December 1984. At the heart of the episode was a leaky valve that let water mix with a dangerous chemical, which led to a violent reaction and a rapid buildup of pressure within the chemical's storage tank. At 12:40 A.M. the storage tank cracked open, and the poisonous gas that escaped formed a low cloud that drifted into the nearby city and killed more than 2,000 people, injured 200,000 more, and also killed thousands of animals.

A shift changeover had taken place from the evening to the night crew, and its procedure was carried out as planned. Just before the end of the evening shift, one worker checked the pressure for the methyl isocyanate (MIC) in tank number 610. It was 2 pounds per square inch. That was normal, and he entered it in the logbook. A half-hour later, after the new crew came on duty, the senior operator who checked the pressure for that tank saw it was 10 pounds per square inch. He thought nothing of the 10-pound pressure, because it was relatively normal, and entered the figure in the logbook.[10]

In the span of a half-hour, there had been a fivefold increase in pressure in tank 610. But instead of a single, seamless human mind monitoring the situation, the shift work plan depended upon a second mind to take up with an undiluted sense of continuity where the first had left off. The new worker may have noticed the entry just above his own, but he had not made both of them. Perhaps because of that, the significance of the rapid pressure change did not register.

Without any extra effort, one person is mindful of an experience in the passage of time. A team of two must construct that same awareness from several data points. Consider the everyday project of baking biscuits. Compared to two bakers taking turns reporting to each other, one baker looking repeatedly has a better sense of how fast the biscuits are browning in the oven. It makes a great difference whether a person acquires memories through actual experience or receives them secondhand. Memories that are created directly fit immediately into one's working thoughts, and lessons of personal experience stick longer and have more power over how one interprets current events.[11] In a rapidly developing situation, some of the risks may not be recognized by persons who monitor only a portion of the facts that have to be merged to understand what is going on.

Many conditions at the plant in Bhopal were faulty at the time. Equipment was in disrepair, personnel lacked training, and gauges were hard to interpret. A number of things contributed to the catastrophe. The safety equipment on hand malfunctioned. The personnel sent confused messages. Even after knowing of the leak, the employees decided to take their tea break before attempting the repair. The accident is grim testimony that in a complex system multiple failures, which begin independently of one another, can combine in unanticipated ways to aggravate a risk and result in an accident.[12]

The early signal of rising pressure, which was overlooked during the shift changeover, must be counted as one of the failures. Along with it, a second lapse that allowed the rupturing of the tank was also part of the relay procedure. Someone from the preceding shift left a note in the daily maintenance log to wash the water pipe but wrote nothing about inserting a metal disc called a slip blind into the pipe to prevent water from leaking through the valve. When the supervisor on duty learned of this later, he commented, "But the daily notes are always vague."[13] Logbooks accept whatever they are given; they do not ask for an explanation.

Ideally, like a crystal that stacks its atoms to fit in several directions, incessance would have the symmetry of identical workers replacing one another on the job. Staffing is more easily managed if the personnel are standardized.[14] Then the substitutes' actions are likely to be harmonious with those of their predecessors. Since people are not so similar, the roles they fill will be modified so that all may perform them consistently around the clock. Incessance promotes group practice in this way. One cannot guard a political secret, maintain a psychiatric confidence, or tuck operational data in a mental pocket at sundown if someone else is going to carry on in the evening. Spokesmen dealing with the press about an ongoing crisis must align their statements with what their predecessors have said. Doctors must curb their knack for an esoteric treatment style, because other physicians will step into their roles on the next shift. Autonomy, so dear to professionals because of their special knowledge and working styles, becomes disruptive if several incumbents of a role express their individuality over the cycle of the day. Compared to others who have sole responsibility for their work, shift personnel must behave with their replacements in mind.

Some of the strains that arise when people share spaces now appear when they share time. Each group inherits the circumstances left for it by the shift before. Tasks should have been completed, machines left in working order, and the work station tidied. Hospital housekeepers should have bagged the dirty laundry and sent it on its way rather than leave the task for their replacements. Cab drivers who work in fleets are uneasy that cabbies during other hours will mistreat their favorite vehicles. Truckers are averse to sharing their rigs because of their own elaborate seat adjustments and other personalized outfitting of the cabs.

The permanent staffers on any shift are the most disapproving of jobs left undone. A mood of dependence-with-resentment grows. Minor sabotage starts, such as hiding tools. At a company dealing in crushed stone, if a driver had to share a rig with someone on another shift he would tighten the clutches on the crane so that it would be harder for the other to use. In a department store, the daytime regulars make a practice of hiding goods from the evening personnel so that they would have the most desirable merchandise, in popular sizes and colors, to sell the next morning. The transition ritual itself may become a minimal communication event. Instead of reviewing the current status of tasks, departing staff may let the replacements find out for themselves.

Broad responsibility for the conduct of affairs and vital matters are the provinces of the upper end of the hierarchy. Something must be done at higher echelons for decision-making around the clock. Since relays are not practiced at executive levels, some authority and accountability will be placed in other hands. All top officials and their subordinates face the question of who will be in charge while the boss is out and how much discretion they will have. In the military it involves generals and officers of lower rank, in the hospital physicians and nurses, in factories superintendents and foremen, in cities mayors and heads of departments, and in commercial organizations presidents and managers.

Some matters will be deferred without harm till the following day. Long-range commitments in planning, finance, hiring, policy, and programs are accomplished almost wholly during daytime hours. Other decisions cannot be postponed. Our civilization abbreviates the tolerable reaction time for dealing with important events, and night is no longer an excuse for delaying an action. So chiefs who want to sleep undisturbed issue contingency orders—action plans that deputies should follow in situations that can be anticipated. Like laws, contingency orders are abstract guides to conduct, formulas for responses to potential emergencies. They are not necessarily an inferior way to cope; ready-to-use plans are as useful to organizations as habits are to individuals.

In other matters the unavoidable need to act forces a transfer of power downward. Leaders delegate authority to their deputies. This is often a comfortable arrangement, for leaders consult subordinates in making decisions, and some of those aides have occasionally taken over the job of an absent chief. Deputies, assistants, and lieutenants act on their own and are always making judgments about what information to pass on upward. Although they must have approval from the top for their decisions, most such checking can wait until morning.

After all those maneuvers, the utmost crises still require the leader's immediate attention. Such crises carry potential for great harm; human lives or fortunes hang in the balance. Medical shock, technological catastrophe, sudden change in economic circumstances, threat of war, overthrow of a government, a natural disaster—all bring imperatives for a high-level rapid response. The news must reach the person who has both power and ultimate responsibility for action. Crises may happen during any period of running a system, and a portion of them will occur at night. They may take place nearby or in another part of the world in the daytime, so that news of them arrives locally at night. Modern communications technology sends bulletins of all events around the globe into each time zone. After sundown personnel continue to scan for signals of crisis, whether they are keeping tabs on a patient who has just had surgery, an industrial process, or a political hot spot. News of vital events that happen anywhere will be received somewhere at a time when relevant parties are asleep. The chief must be awakened. A crisis says ignore the surrounding dark and behave toward a leader as if the alarm has come in at high noon.

Even in the face of an alarm, however, people have a frame of mind to honor sleep. In the past others would not disturb a sleeping person because they believed his soul was away and it would not have time to reoccupy his body if he were suddenly roused. If waking the sleeper were necessary, it had to be done very gradually so that the soul would have time to return.[15] In some cultures awakening a sleeper brought on punishment. Although our understandings about the soul may have changed, there is still a hallowed norm that a sleeper has the right to remain insulated from the ordinary claims of society, to receive deference from family and outsiders, to be shielded from anything that might disturb that dormant state.[16] Add the condition that the person is the boss, and one's reluctance to waken the sleeper becomes intense. If someone has to be roused, the privacy of a lower-ranking deputy will be invaded first.[17] As the Bhopal disaster unfolded, the plant's administrative superintendent on that shift was summoned at 12:50 A.M. The assistant factory manager was telephoned at 1 A.M.[18] The factory manager was called after 1:30 A.M.

Personal styles of executives affect what deputies will do. Some chiefs are more accessible than others. One army general's order to subordinates used to be: "You must wake me up about any matter out of the ordinary and let *me* decide whether or not it is important." Other higher-ups resent having their sleep disturbed and growl about interruptions for a matter they would address immediately during the day. It is embarrassing for a conscientious deputy to hear a superior say it is not worth losing sleep over. A nurse hates to waken doctors on overnight duty; usually they are grumpy. Often she delays and agonizes over whether a call is warranted. Watching a patient, she cannot make decisions about treatment changes without consulting the doctor, but when she does call, the doctor is likely to rave about being waked; and she feels she has been chastised for doing her job.[19] So night nurses avoid waking physicians on duty because they get piqued at being disturbed for "minor problems."[20] Shift supervisors also choose not to bother the plant manager on the same grounds. The chief who punishes a subordinate with annoyance when awakened creates a dilemma unique to incessant organizations. The paramount reason anyone would want to awaken a leader is to convey bad news. Even the happiest tidings can wait till morning. A crisis cannot. To subordinates, any time is an unseemly time to transmit bad news upward. The normal tendency to avoid reporting that something is going wrong is strengthened by attitudes toward sleep and by higher-ups who are peeved when awakened.

With the arrival of incessance, some blatant instances of the inaccessibility of the leader have taken place, occasions on which the chief was left uninformed of grave news that would have been delivered promptly in the daytime. The most outstanding episode is the sequence of events culminating in the bombing attack on Pearl Harbor on Sunday, December 7, 1941.[21] It has been a focus of inquiry and analysis from many points of view and used for purposes of blaming, scolding, and reeducating. A great deal of information has been combed, interpreted, reshuffled, and reinterpreted. Something can be added, however, by looking at the organizational plans for reaching top leaders under conditions of incessance. At the beginning of the 1940s most people saw nighttime as an intermission. Even urgent business could be suspended. They used only a portion of the twenty-four hours for active habits, so their mind set was to treat the other portion as a period in which nothing happens. United States military headquarters, however, had watch officers on duty around the clock. Thirteen portions of a message from Japan to its envoy in Washington had been intercepted and decoded over a ten-day period from late November through December 6. From its contents government leaders knew that trouble was brewing fast and that a rupture in relations with Japan, meaning war, was imminent.[22]

In the very early morning of Sunday, December 7, Washington time, another intercepted message revealed that the situation was critical. After this fourteenth part of the message was decoded and found to include instructions not to communicate with American authorities before one o'clock in the afternoon on Sunday—an unprecedented and extraordinary stipulation in a diplomatic message—Colonel Rufus Bratton of the Far Eastern Section of Army Intelligence concluded that a surprise attack was coming somewhere in the Pacific.[23] Early that morning the intelligence aides,

who then hurried to show the message to someone with the authority to send an urgent warning to field commanders, found that
no one on duty would have the power to act until Army Chief of
Staff General George C. Marshall reached his office.[24] Marshall was
finally contacted at mid-morning on Sunday.[25] Ultimately the general sent a message alerting the garrison, but it arrived too late.

A number of separate mistakes and coincidences contributed to
the amount of damage wrought at Pearl Harbor that day. For example, a message sent ten days earlier to the commanders at Pearl
Harbor ordered the Navy into appropriate defensive deployment in
preparation for combat. The Washington staff on December 7
thought the fleet was dispersed, but the commanders had received
vague warnings regularly, masking their urgency so as not to alarm
American civilians or alert the Japanese, and a sizable part of the
fleet had not been ordered out of the harbor.[26] By coincidence a
contingent of U.S. B-17 bombers was due in Hawaii that Sunday
morning. Again, the details of exact routes and numbers of planes
in a squadron were not disclosed in messages, so the radar station
personnel at the northern tip of the Hawaiian Islands had only a
rough idea of how many planes to expect, and when. Those who
first spotted the Japanese airplanes by radar mistook them for the
B-17s and did not contact headquarters. On top of that, the message sent from Washington that Sunday morning to all military in-
stallations in the Pacific encountered atmospheric conditions that
interfered with its transmission only to Hawaii, of all the destina-
tions, and that message had to be sent circuitously, adding to the
delay.[27]

The relevance of Pearl Harbor to the problem of leadership during incessance is shown by what did not happen after the fourteenth
part of the Japanese message was decoded that night. A clear procedure for subordinates to communicate rapidly with the top command was missing. The board of inquiry found that no one subordinate had been given the authority to act in General Marshall's
absence.[28] Lights were burning all night in the War and Navy departments,[29] but those on duty functioned as message monitors and
had little decision-making power. Colonel Bratton reported that
when he sought to find someone with authority who could send the
urgent warning, no one was available on duty who could or would
act promptly in the Army Chief of Staff's absence.[30] General Marshall testified that he had an orderly at his home to receive calls

when he was away at night, that he could have been reached, and that he was unaware of any effort to locate him at his home or elsewhere by messenger or telephone during the evening of December 6 or the morning of December 7, until he was taking a shower after a ride on horseback in a park.[31] Officers in the War Department asserted, however, that after receiving the intercepted Japanese memorandum they tried to communicate but failed to reach him.[32]

The review of what happened that night became a turning point in attitudes about the night. The lesson learned from its tragedy stimulated intensive attention to government communication channels, which is now exemplified in many nations by the maintenance of twenty-four-hour military readiness and elaborate formats for reaching the heads of state and the top military command at any hour. In the United States missiles are poised for launching around the clock, a fleet of bombers is usually aloft, there is a code to convey the seriousness and urgency of a situation (the worst being "red alert"), and formal procedures are in place for reaching the President and the Chairman of the Joint Chiefs of Staff.

Still, in converting from a cyclic administration to an incessant one, those arrangements refer to only an initial phase. Even with the structural improvements in place an attitude persists to leave a sleeping leader undisturbed. With the arrival of night there comes an unwillingness to contact the chief. On August 19, 1981, while the President of the United States was vacationing in California, a dogfight took place in the Mediterranean off the coast of Libya, and two of that country's fighter planes were shot down by U.S. naval aircraft. News of the clash reached military headquarters in Washington, D.C., six minutes later. At that moment it was after 11 P.M. in California. Presidential aides notified other top officials but chose not to tell the President until nearly six hours had passed. About 3 A.M. the senior aide asked staff members if they thought it would be a good idea to call and inform him of the incident. Their reactions inspired him to waken the President about one and a half hours later.[33]

We cannot be sure that informing the top executives would have made a difference in the outcomes of the incidents described here. The officers who had been in charge at Pearl Harbor claimed in their testimonies that if they had been told of Japan's one o'clock message several hours earlier, which was possible, they would have

avoided the debacle. The broad conclusion of the official investigations was that the commanders in Hawaii made less preparation
than they should have in light of the earlier warnings.[34] What is
certain is that conventional attitudes toward sleep continue to inhibit subordinates from notifying their chiefs.

Important signals were neglected or action postponed on other
occasions too.[35] Each has become part of history, perhaps never to
be repeated in the same setting, but similar ones that we do not
hear about happen all the time. The public is treated to detailed
stories of only the more dramatic moments, tragedies, and near
misses. Most miscalculations in business enterprises, industrial accidents, and financial calamities cannot be analyzed because they
occur within private companies that do not reveal the details.[36] Expansion into the night or multiple shift operation may not be the
only cause of such mishaps, but it contributes in distinctive ways.

Compare what happened in those international crises with the
conduct of personnel at the atomic power plant at Three Mile Island, Pennsylvania, on March 28, 1979. Shortly after 4 A.M. that
morning an equipment failure occurred, and the nuclear fission
process was halted. The pertinent fact in context of this discussion
is that the staff on duty notified the plant manager promptly.
Within minutes of the shutdown the personnel had telephoned him
at his home to report what happened. Why was the behavior on
this night different from the other nights mentioned above?

Dozens of alarms went off in the control room in the beginning
of the accident at Three Mile Island. Flashing lights accompanied
by wailing sirens created a tumult to inform operating personnel
that fission in the reactor had stopped. Several times a year, apparently, a power plant will experience some malfunctioning of
equipment and automatically cease its operation each time. Such
an unscheduled shutdown is called a "routine" emergency, and that
is what the plant manager was told when he was awakened. The
manager treated the shutdown as routine, for initially the problem
was not dangerous. He did not call back until more than an hour
later to check on how matters were proceeding.[37]

Other conditions help explain patterns of nighttime unpreparedness and inertia, just as they do instances of fumbling urgent
matters in the daytime. None of them, however, alters the circum-
stance that is absent during the day: The person of appropriate status, power, and responsibility for decision-making is asleep. Mat-

ters that in other hours would be conveyed directly are left with subordinates when the chief is made inaccessible by slumber and a wall of norms.

The organization once reflected the tempo of the people who founded it. The timetable of the single-shift organization had its details finely suited to a diurnal species. Its personnel, whatever their rank, participated in the same hours. Everyone began together, halted concurrently for lunch, returned in unison to their undertakings, and together called the busy day to a close. The daily rounds for members and organizations were such that if you knew the schedule of one you knew it for both. The same people who shut down the enterprise one day started it up the next. They returned and put the system in motion again without much concern for the interruption, because the same minds carried the knowledge of what was going on. If they knew the system's affairs when departing for the day, they would know them tomorrow.

Before the last two centuries it was rare to find relays of the same personnel in the same roles replacing themselves daily.[38] It is one thing to quit never to return, knowing that someone else will take your place. It is another thing to depart knowing someone will become your substitute, that you will come back to supplant the other, and that this will happen over and over again. It forces the acceptance of shared responsibilities and sharing credit for achievement. It subtly offers chances to blame a predecessor or a replacement if something goes wrong. It is true that most relays are designed for standardized jobs, so shortcomings in work performance are likely to result in local, temporary failures on tasks. Yet there is a general trend for more division of labor and more interdependence among the staff of a work team. Now, along with dividing a project into jobs, the relay policy divides jobs into shifts.

Individual responsibility is already blurred in modern organizations. Personnel at all levels carry out a program. As organizations become more complex, with messages sent for recipients to act on and orders carried out by others, it is harder to pinpoint who is responsible for error. As personnel also perform in relays, it further dilutes the identity of who made what decisions and who carried out what actions. The principle of relays contradicts the idea of the leader role, and interchanging them is rarely done. Where can accountability be lodged? To some extent laws and legal practice assign responsibility toward the top of the hierarchy. But with the leader not regularly on duty at night, is the deputy answerable even if not given decision-making power? If a major crisis is mishandled, who is to blame if deputies followed contingency orders? How reasonable is a chief's excuse that "I was sleeping and they didn't wake me up"? It becomes harder to know who is liable as well as to understand what went wrong.

The incessant organization, an explicit twenty-four-hour institution, is incomplete in its ways of maintaining continuity. Something is being lost at the changeovers. Ordeals involving incessant operation are disclosed in the serial reading of gauges at the Bhopal factory, in the staffing omission at Buckingham Palace, in little acts of sabotage from one shift toward another, in the record of surgical ward mistakes, and in the inaccessibility of General Marshall the night before Pearl Harbor was struck. Some omissions have been averted, but the transition rituals and updating have not been enough. The modern usage of the word "relay" emphasizes transmission and replacement, but it comes from old French and Latin words meaning to leave behind and to loosen. The old connotations still apply, for relay outfits can come apart at the seams.

Perhaps over a long period administrators will become aware of what procedures are effective. Some of the incessant organization's difficulties reflect the early stage of its existence and meager experience with the form. Ultimately the cyclic format and its conventions will be dismantled and replaced. But the recurrence of fumbling problems at night suggests that our style is to revise the measures only after harrowing events drive us to do so. We survive disasters and breathtaking near misses in one predicament after another while learning how to function after dark. An official in the nuclear power industry made a similar observation: "[W]e have had too few accidents. It's expensive but that's how you gain experience." He was willing to depend on trial and error even though error gives rise to such anguished trials.[39] Organizations shed their intermittent forms little by little. At that slow pace of change they appear to be submitting to a form of natural selection: Catastrophes will remove the wrong organizational designs.

In one sphere, a trend that incorporates the lessons learned is noticeable. The need to respond to important events obliges leaders to give up sleep in emergencies. If an incessant organization has a chief who manages to be left asleep consistently during night hours, it is in a beginning phase of converting to twenty-four-hour functioning. The absence of top managers raises the threshold to be crossed for communicating news to them. They are less accessible, and it is uncertain who has the authority at that time. Partial decentralization is ordered; otherwise decisions are postponed. If the chief is known to be bad-tempered when awakened, underlings draw back more. Outside events go on their course, and matters have to be very grave if they are to overcome the tendency to let sleeping leaders lie.

As the network of world events and their consequences tightens, as news of them speeds to us, and as we continue to design and try to manage ambitious systems, the arrangements made by high-level officials assume an intermediate form. The chief tries to maintain control through contingency orders. As a surrogate for the chief, however, contingency plans have a basic defect. On one hand because they are produced in a relatively unpressured atmosphere, the deliberate review of pros and cons and choice of tactical priorities favor their soundness. On the other hand, the orders are readied for anticipated situations. They are better substitutes for middle-level executives than for the top level. Decisions at the top fall into two groups. One contains long-range planning and policy formulation, which are easily allocated to the daytime. The other group is not operationally routine. It includes events erupting in uncertainty and involving unknowns. Those problems, rare and knotty, are also the direct concern of high echelons. Although we traditionally understand top management roles as centered on long-term perspectives,[40] they must also tend to events that are irregular, unanticipated, and compelling. Day-to-day matters are not problematic while the chiefs sleep. They will be needed mainly for situations of uncertainty and crisis, and in such cases contingency orders are lame.

The combined weights of experience, judgment, power considerations, and responsibility ultimately press down the threshold for access to the top. Facing a choice between repose and exercising the authority that belongs to them, leaders surrender sleep rather than power. At the same time, experience with the incessant community is softening the prohibition against awakening sleepers. Chiefs become defined as accessible, and they will permit themselves to be awakened. They too will be harnessed to twenty-four-hour activity.

This is the order followed in the conversion to incessance. It is not a strict chronology that counts but the accumulation of experience within particular organizations. The cases described in this chapter show the transition. First there are partial gestures toward night's wakeful potential, but administrative arrangements remain confusing (Pearl Harbor–Washington, 1941). Then, acknowledging the need, procedures are clarified, but there is still deference to sleep and a hesitation to intrude (Libya–California, 1981). Finally, breaking through the barrier of sleep, the plans are unhesitatingly used (Three Mile Island, 1979). These steps will be taken in this sequence whenever organizations expand their wakeful hours. Society first alters activities at night, then it changes attitudes about access to sleepers. In two of the occasions there were delays in reaching the leader. It happened despite plenty of signs and news about preparedness and talk of war in 1941, and also when the trigger of war was pulled by shooting down foreign fighter planes while at peace in 1981. Surely if the final part of the 1941 message had been decoded at eleven in the morning, a person with authority would have been accessible and would have been contacted quickly. On the 1981 occasion, again it is fair to surmise that if it were daytime an aide would have told the President right away. The exception occurred for the familiar problem. At the nuclear power plant, breakdowns at any hour have become routine, so is the rule to notify the person in charge. Once crises become routine, the norms protecting sleep can no longer withstand the news of them. Having recognized a breakdown, the staff at Three Mile Island knew the appropriate thing to do. They roused the plant manager right away. Incessance had arrived.

7

Shift Workers

If incessance develops in the workplace, it will soon invade workers' bodies and households. Each sphere of life follows a timetable, and all must come together in some way. Change the clockwork of one and a series of readjustments is set off in the others. In the transition to an unremitting schedule at least four spheres will be recast. The first is the nonstop organization. It introduces relays to cope with its staffing needs and rearranges decision-making in the absence of its top executives. The second is the community, whose inhabitants simultaneously enjoy more access to goods and services and are exposed to intrusions of light and noise. The third is the human body, whose physiological functions lose their customary rhythms and coordination. The fourth is household life, whose members' timetables are scattered. We still do not have a grammar of ecology and must discuss the rearrangement within each domain separately.

There are multitudes of shift employees in the United States alone. At midnight more than 7 million are at their jobs. They commit themselves to a schedule that is out of phase with most of the population, and by doing so they become dependable users of the night, perhaps the prototype of individuals who will live in an incessant community.

It is not the best of times. Early settlers of a region have never found it so. Pioneers are transitional figures. They set out with their biological and cultural makeup and find themselves tested by the demands of the new milieu. Comfortable ways, ingrained habits, and old understandings are wrested from them. The frontier takes its toll through discontinuity, bafflement, and stress. Maybe we esteem the Western pioneers for that reason. They struggled with bedeviling circumstances and a marginal life, working strenuously, making sacrifices, and through myriad trials they fashioned a style for surviving in the new environment. They subsidized the rest of society by devoting their bodies and social life to the frontier experiment, and we admire them for the hardships they endured.

Now shift workers strive after dark. They bear most of the load for developing that region for society. Personally they absorb the costs just as settlers on the land did in their day. Their schedules take two typical forms. One is to work regularly in the evening or at night. The other is to rotate among day, evening, and night shift assignments. To those schedules they adapt their outside commitments, though their life-styles vary with differences in age and sex and according to whether they live alone or in a household with others. But three things stand out as almost universal for the group, and these shape a similar existence.

First, a particular habit is so widespread among rotators and regular shift workers that it unites them in a common lot regardless of the different work schedules. On their days off they switch to the normal daily cycle. Whether they follow one fixed shift in the evening or night or a rotating plan in which work times change repeatedly, most of them regularly reset their schedules on days off to participate in the main community. They stay awake in the daytime and try to sleep at night. Even the regular evening and night workers rotate twice a week, once at the start of days off and then from days off back to work. In switching the timing of sleep and activity they muddle their bodies' physiological rhythms. Most shift workers follow the practice of staying awake in the daytime on their days off, so most of them are subjected to those upsets and carry an abiding malaise. They feel sluggish on weekends and abstracted on the job.

Second, because their work is in the off-hours, the timing of other events are pushed around. Waking hours, meals, moments of recreation, and spells of sleep are governed by the routine of employment. During their work week they are out of phase with family and friends. Unable to switch all their other interests to different hours, they have to deduct from how much they attend meetings, see other family members, and engage in sexual love. They will give up sleep to recoup some of these losses. They will sit down to dinner with their families when their stomachs say it is breakfast time. Inasmuch as their schedule keeps them from joining in, they concede the loss of a part of family and social life.[1]

Third, for those who are members of families, their novel timings affect the lives of others at home. The household becomes its own little incessant community. Different rights of dwellers collide as family schedules and work schedules conflict. The struggle to sleep at night that bothered people in the neighborhood and that caught up leaders of organizations is repeated for shift workers in the daytime. Whereas daytimers clash with nighttimers over noise after dark, shift workers complain to their families about peace and quiet while the sun is shining. Sleeping or awake, the shift worker imposes upon others. Family timetables are elbowed away from the community rhythm. The family's routines are reordered around the workers' comings and goings. Mealtimes are chronically changed. There are disputes over making noise while shift workers try to sleep, and recurrent debates over whether they will participate in recreation with spouses and children.

Those three conditions apply so widely that the terms "shift worker" and "night worker" can be used interchangeably. Both rotators and regular off-hours employees alter the timing of their wakefulness at least on each side of their days off, are personally out of phase with the main community, and live in a schedule-turbulent household.

Within the organization, the assignment planner first gives priority to staffing needs. To fulfill those requirements personnel will be treated as interchangeable, and their timetables will be juggled across the hours and days of the week. In this paper-and-pencil era of solving the task, the current methods for accomplishing a well-fitting schedule are clumsy. The mathematical principles behind it reside in a class of problems called the theory of computations, and it is still not fully realized. The supervisor often ends up with a plan that is flawed and then makes last-minute attempts to achieve coverage by moving staff members around. The results for workers are unpredictable and erratic assignments. Even after posting the schedule, the planner breaks pencil points and wears out erasers on the worksheet in reshuffling personnel.

While most people know their daily timetables as soundly as sensing where they are, shift employees cannot take theirs for granted. They continually invest effort to learn when they are expected at work and in other places, when meals will be taken, if social invitations can be accepted, and whether long-term commitments may be made. It crops up in virtually all arrangements with friends and family. They cannot forget the timetable. Whenever looking at future plans, they peer at an inconstant schedule.

Rotators, especially, are unsure of their assignments. No band of time per day is reliably free from the potential claims of their employer. Sanitation men in New York City were chronically anxious about reassignments because they happened so often.[2] Middle managers on the railroad were expected to be on call to meet trains, and last-minute changes trumped their personal plans.[3] A source of tension among police officers is not knowing what shift they are going to be on the next day. Employees in the television industry live with the same uncertainty. Many such workers feel that not knowing what their hours will be from one day to the next is the worst part of their job. Relaxing at home, the junior pilot tenses as the telephone rings, because he fears it is a call from the airport saying he is needed to fill in. The nurse, completing an evening tour of duty, listens in dismay as her supervisor pleads with her to continue through the night shift, or come in tomorrow on her day off because "we're short."

Being able to anticipate future assignments is more important than stability of the assignments themselves. Employees can adapt if they know what to expect. As long as work obligations are predictable they can arrange their outside lives and make other commitments in advance. They grumble about the uncertainties to the scheduling supervisor, and the supervisor, sensitive to the complaints and apologetic about having to change assignments, usually grants a worker's request for a further change. Yet it cannot be granted simply. If someone wants to move from one time slot to another, there must be a compensating move. So the planner allows the workers to trade among themselves. It may be bothersome at the time, but other co-workers feel obliged to cooperate and accept an exchange, for they know that doing so creates an obligation in turn. The day will come when they will want to revise an assignment after the schedule has been posted and can call upon others to repay the favor. Between the planning supervisor's last-minute changes and the trading conducted by the staff, the schedules stay volatile. Last-minute reassignments force them to cancel appointments and to miss family outings. Friends have trouble keeping track of them. Spouses do not know when their partners will be free. It becomes so vexing that spouses and friends urge shift workers to find work elsewhere. The wife of a policeman felt so strongly about having to put up with the calls at night, which were part of her husband's job, that she refused to introduce a bachelor trooper to her girl friend.[4] Lonely wives give their husbands ultimatums: Either leave the shifts or leave the marriage.

The wear and tear from uncertain schedules drives workers to abandon their jobs. Absenteeism is higher among workers subjected to rotating shifts than among those on permanent shifts.[5] Hospital personnel who have undergone erratic schedules have higher rates of absenteeism and turnover, and rotaters among them are the most likely to quit.[6] Since the departures aggravate the staffing problem and force more reassignments, incessant organizations find themselves trying to achieve coverage in the face of absenteeism and turnover generated by their own scheduling practices.

There are, in addition to the burdens of unpredictability, physiological hardships in repeatedly switching work hours. Long ago a rapprochement between timetables of the environment and of persons evolved. Body functions keep in step with the natural alternation of light and dark and are harmonious with routines of work and rest. For example, cortisol, a hormone produced by the adrenal cortex, which acts on organic metabolism and in an individual's response to stress, is usually at its highest level in the blood at the onset of the active period and lowest during sleep. The physiological functions are also synchronized among themselves. Active phases of many of them coincide, and they subside together along with a lowered metabolic rate and lower body temperature. Ordinary daily rounds are so nicely suited to that natural cadence that most people pay little attention to the ebbs and flows of body rhythms. During the day they perform competently at both physical and mental tasks.

If they change the timing of their activity, the rhythms are disturbed. Upon leaving diurnal routines to labor at night, shift workers overthrow the normal biological beats. Hormone production, heartbeat, brain waves, sensitivity to certain drugs, metabolism, and breathing stagger in their tempo. Functions lose the coordination they had among themselves. The heart does not pump with its customary steadiness. Cortisol production becomes erratic and is not sustained at any level for long. It is harder to synchronize thoughts with fine muscular adjustments. Metabolism of digestion is not synchronized with eating. The body is an elaborate society by itself, and having been buffeted by eclipses, sudden shortages, quakes, storms, and floods in the wrong season, it is not about to continue its collective life as if nothing happened.

Rotating workers are affected most, but others who have fixed off-hours schedules are bothered as well when they switch to the community's routine on their days off. In this way permanent shift workers become rotators on their own initiative. They submit to the turmoil twice a week, once at the beginning of their days off and again at the beginning of the work period that follows.

A hormonal flywheel keeps evening workers up when they want to retire upon coming home from work. It takes them time to unwind.[7] The body cannot drop quickly to its physiological lows after being so energetic. Glands like the adrenal, whose output while at work was so helpful, may stop secreting their juices when the job is over, but the hormone concentrations in the blood are still high. The body must wait until the somatic effects wear off. So evening workers are restless past the bedtimes they desire, and they look for some mild recreation instead. They watch television or write letters or read books. A few clean the house lightly. All try to insert some diversion between their work period and the time they can close their eyes.

The workers feel disoriented and vaguely unwell. Most commonly they have difficulty falling asleep and staying asleep. They turn in and slumber for a while, only to begin tossing and turning, and are soon awake again. They try once more but sleep erratically. Some come home so tired in the morning that they drop off, but wake up after a few hours. They take brief naps at various times if unable to log long stretches. Even when they accumulate enough time in bed, they feel they have not had enough. When the rhythms are disturbed many functions go astray, but sleep disorders are the most common of all health problems among shift workers and are felt soonest. It is the main symptom of the general riddle of adjustment, because sleep is not one stilled voice—it is a quieted chorus. Numerous well-defined slowdowns occur: heart rate, oxygen consumption, breathing, and selective hormonal abatement. Sleep occurs when those functions are subdued.[8] Sleep is more restful if it happens during the low points of most of the important rhythms and of body temperature.[9] A general study of poor sleepers found

that they were physiologically more active. They had more frequent heartbeats, higher temperature, and higher skin resistance.[10]
Rotated shift workers who have to sleep out of phase with their
circadian lows show these attributes too. They are going to bed at
the wrong time on their body's clock, for inside there is no consensus
of inactivity. Airline pilots who sleep out of phase from the lows
sleep fitfully. They awaken unrested even if they have been sleeping
many hours.[11] Night workers sleep the least and nap the most. Rotators sleep the least when on night shift. They complain of too little
or of irregular slumber and of feeling tired afterward.[12] The shift
workers' typical resting problem is not getting enough sleep, and
what they get is of poorer quality.

The upsets do not last. The rhythms can be resynchronized. If
a different phase of activity such as working at night is maintained,
the revised job hours tug at the physiological processes to correspond to the new timing. Accepting the schedule imposed on it, the
body's clock begins to reset itself, but it does so sluggishly. The cycles
reestablish themselves at different rates.[13] Rhythms for urine excretion and for the presence of amino acids in the blood readjust
readily and follow the new schedule in a day or two.[14] The heart
takes four to eight days to be steadily rhythmic again.[15] Adrenal
cortisol production is slower to change, requiring from five to ten
days to locate the new cycle.[16] Sweating tempo reappears in eight
days or more. More time will pass before body temperature moves
in step.[17] Body temperature settles down so slowly because its pattern depends on the various rhythms being coordinated with one
another. Two weeks will go by before all the functions are resynchronized.[18] By then, however, other rotations have occurred, and
many shift workers live in a state of ongoing physiological confusion.

Feeling poorly often, it is not surprising that employees bring
their languor to the workplace. They labor when their bodies are
unable to perform best. Night work asks a greater expenditure of
physical and mental energy to match daytime performance.[19] Many
night workers take amphetamines to keep going on the job. They
are beset by the difficulty of staying awake.[20] Some doze off. An
inspector acting on a tip visited three hospitals after midnight and
found twenty-two employees sleeping.[21]

Without adequate sleep the staff members are less alert and less
coordinated, and tend to rely on fixed habits. They work with di-

minished capacity, are insensitive to minor problems, and their performance is punctuated by more errors.[22] Visual sharpness is lower.
Meter readers in a gas works make most mistakes at night.[23] Response time is slower. Telephone operators lag in answering calls
around 3–4 A.M.[24] In manufacturing, the grade of workmanship
falls.[25] Workers turn out more defective goods and damage more
equipment.[26] It is a period of more accidents in the machine and
motor industries.[27] Nighttime blunders are more serious.[28] A much
higher rate of airplane accidents occurs then than in the daytime.[29]

Onlookers see fatigue as the reason for listless work and poor
performance, and blame the mistakes and accidents on operator
error or human error.[30] Tiredness may be involved, but an observer
may misinterpret the body's physiological upsets and unsynchro-
nized state as only fatigue. In a large organization, the complex
division of labor must achieve synchrony among its parts to operate
well; if they are not coordinated, the system malfunctions. The same
principle applies in a person. One's effectiveness rests on a high degree of integration among body rhythms. In an industrial accident
attributed to human error, the error may be the last event in a sequence that began with shift rotations, which caused physiological
disorder, which left the person less capable and in turn led to the
mistake. We know that night personnel have been subjected to erratic schedules and that performance is more flawed at night. The
cause is not forged only in the last link of a chain of influence.

Several reports about the accident at the Three Mile Island nuclear power plant in 1979 overlook the possibility that body upsets
could have contributed to the operators' performance. Instead, the
culprit is made out to be poor training. At the plant, when several
water pumps stopped working, the heat in a tank caused the pressure to rise past a predetermined risky threshold, and the nuclear
fission procedure was halted automatically. The investigators concluded that a series of equipment failures, human errors, and inappropriate procedures then escalated the problem into danger of
a meltdown in the reactor core.[31] Acknowledging the equipment
failures, the manufacturer who built the reactor still argued that
the accident developed because operators on duty did not follow
correct procedures after the breakdown. The official report and an
analysis prepared by outside consultants for the Nuclear Regulatory
Commission both concluded that the faults lay with inadequacies
in equipment design, in the way information was presented, in the

emergency procedures, and in the training of plant operators. During the first two hours of the accident, the President's commission said, the operators ignored or failed to recognize several signs that should have warned them that there was an open valve starting a loss-of-coolant problem. "The fact that they failed to realize . . . these conditions . . . indicates a severe deficiency in their training to identify the symptoms of such an accident."[32]

The plant operators did not cause the accident by themselves. Equipment malfunctioned. The investigating commission may have been right that training was inadequate, but given what we know about disrupted physiological rhythms and the connection between such stress and dulled abilities, it is likely that the shocks of erratic work schedules played a part. The control room operators did not correctly interpret temperature gauges that told of superheated steam and an uncovered reactor core. They also failed to notice two lights which indicated that valves were closed on emergency feed-water lines, so that no water could reach the steam generators. "One light was covered by a yellow maintenance tag. No one knows why the second light was missed."[33] The commission could not say why they did not notice it, but the indicator light could have been missed because of the lowered alertness that followed from bodily upsets.[34] The crew had just rotated onto the night shift. The accident began at 4 A.M.

Corporate administrators know that their esteemed managers may falter in business negotiations after being subjected to jet lag. No one imagines that lack of training explains lapses in their performance. Several of the largest corporations have issued memos advising their executives who travel abroad not to do business on the day after they have sped across several time zones. That insight applies at lower levels too, where industrial timing is often at odds with the clocks inside workers' bodies. The evidence of poor performance across so many occupations, along with what we know about the adverse impact of phase shifts, suggests that it is part of the explanation for mishaps.

In a number of calamities that occurred at night, what were the physiological states of the personnel? In a suburb of Mexico City a gas storage and distribution plant of the Pemex Company exploded Monday morning, November 19, 1984. In the evening several days before, a gas flare had gone out, and gas began seeping into the surroundings. Then, about five o'clock in the morning,

workers who were transferring liquefied petroleum gas from a pipe-
line miscalculated and overfilled one of the huge storage tanks. It
failed to withstand the pressure and ruptured. The escaping gas
found an ignition source, perhaps an engine spark from a passing
vehicle or a cigarette ember, and burst into enormous boiling liquid
and vapor explosions. The brilliant, burning flashes incinerated
hordes of houses in the surrounding neighborhoods, killed more than
a thousand people, and displaced two hundred thousand more.[35]
In the late spring of 1985, in Louisiana's channel waters called
Bayou Chene, which lead to oil and gas fields offshore, a barge with
an oil rig on it that was being towed by three tugboats to a new
drilling location capsized about 1 A.M. At least ten of its twenty-
two-man crew drowned. The company balked at making other details public, but the time of the accident could not be concealed.
Shortly after midnight in central France, on August 31, 1985, an
experienced engineer driving a passenger train failed to reduce its
speed on a curve. He saw a signal telling him to slow down, for he
pressed a button that indicates the driver has seen the signal; otherwise automatic brakes would have been activated immediately. The
racing train derailed as it traversed a section of track being re-
paired, and minutes later some of the end cars were smashed by
another train that followed. Forty-nine persons were killed, and a
hundred were hospitalized.[36] The preliminary statement of the
causes of the nuclear power plant explosion at Chernobyl in the
Ukraine on April 26, 1986, referred to human error, specifically
noting that "a number of consecutive incorrect actions" were taken
by the technicians while moving reaction control rods during a
shutdown.[37] The Chernobyl disaster took place at 1:23 A.M. Those
events are recent, and information about them is incomplete, but
their occurrence after dark argues that systematic attention to the
timing of such calamities is overdue.

Work scheduling is the pivot around which other components
of the community timetable turn. If work shifts can reach inside
the human body and unsettle its functions, they surely affect routines in workers' families. The employees of incessant organizations
conduct the change into their own households. At night community
activity infringes on daytimers' sleep. At night in the household,
other persons are affected by the shift worker's comings and goings.
His wife stays up later to greet him or, when the alarm clock rings,
gets up to chat while he prepares to leave. The bustle, clatter, and

noise of running water sometimes awaken the children. The shift rotations of married male workers scramble schedules for their wives. They have to change the hours they prepare meals as well as having to cope with separate cooking efforts for husbands and for others in the family.

Home routines are affected by the workers trying to sleep in the daytime. The norm of honoring sleep is as potent in the house as it is for chieftains of incessant organizations. "If he sleeps in the morning or during the week," one wife said, "I don't do housework because I can't run the vacuum cleaner or dust. I do quiet things." Another commented, "I have to wait until he gets up to do my daytime chores. . . . I always worry that when I clean I might wake him up." The children cannot move around freely because the bedroom is put off limits to shield the sleeper. Mothers tell their offspring to play quietly, not to slam the door, not go near the sleeper's room, and not to bring home many friends after school. They send them outside when possible.[38] Sleep is interrupted more if there are more youngsters in the family and fewer rooms in the home.[39] The would-be sleeper complains about boisterous children and housekeeping noises and insists that the others should be quieter or do something else.

For the most part these tales are about men because more full-time shift workers are men. The traditional inequality between the sexes leaves it harder for the female to win the same cooperation from family members. A surgical nurse working full time on the night shift said her husband and teen-aged children could not understand her need for sleep. The children were always saying, "Mom, all you ever do is sleep all the time, and every time we see you, you're sleeping."[40]

But sleep is also attacked from outside the home. It is pestered by the bustle of others while the sun is up. Trash collectors move dumpsters and garbage cans. Noises of hammering, of music on radio sets at high volume, voices of lively children, and the sounds of lawn mowers, all travel into the bedroom. In the middle of the night one can march over to a noisy neighbor and indignantly demand quiet, but that is inappropriate in the middle of the day.[41] Night workers try various devices such as ear plugs and heavy muffling curtains to insulate themselves. It is hard to say which telephone calls annoy them more, those from strangers selling something or those from friends who ring up when they should know better. "No one will call someone at 2:30 in the morning," one man fumed, "but they won't think twice about waking me up. I answer the phone and they say, 'I'm sorry.' . . . They can't get it through their heads."[42] And when the bell tolls for another member of the household it is heard by all. If living alone they are still disturbed by ringing telephones and doorbells. One man pinned a sign saying "DAY SLEEPER" to his front door in an effort to ward off casual visitors and door-to-door salesmen.[43] Sometimes that turns out to be an invitation to pranksters rather than a restraint. The sleep of all who are exposed to incessance is hunted at all hours. No one is spared. Sleep, more than particular individuals, seems to be the prey.

Tired much of the time, the shift worker would rather lounge than go out with his family. "You go," he says, "I'll stay home." If he laments about the trials of working off-hours, his children tell him to get a daytime job. If he tries to participate in their normal schedule on his days off, he ends up worn out and grumpy. In the heyday of the railroader, unless he could manage to have his meals coincide with those of his children he might not see them at all.[44] Evening and night employees often do not eat with their families, and admit that they see less of their youngsters.[45] Police wives feel cheated of the companionship they view as their entitlement; they complain that their children are unfairly deprived of the company of their fathers. Unhappy at her husband's being so rarely available, one police wife feared that the telephone ringing when he was off duty meant the chief was calling him in for urgent service, so she avoided answering it.[46]

In shift worker families, couples often go to bed at different times. In one instance "the cycles of the couple were so out-of-phase that they saw little of each other except for weekends; since the wife worked by day and the husband by night they could have shared a bed, but not together."[47] Ordinary bedtime is an adjournment of practical duties, an easing of the daily pace, and a moment of reunion for partners. When they meet in bed their mood is softer, other responsibilities are put aside, and scrutiny is diminished. They are not in a hurry, and they are available. Intimacy, like everything in social life, has its routines. Even if they did not lie down in passion, their desire is enhanced by talking things over, telling of a pleasant moment or rekindling a memory, expressing the day's worry, making plans, realizing physical closeness, touching, and gently synchronizing their psychological and biological states. The cloak of night also covers persons who might otherwise be embarrassed to show erotic interest. A couple's loving develops a regularity suited to their concurrent emotions and their bodies' clocks. But if one is a shift worker, there will be more absent passion as well as total absence. When in bed together the two may be physiologically out of phase, one partner fresh and rested, the other not; one interested in sex, the other not.[48] Night is for lovers, except for shift workers.

Couples make special efforts to fulfill themselves on weekends or when the children are away. One wife says, "We have sex on weekends. We can't get together during the week." Another remarks, "When you're living parallel but not necessarily congruent lives, you have to plan for it. You don't always make love at night." A husband adds, "You probably tend to have relations less frequently because you have to think about it, to plan strategies. You find you're no longer totally spontaneous."[49] If they try in the daytime, it is less gratifying because they hurry more. Some are averse to making love in daylight. Shy, traditional, or religious, they find it awkward and less enjoyable. Daytime is also a period with higher risk of interruptions from one's children, neighbors, relatives, friends, doorbells, and telephones. A wife explains: "We get together a lot fewer times . . . we have had certain problems. We've had the doorbell ring. My mother came over one afternoon and we were upstairs. But it seems like a rush. You haven't much time to stay in the bedroom. You have to worry about the baby or someone coming. It is more of a hurry-up deal."[50] Since the opportunities are less frequent the couple may feel extra pressure to make the most of each event, in the same way that people compulsively take full advantage of vacations because they come so rarely.

As the job separates night workers from the main community rhythm, it also hinders their ordinary social life. Near as the workers are to their neighbors, they are less accessible. Friends do not pay visits if they expect their host will leave them shortly to go to work, or if they cannot be sure whether he is sleeping or working. Since many wives will not go to gatherings without their husbands, the isolation is imposed on them too. Rotating workers have fewer friends than do employees who are steady on a shift. After a while they mix less and lose touch with some of them. Friendships, however, are not regimented by a timetable. Although the absolute chance of seeing friends and relatives may diminish, it remains greater than the chance for formal recreations. It is harder to be an active member of a club, sports team, union chapter, or fraternal order. Shift workers cannot attend meetings regularly, and they belong to fewer voluntary organizations than do day workers.[51] Instead they indulge more in leisure that does not depend as much on coordination with others. They take up solitary hobbies and do-it-yourself projects and turn to domestic tasks like gardening or house repairs when they feel energetic. Loners may move to the nighttime, but the nighttime also creates loners.

Persons who live alone have a less structured routine, but off-hours work cramps their social life. They reply to invitations with "I have to check what shift I'll be on." The uncertainty persists, because when the new schedule is posted it is still vulnerable to last-minute changes. Offers from others dwindle after several invitations are turned down because of having to work. The lone shift workers sigh and tell themselves, "I'm left out a lot of the time." When able to join a party, they cannot be there from start to finish. Those who work evenings will miss the first few hours. They arrive late and, having to mix with friends who have been drinking and laughing together for several hours, feel conspicuously sober. Guests at one chic gathering received a visual shock when three nurses in white uniforms suddenly appeared in the company about midnight. They had just finished their evening stint and had hurried to join the party without taking time to change their clothes.

If due on the night shift, the workers have to watch the clock and leave just as the party is going strong.[52] In order to be sober on the job they must be very prudent in drinking. Knowing they will have to leave early, they are less disposed to join friends for a dinner or a show. "Going out with girls is something else," says a man who works as a dispatcher at night. "A girl has to be very understanding. . . . She also has to not mind being taken home at 10:30 P.M."[53]

In the workplace after dark, the most noticeable difference from daytime is the easier pace. Portions of the organization have shut down. Office machines stop clacking, and telephones go dumb. Fewer people come and go. Interruptions dwindle. Mail deliveries stop. There is less need to hurry. With the hubbub diminished, places that were too distracting for small talk in the daytime become amenable at night.

The atmosphere is freer with few managers around. A dearth of bosses may make top-level decision-making problematic, but it also leaves lower-echelon workers with more responsibility. They feel trusted, and proud to be on their own. They work at their own pace, have more personal control over tasks, and take breaks without worrying what the boss will think. They come to work dressed informally. The few supervisors on duty behave otherwise than they would in the daytime. They walk in wearing open-collared shirts and are on a first-name basis with everyone.[54] All feel stronger ties at work and develop warmer friendship circles than are found among daytime associates.[55] They may have fewer involvements with neighbors where they live, but they have more co-worker friends.[56] It is a solidarity encouraged by the sense of sharing an unconventional timetable and of having a different life-style from day workers,[57] and expressed when the night workers rally together in any case of conflict among the shifts.

Even commuting to and from work is less stressful. Shift workers travel during off-peak hours or move in opposite directions from everyone else. They speed along emptier roads, congratulating themselves that their travel takes fewer minutes than the journey in heavy traffic. Others ride in empty subway cars or uncrowded buses. Among passengers on public conveyances, those who board at the first station secrete less adrenalin than those who come on after seating is more restricted.[58] The presence of that hormone, which raises one's blood pressure, is much greater under crowded conditions.

The lenient pace pervades other parts of night workers' lives. They often mention the pleasures of being out of step with the society that goes hurly burly around them.[59] They need not dash to the post office or to the bank along with grabbing a meal in the lunchtime break. They shop in the daytime when the stores are unpopulated, lunch with friends, arrange doctor or dental appointments without having to ask for time off from work. Errands do not pile up for the weekend. Of frequenting dining places outside regular meal times, one worker said "It's nice to be able to eat without someone breathing down my neck waiting for my seat." They go to the beach on weekdays, when there are no crowds. Those who live in apartment houses discover they have an adequate supply of hot water when they want it, instead of settling for a trickle at the same time all the other tenants are bathing.

Despite the boons in easier commuting, errand-going, and ca-maraderie on the job, few persons like shift work unreservedly. Rather than embrace it, most simply do not mind it. In Great Britain, when employees in an organization having twenty-four-hour staffing requirements were asked what they would like, three-fifths preferred permanent days and only 12 percent chose to rotate.[60] In the United States night workers in both a mental hospital and an electronics plant, in each case doing the same jobs as day workers there, rated their own jobs lower in prestige.[61] A survey of wives in another setting found only half of them saying they were satisfied with their husbands' job schedules.[62]

All that affects them, whatever the details, is rooted in the schedule. A body that cannot sleep, a spouse who is not there to love, a family routine astray, an unattended club meeting, a friend missed—all follow from having moved to the other side of the com-munity timetable. They step into job demands that know no hourly boundaries. Their minds know what is coming, but they cannot warn their bodies. Family life is ordinarily thought to be a refuge from the hurts suffered outside. The household's communal mood is supposed to soothe the alienated laborer and rehabilitate him from the harsh impositions of the workplace. But shift jobs disrupt house-hold routines, and families absorb the confusion. The bonds and involvements of home, already loosened by industrialization, are further frayed by off-hours work.

For the workers there are few special ballads and yarns to cel-ebrate their venture into the night.[63] After their duties some hands gather to drink and exaggerate their experiences, yet no tales burst-ing with comic exuberance about night work have come to the fore. In our culture the word "pioneer" implies a courageous spirit, but few night workers feel akin to the bold explorer. Tell shift workers they are modern pioneers, and you remind them that they live on the fringe of the daily round. They become preoccupied with jus-tifying their life-style. They recite the benefits of shift work and call themselves voluntary misfits who choose to be outside conven-tional society.

8

Coinciding Trends

We already know the destiny of the night frontier. It began hundreds of thousands of years ago and burgeoned in the last two centuries. The long record of adding to wakefulness and deducting from sleep leaves no doubt that it is well along its course. Its benefits are so familiar they are taken for granted, its discomforts so commonplace that many of them are suffered by habit. What clearer criteria are there for deciding that a frontier has taken hold than its durability, growth, and consent to benefits and costs alike? Since our nighttime venture is part of the ongoing affairs of society, other patterns bear on it. Incessance has a life of its own but is also enmeshed in the rest of life. Other social, biological, and psychological conditions resist, withstand, and augment the night frontier. That broader set of circumstances is not as coherent as those already reviewed, for they occur as part of a general course of events and without an overall plan. But a main social trend is successful because it adapts from what is at hand, joining compatible circumstances whose origins were at first independent of it. Our wakefulness after dark also encounters trends that began separately from concerns for expansion, and their effects add up to some unexpected confirmations of the night frontier.

One of the most telling trends is the failure of efforts to quell shift work. Opposition to it arose almost as soon as around-the-clock manufacturing was introduced. The perception that night work is unnatural inspired the sentiment that it should be banished. But workers, individually and in groups, demonstrated that they preferred job chances more than they regretted abnormal hours.

Once gas lighting was introduced, economic ·pushes and pulls were foremost in expanding activity after dark. Entrepreneurs took advantage of factories and equipment that had been left idle overnight. Cotton, steel, glass, and paper mills, even when not employing personnel around the clock, would have them come in at sunrise and stay till near midnight. In some places workers labored until two in the morning, then slept in the factory until 5 A.M., when they rose and resumed work.[1] Where shifts were practiced, the absence of one employee was counteracted by asking another from the turn just ending to continue on the next. Some people toiled three twelve-hour shifts in a row. Lawmakers, unions, and other citizens protested the nighttime's effects upon labor. They declared that work after dark was injurious and that women and children especially were being harmed by it. The most obvious impairment was that night workers could not get proper sleep and recovery in the daytime. A child needed rest at night. A woman should not be out then because of the risks to her health, her family life, her household duties, and her virtue.

England's Parliament enacted law after law to shield women and the young. Every few years, beginning in 1802, it passed new legislation with those aims in mind.[2] Its statutes barred night work for apprentices, who were usually younger persons. It banned workers under eighteen years old from labor at night and children from working after 7 P.M. It prohibited night work for women and imposed caps on the length of their work spans. Even the shift work system itself was annulled several times.

As overnight enterprises multiplied in the United States, diverse groups on this side of the Atlantic voiced the same objections. Legislators passed statutes resembling the English laws. Hiring supervisors asserted that the factory was no place for women at night, when the work was too hard. An official of a labor group said that "our women and minors ought to be taken care of, and . . . when they get to 6 o'clock at night it is late enough for any woman or child to be found in a cotton mill." Other men opposed giving females jobs at night because it permitted more immorality. When Massachusetts passed a law restricting night work in 1890, it was seeking to stop textile mill employers from hiring for a second shift the women who had already completed a ten-hour stint in a nearby plant. The women sought the jobs because their wages were low. The National Consumers' League, an organization formed by women to improve their working conditions, denounced the weariness imposed on women who slept few hours and the consequences of neglected children and squalid homes.[3] Supreme Court Justice Louis Brandeis joined to write a public tract making the case against night work for women.[4]

The legislation was repeated decade after decade, which attested to the futility of trying to confine night work once it was started. England could no more curb labor after dark than it could repeal the machine age. Employers declared their urgent need for labor. Industrialization's engine roared too loud for them to heed the laws. Entrepreneurs claimed that there was no difference in health between day and night workers and that children did not suffer. They spoke of the increased expense of production: It would be costlier to employ adults if youngsters were barred from working after dark. They introduced split-shift assignments when the lengths of shifts were bounded. They disregarded the ages of youths who applied for jobs. Parents' objections were muffled by the extra income their offspring brought in.

Karl Marx knew of the laws on the books when he declared that night work was another mode of exploiting human labor. He was incensed that Parliament had not voted a penny to have the code enforced.[5] Unions underscored the long hours as one of their prime concerns. The American Federation of Labor undertook to reduce the hours of work in the late nineteenth century by campaigning for an eight-hour day. In the same period some managers in the steel industry independently recognized that twelve hours was too much to ask from the workers, and decided to institute three turns of eight hours each. This, the managers affirmed, would enable the men to work harder constantly.[6] In New York State, an association of street and railway employees lobbied for laws protecting women, but when it went into effect in 1919 eight hundred dues-paying female members of the union found themselves unemployed. Female workers began fighting such legislation or seeking exemptions, because thousands of them were losing their jobs.[7]

Women challenged the restrictions as part of trying to eliminate discrimination between the sexes. To the U.S. Supreme Court they objected to a New York State law that prohibited them (exempting singers, actresses, cloakroom attendants, and hat-check girls) from working in restaurants after 10 P.M. That campaign failed. The justice who spoke for the majority upholding it in 1924 wrote that "night work so seriously affected the health of women, so threatened and impaired their peculiar and natural functions, and so exposed them to the dangers and menaces incident to night life that the State felt impelled" to enact the law.[8]

The International Labor Organization long sought to impose bans on night work for females and for all persons under eighteen. Labor unionists, sociologists, and biologists argued for reducing shift work because of its harmful physical and social effects. Health is not for sale, they said, and the worker's family life must be protected. In recent years they tried to place legal limits on after-hours work in France, England, and Japan.[9] Others retorted that if a poor person could rescue himself and his family from malnutrition through taking a shift job, he would gain more in health than he might lose through upended physiological rhythms.[10]

A broader refutation has come in the behavior of workers themselves. They accept shift work because it is employment. Employment stands higher in their priorities than many other considerations. They disperse to hunt for job opportunities, and they accept them at night if the alternative is no work at all. They suspend ordinary social life and do the best they can to persevere. Coincidentally, the spirit of the drive for parity between the sexes led to new legislation avowing the principle of equal opportunity; adult men and women were given the right to make a personal choice about the times they would work. As long as the population of seekers exceeds the population of jobs, the prohibitions of night work will be overruled.

In several ways, in the various settings of society, people are socialized to the timetable and conditions of the incessant community. A portion of the children in the population live in households where one or more adults are active beyond midnight. If older persons follow after-dark schedules, as where a member of the family is a shift worker, the children are inducted into routines that prepare them for a more wakeful nighttime. They are in contact with elders who are up and about, taught to comprehend a diffused timetable, and reassured that a parent who works at night is doing something ordinary and acceptable. By the time they are grown they are more prepared for it. Somewhat more favorable attitudes and a better adjustment are found where shift work is common and has existed for a long time.[11]

Our society also prepares its people to be more capable in making and unmaking social ties. It is a capacity that turns out to help withstand some effects of reassignments in incessant organizations. In traditional, well-settled areas, persons raised and living in enduring groups are comfortable with their own kind and are otherwise reserved in social contacts. That outlook changes with modernization, in the course of which they learn to combine, break up, and recombine with others repeatedly. Increasingly, individuals are transferring more among dwelling places, jobs, friendships, and intimate social relationships. Their informal training begins with meeting different babysitters and steps up soon afterward at school, as the child is exposed to sundry teachers, classes, and schoolmates. The administration in an elementary school deliberately reshuffles pupils from one year to the next with the aim of developing their abilities in appropriate social environments. In high school the bell that rings at the end of the hour signals a transfer to another social group as well as to another academic subject. By the end of a day a student has joined and left friends in classroom after classroom while moving from one study topic to another. College-educated persons undergo four additional years of intermixing repeatedly with classmates in different courses.

In the years that follow the reshufflings continue, because young adults change jobs often. They meet new co-workers and become accustomed to departures from their work groups. Executives transferred by their firms join the reshuffled hosts. Making and breaking relationships is practiced in the community through social dating before marriage, and today's marriages are followed in increasing ratios by divorce. The high divorce rate is a sign of recombining more than of the breakup of the institution of marriage, for remarriage rates almost keep pace with divorce rates. People are changing partners, not the institution of partnership.[12]

Each person is not alone in encountering replacements among parents, caretakers, teachers, classmates, neighbors, co-workers, and friends, for each meets others doing the same. All undergo removal from one group and splicing into another. By generating a series of unstable social environments, the culture produces a personality that may be called a recombinant individual, a person more effective in suspending involvements and reestablishing other ones than the type who did not travel far from home, who knew one set of kin and a circumscribed neighborhood, and who was shier with outsiders.

The recombinant individual does not give up ties without re-
gret, but has skills to adapt socially and become involved more
readily upon moving from one group to another. At one time we
thought that socially fragmented environments bring on alienation
and inability to achieve personal involvements. But studies of children in day care centers, and of social life in urban areas, show
that is not inevitable. Comparisons between children who were
largely reared in their own families and others who were placed in
day care or nursery school programs consistently find that the latter
are more socially skilled, less anxious, and more confident in their
interactions with others. Compared with youngsters who have not
participated in programs away from their families, those who have
are more interpersonally competent and mature. They are more
gregarious, friendly, responsive, and leaderlike. They develop the
various social abilities that one acquires in becoming an older
child.[13] In adult life, the more people move about, the more similar
the general social environment becomes, and the easier it is to move
about.[14] Subjected to transfers of affection and involvement, they
become more accustomed to them. They grow adept at striking up
acquaintances rapidly. Researchers have found that inhabitants of
large urban communities have more numerous social ties than do
rural residents.[15] Urban dwellers do not lose the capacity for deep,
multifaceted relationships; instead they gain ability for more modest involvements as well.[16]

Friendship, like many human skills, benefits from training and
experience. The readiness to disengage and reshuffle social ties could
be interpreted as the shallow style of a personality bruised by the
disappointments of repeated losses of intimacy. But instead of a contrast between superficial and deep involvements the two may be
seen as successive stages of social relationships. An attachment pro-
gresses in degrees from getting acquainted to more intimacy. A casual friend would be a meager achievement only if one's capacities
were blocked beyond that phase, but the capacity to be superfi-
cially involved is a prerequisite for deeper ties. The recombinant
individual has an interpersonal style of being more flexible, affable,
open to a wider range of alliances, and, along with being more
capable of entering new relationships, a greater confidence when
leaving them.

The incessant organization's reliance on shift relays leads to social disruptions. Work groups are not moved as wholes among the

shifts; individuals are reassigned. Each rotation calls upon the person to let go of attachments to some co-workers and join with others willingly. The setting is a kaleidoscope of people tumbling in and out of temporary contacts with one another. Its employees do not welcome being pulled out of work teams and inserted into other ones, nor is it accepted without a sense of losing co-worker friends. The scheduler does not ship along the special human relationships. Romances are not transferable. Neither are the nuances of what to expect from the supervisor on duty. Nor can workers carry from one time slot to another the informal arrangements for who brews the coffee and who unofficially decides disputes. But the quality of the effect is not new. The reshuffled groups are made up of people who know a lifetime of interchanging and are partly inured to it.

In employment and otherwise, more chances to withdraw and to enter new relationships are offered by the incessant community. Some separations last only until the persons' orbits coincide again. Shift work does not have the character of having pulled up stakes and moved permanently to a remote outpost; members of the nighttime labor force are always transferring to the daytime. Similarly, for emotional reasons people may retreat fleetingly instead of severing a tie for good. The night affords temporary social distance. It is more affordable for those who cannot bear the costs of moving away. It is cheaper than geographic travel, and one can return to the main schedule fairly easily, affording chances to renew social ties.

This coinciding trend of recombinance is relevant to psychological adjustment. There are, as well, pertinent biological trends. Some compatible effects are being wrought more subtly by lighting itself.

Light, in addition to enabling a venture at any hour, dispels drowsiness. In doing so it conditions people to be active at night. Since early in the nineteenth century, when gas lighting was introduced, people have subjected themselves to far more illumination indoors than their ancestors ever encountered. Not only are households bathed in luminous intensities many times that of candlepower or oil lamps, but the photoperiod is also extended.

Longer exposure to light renders individuals physically fit to stay up later. It does so by reducing the presence of the hormone melatonin in the blood. A high concentration of melatonin in the bloodstream is connected to drowsiness.[17] It seems to have sedative properties, for when doses of the hormone were given experimentally to a number of healthy men, they reported feeling sleepier.[18] Melatonin is present at higher levels in children, and perhaps that is a biochemical reason why they sleep longer than older persons. The hormone is secreted by the pineal gland, but the gland's production of it is skimpier when a person is immersed in light. Indeed, the synthesis of melatonin is coupled to the light–dark cycle, and the hormone's rhythmic presence in the bloodstream reflects the cycle with a much lower level in the daytime and its highest concentration at night during sleep.[19] Experiments clarifying the effect relied on drenching subjects in illumination several times greater than ordinary indoor levels, but other research indicates that creatures also respond to the duration of the period of light and that melatonin levels drop after prolonged exposure.[20] Exposure to both natural and artificial forms of illumination inhibits the pineal gland. Since people switched from an agricultural to an indoor industrial way of life, they encounter less intense light through artificial illumination, but for much longer periods. Since a consequence of lower melatonin levels is that people do not feel as sleepy, the extended illumination is conferring a greater capacity to postpone sleep and is therefore an ally of wakefulness in modern times.

Light has still another, longer-term effect, because the hormone melatonin is also involved in the process of puberty. The hormone holds back the rate at which this maturation occurs. Light, by decreasing the amount produced, therefore hastens puberty indirectly. The completion of puberty brings a tidal change in the behavior of others toward the adolescent, including conceding the privilege of staying up later. Since being allowed to postpone bedtime is an entitlement that comes with being more physically mature, the average amount of wakefulness in a population will rise if its average age of puberty drops.

For the past century and a half children in many industrialized nations have been starting puberty and undergoing the transformation to sexual adulthood at younger ages. It now comes about three years earlier than it did in the mid-1800s.[21] Changes in nutrition have played a role. A poor diet and being underweight will delay one's growth and maturation, whereas children who are better fed and have adequate body weight start the changes of puberty sooner.[22] Sexual development came at an earlier age in countries where the gain in prosperity accompanying the Industrial Revolution brought better food supplies and improved nutrition. Moreover, within those nations, children from well-off families reached puberty at a younger age than did those from the underprivileged.[23]

Along with being better fed, the higher standard of living enjoyed by prosperous populations includes dwelling in households that are more amply lit. The settings where children reach puberty earlier are also settings in which persons are exposed to more light. Menarche (the most reliable signal that puberty is under way) arrives earlier among girls in just those places where people use more electricity and keep lights on longer every day: in industrialized rather than unindustrialized nations, in the city rather than in the country, and among the more prosperous classes.[24]

The effect of extending the daily length of light was first recognized in nature in relation to sunlight. It hastens growth in living things, for they respond physiologically to the span of day length relative to darkness. But natural and artificial illumination work in broadly similar ways.[25] Farmers regulate the photoperiod of domesticated animals to stimulate their development. In commercial chicken coops extra lighting has been used for decades to regulate body growth in hens and to increase their egg laying. By exposing some large animals to light for longer periods daily, farmers hasten their breeding timetables. Cattle do not have a special breeding season. Like humans, they ovulate and conceive throughout the year. But heifers born in seasons of increasing daylight reach puberty about two months earlier than those born when the photoperiod is contracting. Stock breeders deliberately expose heifers to longer periods of illumination. As a result, even when feed intakes are restricted, dairy animals undergoing sixteen hours of light daily show higher rates of weight gain than those subjected to twelve hours or less.[26] Those successes demonstrate that extending the daily length of light can be used to escalate growth in living things.

Are human beings also influenced by lengthened photoperiods? Scientists are cautious about transferring conclusions from other species to our own, but we are physiological kin to the mammals that show faster maturation in longer light.[27] That result favors recognizing a role for illumination in the growth and development of humans too. Its effect on puberty was not studied systematically at first, because researchers' attention was drawn to other possible influences. For example, in the past children in the tropics seemed to arrive at puberty at younger ages than those in temperate zones.

Scholars believed that temperature was the compelling influence, but careful studies failed to demonstrate a connection. Temperature and light, however, accompany one another; the days grow balmier as daylight lengthens. Another reason why the influence of lighting was not discerned is that researchers may have attended to natural light alone, for that is how the photoperiod was initially understood. The level and the duration of sunlight fluctuate daily and over the course of the year, and if a study were limited to natural light it would underrepresent actual exposure. Natural, tungsten, and fluorescent light differ in their spectral lengths; although we do not know the precise effects of each, the overall pattern of exposure must be taken into account. In modern times, especially in winter, artificial light would add generously to the daily length of the photoperiod.

The body begins puberty with an elaborate array of conditions in place. When the hypothesis was first made that increased light stimulation is directly connected to faster bloom in children, it was accompanied by a proposal that the pineal gland and its hormone melatonin play a role in the process.[28] Melatonin guards the pace at which sexual development in adolescence will occur. It probably provides a signal to other processes in the body and controls the release of other hormones that foster rapid body growth and changes in reproductive organs.[29] Its effect is to impose an upper limit on the speed of development, and it controls the process by acting like a braking device. For example, with a governor installed in a car, one cannot go faster than a predetermined top speed even while pressing on the drive pedal, whereas once the governor is removed the system accelerates in response to the other forces pushing it forward. By checking the rate at which some functions for puberty occur, melatonin governs the pace of maturing.[30] Once the hormone's presence is diminished, other processes have swifter effects. Its retarding power slips away, and growth surges ahead.[31] Thus two negatives make a positive: Light suppresses the work of the gland that produces melatonin, and when the concentration of that hormone is reduced, the physical changes in puberty speed up.[32]

This advance along a biological path then takes a turn into a social realm, for other persons adjust their behavior to the appearance of more physical maturity. Even parents, who know the actual birthdates of their children, are affected. Being physically mature is interpreted as being more socially mature, and the child who looks older will be treated older. A study of the interaction between parents and their adolescent children found that the parents did respond in that way. Conversations between parents and child were related to the child's physical appearance, independent of his or her age or reasoning abilities.[33] Among other things, being treated as an adult sooner in life allows youths to stay up later if they choose.

Therefore, light exposure grants environmental, biological, and social conditions for more wakefulness. By illuminating the surroundings, it enables people to be effective after dark. On a long-term basis, it brings people earlier to the social status that permits them to stay up later after dark. And it puts off their drowsiness so that they can keep going. On the brink of adulthood, an individual in our culture is ushered toward a mature body that can be less sleepy in a community offering more opportunities at night.

No mastermind is at work, no deliberate program or guiding principle operates, and yet in the long term several other conditions have joined with the causes of colonizing the night to improve personal adaptation to it. Our characters and our bodies are changing and becoming suited to the particulars of incessance. Being reared in a more wakeful household, accelerating the timetable of maturation, hormonal levels in the blood being less conducive to drowsiness, and practices of repeatedly recombining in personal relationships all contribute to a better fit between persons and nighttime undertakings. Social, biological, and psychological processes have combined to transform us in ways to fit the environment we refashioned, and the community is being stocked with people who are more comfortable with its timetable. Along with altering our milieu, we are altering ourselves.[34]

What the transitional group finds harsh about incessance will be felt as more natural by the next generation. It will not know the past or feel a loss of what it did not experience. It will have less of the sense of discord that the pioneer generation had in trying to bear up under the transition. Reared in the changed environment, our children will take incessance for granted.

9

Future Times

From year to year our expansion in time may seem drawn out. We live in the midst of the growth and it appears piecemeal, until one day we look back and notice how much has happened. If we realize that most of the dark hours were converted to activity in less than two hundred years and consider how small a fraction that is of the time we have been on this planet, our pace of colonizing the night is spectacular. The earth continues to rotate, light and shadow take their turns passing across its face, but human affairs no longer revolve as much as they used to according to those cues. Along with spatial ecology, think of temporal ecology. Along with densely settled areas, think of incessance. Along with landscape, think of timescape.

The sun and our spinning planet gave us an environment of alternating light and darkness, which once completely ruled our daily round. We adapted to it in body functions, behavior, family routines, and organizational forms. All were fitted to a cycle of activity and quiet. The separate phases were marked clearly. Projects were bounded by dawn and dusk, and the dark interval was a haven from daytime demands, a rejuvenating retreat. We took it for granted that it was the natural way to live. It was.

Yet in the distant past we began to modify that schedule. The change started with using fire as a source of illumination, and in the same way that our feats of navigation and making fur clothing enabled us to reach across spaces, gaining control of light enabled us to reach across the hours. The advance proceeded slowly until William Murdock made a decisive contribution at the beginning of the 1800s. His gas lighting device and later Edison's electric version enabled us to produce a semblance of daytime around the clock. Our affairs began to spill over into the dark, and we reached for the relief and productive opportunities that the additional time allowed.

Activity at night also fulfills demand for more public access to goods and services. It holds out jobs for the disadvantaged, whether they are young or of a minority group or just plain poor. With store hours open so long, the weekday pace is eased. People more easily tolerate having forgotten a purchase and revise plans. And although the community resents some night intrusions, the poor, the working class, and the middle class benefit most, because the rich and the powerful could already command goods and services at any hour.[1] By spreading all facets of our lives over more of the day, we have created a more complex community, in which the diffusion gives each person more freedom in how to participate and also brings uncertainties into relationships, like family life, that once were close-knit.

It is a new realm with novel experiences, but the pattern of expansion is not new. We have long had a tendency to grow and to fill and exploit our milieu.[2] Whenever we approach the limits of the environment, we intensify efforts to pack it more densely, and as we feel more scarcity and oppressiveness in its bounds, the prospect and meaning of a frontier begin to take shape. It is a way of solving the limitations and shortcomings we encounter, by drawing on the frontier's natural resources and having it relieve the main settlement of some of its burdens.

There is a circular effect in our frontier achievements, for if they are successful the new abundance invites further use of the milieu, and ultimately we will approach the limits of our new environment. In a finite realm, growth itself inhibits further growth. In the case of nighttime, the reasons for using it more continue to be strong. There are still profits to be made by doing something speedier. There is no letup in daytime hubbub, and congestion increases as the population grows. In a service-oriented society amenities are sought in more hours as well as in more places. The emphasis on rapid accommodation to events stays with us. Firms deal with peak or slack seasons of demand by flexibly timing their use of labor. Shift work rises and falls accordingly, and to that extent the use of night hours fluctuates with the economic fortunes of society. In hard times, however, when a nation or region was short of capital, it turned to multiple shifting as a way of reducing unemployment and strengthening its economy. It may do so again. The pushes for worldwide monitoring of political and scientific affairs continue to increase. All dealings across time zones foster more wakefulness. From one era to the next there may be a shift among those priorities for using the night, but if its attraction wanes for one purpose it will be offset by the resurgence of another.

And so the chances of coming up against the limits of this frontier are good. We are bound to confront checks to further growth. One of the most common limitations is diminishing returns for profit-seeking enterprises as markets become saturated. Early in this century an industrialist complained about the folly of manufacturers who resort to multiple shifting as soon as a little profit could be made "and begin to run their mills night and day, thereby heading at once for an overproduction that knocks the bottom from under their market."[3] Recently, in a Boston neighborhood that already had two twenty-four-hour supermarkets, a third store began to stay open. It soon found that there were not enough customers to sustain its schedule, and backed away from nighttime hours.

Another limiter on the use of the night is the loss of a needed resource. Energy in various forms is required to feed any level of activity. When in the waning weeks of 1973 a shortage of fuel oil befell nations in the Western world, resulting from restrictions in shipments of crude oil from Arab lands and sharply higher costs for the amounts still available, the shortage was felt at night as well as in other ways. Following intensive international negotiations, the principal oil exporters resumed shipments four months after the crisis began, but higher prices for gasoline and heating oil and the deliberate withholding of supplies for emergencies had already had their effects. Organizations open to the public after midnight had cut back their hours. Understandably, automobile service stations curtailed their activities. Some restaurants, fast food eating places, and such recreational enterprises as cinemas and bowling lanes did so too. Custodial work in office buildings was switched to daytime schedules to permit a shutdown of heating at night. In Italy, movie houses, restaurants, and night clubs were told to close earlier than usual. By decree British television broadcasting had to stop at 10:30 P.M. to save electricity. Lights in the downtown districts of cities throughout Japan were doused, and the late late show on television was canceled. In other nations lighting displays were turned off, autos were driven less, and activity slackened. In energy-saving moves a year later, the Spanish Interior Ministry ordered cinemas, theaters, bars, cafés, restaurants, and night clubs in Madrid to close earlier than their customary times. The Greek government imposed similar curfews on the tavernas and bouzouki nightclubs of Athens.[4]

In Boston during that period, no cutbacks in active hours were made among indispensable agencies such as medical care units, hot lines, emergency services for households or businesses, utilities, veterinarians, or even retail food and merchandise outlets.[5] Also, twenty-four-hour enterprises withstood the oil embargo better than intermediate-length enterprises. Organizations that had stayed open fourteen to twenty-one hours a day succumbed most to the fuel shortage's effects. In general it was as if the schedule of an incessant organization functioned like a ratchet. Once it advanced to that point, it did not slip back from that level again. It held, not only because it had a useful function, but also because of its time role. It rests its reputation on access; it makes a commitment to availability at all hours. That was potent enough to enable it to resist the initial blow of the energy shortage.

The 1973–74 fuel crisis was not severe or long-lasting. Many of the curbs were eased by the 1980s in the face of a glut of oil and lower prices, and expansion in the use of night resumed. In the future a new shortage of energy may force a retreat again. Its outcome will be based on how much a society is willing to spend for the activity it wants. If we choose to put aside our ideals about other matters, the Rocky Mountains could be leveled and more than a trillion barrels of crude extracted from their oil shale.[6] We can attain one goal if we are willing to concede others, and these choices are often present when we face shortages.

The ultimate limit to the night frontier is set by available time itself. It is delivered in a fixed amount each day. Since night's capacity contains just so many hours, the increase in after-dark activity will stop as it exhausts the supply of time. When settling the West, our nation held onto a myth that it possessed a boundless land. In settling the night we are aware that it is hemmed in. We ended the nineteenth century alive to our vast country, and we shall end the twentieth knowing that in colonizing the night we can go only as far as the dawn.

Audiences chuckled early in this century when Will Rogers advised them to "buy land, they aren't making any more of it." As the century draws to a close, they are wondering how to buy more time. Land fever is being replaced by time fever. We can tell which dimension is society's main concern when its members consult clocks and calendars more often than they look at maps.

People throughout the world try to take advantage of available time. Commercially vigorous Singapore, sitting almost astride the Equator, within a band around the earth in which people typically take a siesta, has put aside that midday custom and conducts its affairs as if it were located 50 degrees farther north. The State Council, China's governmental cabinet, decreed that government employees must take only a one-hour rather than a two-hour lunch period. The regulation applies only to state employees in Peking, but this attack on the traditional two-hour lunch break for Chinese workers is a sign of the beginning of changing time use in that nation.[7] In Moscow, where customers queue up to purchase goods, some people make their living by charging a fee to stand in line at a shop in order to save the place for other persons with no time to spare.

Time seems ever scarcer in the United States. In the fashion of our era a small industry of consultants on its use has developed. They all begin in the same way if they write on the subject. "To waste your time is to waste your life. . . . I can't give you any more time than you already have."[8] "[W]e realize a startling fact about time—there *isn't* any more of it . . . few people have enough; yet everyone has all there is."[9] "Time is the scarcest and most perishable resource."[10] On the job, the minutes allowed for mid-morning breaks are stipulated in labor contracts. Now an afternoon rather than a whole day is devoted to the company picnic. When a worker is bereaved, company policy usually limits the time off allowed for the funeral and mourning to three days.[11] We take courses in speed reading. We make a list of things to do, carefully plan the day's route for errands, and enjoy a moment of triumph when we scratch an item off the list. We buy instant coffee and prepared foods that need only be heated and served, and purchase time-saving appliances like microwave ovens to heat them faster. We are exasperated when having to wait for a repairman who will call at our house at no special time during a given day, to wait beyond the scheduled start of an appointment in someone else's office, and even to wait for a slow-starting automobile at a traffic light. In efforts to make the most of each hour we develop habits that lead to emotional and mental exhaustion. Half of the sixteen attributes linked to the stressed personality called Type A, which is more prone to heart attacks, are associated with a sense of time urgency.[12]

As the search for more time mounts in ardor, people question the worth of sleeping so long. Sleep is the most time-consuming daily activity. It is already a target of attack from those who would like to use its hours for productive purposes.[13] This gentle restorer, so often sought and welcomed, now becomes something to depreciate as the community expands its incessance. A popular how-to-do-it manual on how to manage one's time includes a suggestion for reducing sleep: "You might experiment with reducing your sleep time by, perhaps, half an hour. . . . If you are as effective as you were before, you will gain the equivalent of a week of Sundays in the course of a year."[14] The average number of hours' sleep for Americans was reported as 7.83 hours in 1972 and was closer to seven hours a night in 1984.[15] Informal reporters say the length of sleep per night is shortening in France too. Ambitious, competent persons in all walks of life wryly complain, "I could accomplish everything I need to do if only I could give up sleep." They swallow coffee and amphetamines to stay awake longer. They are on the move for at least two-thirds of the day, and it is not enough.

People seem to need sleep. The longer it is avoided, the harder it is to keep awake. If people are deprived of dreaming, it becomes more difficult to awaken them during the dreaming phase when they next sleep and the dreaming lasts longer. Growth in youngsters, conversion of short-term to long-term memory, a respite from the heat of metabolism, and muscular restoration are all served by sleep. As a periodic remission it has a valuable function of enabling persons to renounce their consciousness of society. "If it were not forced upon us by nature, we would be obliged to find some functional equivalent for it, for social coexistence would cease to be gratifying—or even bearable."[16] Still, sleep is out of place in a society whose populace stays up beyond midnight to watch a feature on cable television and whose employing organizations call for workers at all hours.

Sleep is a complex array rather than a single entity. Eventually we will unbundle its parts and do away with some of them. Already people keep irregular waking hours. Instead of a full night's sleep some scatter bits of it across the day, dozing if possible while commuting to work, grabbing thirty winks on the job, and taking catnaps at home. Researchers try to isolate some of sleep's elements and discover what might substitute for each physical recovery, for dreams, and so on. They are already investigating the use of specific drugs that may regulate the timetables of certain physiological functions. People want to have the choice of when to sleep and whether to sleep at all. The prospect of dispensing with it is not so far in the future. The feat is within the capability of a culture that learned how to improve fertility in humans, how to prolong their length of life, and how to transplant organs from one body to another, and that now creates new organisms by genetic transfer. A society that can accomplish those things, in which people's attitudes and organizational needs unite to encourage science in the goal, will undo sleep if it wishes.

We shall replace part of sleep in a manner resembling the way we mastered light, by developing artificial slumber. It may include techniques of resting while awake, for some scholars say it is possible to get along without sleep by substituting relaxed wakefulness for some of its functions.[17] People who are deprived of sleep engage in some of the processes ordinarily noted in slumber. Some undergo frequent brief sleeplike episodes, called microsleep, which appears as falling into a semiconscious state for several seconds at a time.[18] Drivers on long-distance trips fall asleep briefly behind the wheel, and we may not realize how common it is on other occasions. Even when awake, people may act with partial alertness, moving and deciding and speaking more automatically without realizing that they are doing so. The social, scientific, and biological issues are formidable.

Dispelling sleep will become an option, not something imposed on everyone. The technique will be available but not used by the entire population. Like air travel, it will be resorted to by some, though not all the time. Nevertheless, all our lives will be different because of it. "We shall not all sleep, but we shall all be changed."[19] The wakeful nighttime will be as much in our consciousness at the end of the twentieth century as the land frontier was for people at the end of the preceding one. If we succeed in reducing our sleeping hours, we may console ourselves with knowing that among different species customary sleeping time is inversely related to longevity. The shorter-sleeping organism is longer-lived.[20] And we may express the sentiment offered by a character in the novel *One Hundred Years of Solitude* when his village was overrun by an insomnia plague. In good humor he said, "If we don't ever sleep again, so much the better. That way we can get more out of life."[21]

We shall not fill the night fully and evenly. The growth of wakefulness will not occupy every hour everywhere, any more than our land settlements have crept onto every desert dune or arctic shelf. Not all climates and terrains are equally hospitable to colonization, nor are all hours. The costs would be too high and the yields too low. We also value night's serenity and retreat and want to reserve some of it in its natural state. Daytimers successfully defend some neighborhoods from many intrusions. The vast diurnal population has limits to how much disturbance it will allow, and most people prefer the daytime cycle. Nor will incessance spread everywhere, because its causes are not uniformly distributed geographically. There will be quiet hours in many places. Our globe will be punctuated with enclaves of after-dark activity rather than blanketed by it.

The panorama of our past successes taught us a lesson. It instilled more confidence in us and reinforced our tendency to disperse as a way of coping with dissatisfaction and scarcity. That is the lesson we learned, to spread out rather than to accept limits. That is the mood we hold. If we complete a frontier without resolving its causes, we will soon be interested in other expansions. And when we reach the limits of night, nothing will have happened to abate the causes that make us expand. The forces for escape, relief, opportunity, and profit continue with us. The same conditions that in the past promoted us to spread afar will once more urge us on. So, stirred by the same resolve, we shall scan for new prospects.

We were clever enough to take advantage of the inexpensive, compatible opportunities first. Other frontiers will be more costly, and the adaptive challenges will be more unusual. As we begin to colonize the oceans and the skies, the necessary life support systems, such as aqualungs and airtight space suits, only hint at the expense required. More exotic realms will also have more radical consequences for us personally. We cannot foresee all that will happen to us as individuals. We revise our environment so much that we affect our own adaptation to it. We are not the same creatures, in mood and body and culture, that first emerged and wandered from

East Africa, first mounted a horse, first sowed a seed, first put ink to papyrus. Now we are changing in ability to be wakeful, curtailing sleep, tolerating physiological upsets, precociously maturing, being uncertain about social commitments, accepting reshuffled work groups, and diffusing family life. When we began simply to use more of the time available after dark, we did not imagine creating an incessant community. It developed from the rough-and-tumble of choices made at different times, independent of an overall plan. But a condition of our ventures is that we must accommodate to the course we set in motion. Now there is much to absorb us in the momentum toward wakefulness.

APPENDIX A

A Time Census

The Domesday Book, the first survey report of the Anglo-Saxon people with their ranks, landholdings, and livestock according to their locales, was compiled nine hundred years ago. Although a realm with kingdoms and baronetcies was in existence beforehand, that census, authorized by William the Conqueror, put a stamp of formal record on the social composition of England and provided information to help administer it. Since then we have become familiar with the census and its value to governments. The United States testifies to its importance in Article 1 of the Constitution by calling for it regularly, and it has been conducted almost every decade since 1790.

The mainstay of that census is its list of people by residence. It is a report of geographic distribution, of where people sleep, and the nature of their housing. Although it includes many types of information, it does not say much about the flow and dynamics of daily life. For that we need a time census. In the literature on human ecology writers invariably mention the spatial distribution of people and usually neglect the temporal one.[1] In ecology time is clock time, the hours of the day (hence of days, months, and years) as part of the container of existence, filled as we fill space, just as space in this respect is what is measured by its lengths in three dimensions.

There are no overall time-of-day censuses of community behavior, nor reference volumes available, and few research reports on the topic. No one keeps regular records that would allow us to compose the picture. We lack knowledge of the scope and amount of activity, especially at night. There is little overall charting of how many people are up and about then and what they are doing. A more complete account of social life would be achieved by augmenting traditional census data with knowledge of the temporal distribution of the populace and its activities. It would complement the format of the spatial census and portray human ecology in space-time. It would lend itself to studies for the sake of legislation, taxation, provision of services, and administering a community. It would tell of social and economic developments and about the needs of citizens. The figures obtained could be used to decide the sizes of markets for commercial enterprises. It would make available background information for other research queries in sociology, demography, anthropology, and economics. It would tell us more about the nature of our society.

The daily spreading of activities in time dissipates some of the spatial crowding implied by a census report. Density, as experienced, depends on the hours people are together anywhere, so congestion as a social problem cannot be adequately understood until we also know the times people are present in supposedly crowded places. A time census would provide occupational information beyond demographic data. If we are to understand family functioning, it is pertinent to know that more minority group persons and more young people work evenings and nights. Their household life will differ from that of the daytime labor force. Shift work converts a two-parent household into a single-parent household after dark, and a single-parent household is converted into one with parent absent. Goals of effective social development, and the good sense of forming plans and policies on the basis of sound information, justify a time census.

Some partial time censuses have been tried already. Vehicle traffic in and out of the central business district of Chicago was tallied at all hours of day and night.[2] Today traffic counts are taken and analyzed to understand bridge and road use and to settle such practical details as how to allocate the directions of lanes going through toll booths during commuting hours. The daily temporal distribution of people in several cities has been logged, including the socioeconomic characteristics of their populations.[3] Similar surveys of activities according to the hour of the day have been conducted in a number of nations.[4] More informal reports have been produced by writers for Chicago, for New York, and for Paris. The report on Paris includes a series of maps for several hours of the night, telling which types of establishments open and close at various hours.[5]

Incessance is spreading. In the same spirit that we would want to map a new volcanic island if it surfaced in the Pacific Ocean, we should try to chart nighttime affairs. Many ordinary citizens are awake then, working and traveling, shopping and socializing. The night's prostitutes and homeless persons may live in more notoriety, but they make up a tiny fraction of the wakeful group.

Here is a preliminary census of people and their activities at night. Details of the method by which it was produced are offered in Appendix B. It begins with people at work, because that endeavor dominates most other spheres of life. Moreover, the soundest data are available about the realm of work. The U.S. Bureau of Labor Statistics, similar agencies in other nations, the International Labour Organisation in Geneva, and scholars worldwide contribute orderly information about this aspect of life after dark. Those data are augmented by information from several other sources (see Appendix B) to piece together a fuller account. This roster should be regarded like a map of an early cartographer, which helps us to explore further even though it is incomplete. It may do until other surveyors add to the inventory and revise its details for a more accurate chart of the timescape.

CATEGORIES OF ACTIVITY

A time census requires a list of categories to organize its information. Any given activity may grow or decline in its rate, reflected by the numbers of people involved, but the category itself will abide much longer. Tallies of the number of people involved go out of date sooner than the classification of their activities. This points up another use of a census. It is carried out at a moment of history. Therefore comparisons are possible by repeating it at regular intervals. It may reveal changes in the variety of activities, numbers of people involved, trends in how the day is being used, and hints of the future. A time census taken today becomes a historical record. If the inventory were conducted again perhaps a decade later, we might learn how our society will have changed.

The activity categories are listed in order of the proportion of

members of the public who take part relative to paid personnel.
People out on the streets, for example, are a mainly public enterprise. The size of the listening and viewing audience is many times
greater than the staff of a broadcasting station. There is also a high
ratio of users to the personnel of a telephone system. Therefore those
activities appear at the beginning of Table A–1. Following people
outside their homes (A) and mechanical and electronic devices
available to the public (B), the categories continue with service organizations, including communications, government agencies,
transportation, wholesale and retail trade, health care, and utilities. At the other extreme, the incessant operations of commerce and
industry (K, L, and M) are not as visible internally to the public at
large. Manufacturing plants operate almost wholly with employees, and few outsiders come there.

This order contrasts different influences upon the level of incessance. Commercial and industrial enterprises establish their rates
of activity mainly according to internally generated plans and formal contracts. The numbers of people involved in manufacturing
firms and the levels of activity are scheduled and staged. Their decisions are based on economic considerations and are sensitive to
current events and narrow, relevant cues. They can respond quickly
because their operations are based on private interests and centralized decisions. On the other hand, more diffuse signals come
from the public. The public imparts an aggregate of individual decisions at an unsteady pace. There are few deliberately coordinated
reactions, and therefore an overall message arrives slowly. Consequently, a potentially steep change in the level of incessance that
could be brought on by actions of private enterprises will be tem-
pered by the more ponderous resolutions of the public. Private undertakings deliver sharper stimuli for change. Public participation
confers more stability.

To define and clarify the categories, here are some details about
events that may be less generally known.

B. Mass-user telephone numbers offer constantly available
recorded messages that can be activated by dialing a telephone
number. Most of us have memorized the number for the local
weather report and for the time of day. There are also special numbers for prayers, jokes, the status of autumn foliage, snow and skiing
conditions, bird sightings (provided by the Audubon Society), earth

Table A-1

PART I: YEAR-ROUND INCESSANCE

A. *PEOPLE OUTSIDE, PEDESTRIANS*

B. *UNSTAFFED INCESSANCE*
Coin-operated machines selling food, ice, cigarettes, stamps, drinks, dry cleaning, etc.
Mass-user specialized telephone numbers
Telephone answering devices that record messages
Bank deposit–withdrawal terminals
Computer information networks

C. *INFORMATION TRANSMISSION*
Broadcasting:
  radio and television stations
  news cable and radio systems
Telephone communications:
  telephone systems, including computer time-sharing networks
  telephone answering service
  telephone order-taking for stores and mail catalog sales
  consumer product hot lines
  travel information and reservation offices
  national medical information network
  public relations staffs (to answer queries, make statements)
Emergency service:
  hot lines (dealing with poisons, drugs, suicide prevention, rape, alcoholism, venereal disease, general health, gender identity, psychological crises, self-help guidance, counseling, runaways, parental stress (child abuse prevention), nursing mothers, poor people's legal assistance, fraud, housing needs)

confessionals in churches
Red Cross (general emergency aid)
mayor's complaint office
Monitoring:
  national, state, and city government staffs on duty
  military commands, monitoring posts, missile sites
  headquarters of corporations
  newspaper and magazine publishing

D. *TRANSPORTATION SYSTEMS*
Ships at sea
Airplanes
Railroad trains
Subways
Buses and trolleys
Taxicabs
Rent-a-car, limousine for hire
Long-distance trucks, haulers
Ambulance service
Package or message delivery companies
Post office (internal mail operations; some public windows)
Harbor tugboats
Bridge and turnpike toll collection booths
Terminals (airports, railroad and truck and bus depots, taxi and parking garages)

E. *RETAILERS*
Eating places (fast food, coffee shops, restaurants)
Shops (supermarkets, newsstands, groceries, pharmacies, books, records, clothing)
Markets (e.g., flowers)
Service:
  auto service (fuel stations and repair shops)
  laundromats

(*continued*)

TABLE A–1 (*continued*)

Recreation:
  cinemas
  gambling casinos
  indoor tennis clubs
  chess & backgammon clubs
  bowling lanes, billiard halls

F. *EDUCATIONAL* (see also T)
Classroom instruction
Computing centers

G. *PERSONS HOUSED*
Hotels and motels
Vacation resorts
Hospital inpatient wards
Halfway houses (on call)
Jails and prisons
Military bases
Geriatric homes
Funeral homes (on call)

H. *UTILITIES, SERVICES*
Electric power company
Gas supply company
Laundries (large, commercial)
Emergency services (on call):
  fire department
  veterinary service
  auto towing
  equipment repair technicians (for
    industrial and residential
    subscribers)
  heating service (oil burner repair,
    fuel)
  plumbers, flood drainage
  sewer and drain clearing
  plate glass and auto glass installers
  locksmiths
  electricians
  television and appliance repair

diapers (for subscribers)
insurance claims office, assessors

I. *PROTECTION, GUARDING*
Police stations, patrols
Watchmen, security guards,
  apartment house doormen
Border and coast guards; customs
Private vault companies
Detectives, investigators

J. *PROFESSIONAL SERVICE*
Physicians (on call)
Dentist on duty
Hospital emergency ward
Bail bondsmen (on call)
Law offices

K. *OTHER COMMERCIAL*
Large offices and data processing
  departments (e.g., in banks,
  insurance companies)
Brokerage houses
Printing and publishing
Rush typing service

L. *MANUFACTURING,*
   PROCESSING
Factories: smelting primary metals,
  fabricating and assembly (vehicles,
  electrical equipment, machines,
  munitions, appliances), stone and
  clay (ceramic, brick), glass (bottle,
  sheet), paper, plastics, textiles,
  chemicals, rubber (tires etc).,
  refineries, breweries, plants for food
  processing (canning, baking)

M. *EXTRACTING*
Mines
Oil drilling rigs (on shore, offshore)

PART II: PERIODIC AND SPORADIC INCESSANCE

N. *FUNDRAISING*
Marathon appeals via broadcasters
Evangelical prayer crusades

O. *RECREATION*
Sightseeing and tourism
Golf courses

TABLE A–1 (*continued*)

Ice skating rinks	Order and shipping departments of
College student gatherings in beach	stores before Christmas
resorts at spring recess	Shop and factory busy periods or for
	special orders
P. *CULTURAL PERFORMANCES*	Consulting and architect firms
Mardi Gras in New Orleans, Rio de	preparing proposals
Janeiro, other pre-Lenten fests	
(e.g., Tarahumaras, Mexico)	S. *SPECIFIC VENTURES*
Annual folk and jazz concerts	Aerospace projects
Marathon contests (e.g., dance)	Research laboratories
Film and theater festivals	Construction projects, tunneling
	Emergency efforts in reaction to
	disasters and major accidents
Q. *FORMAL CONVENTIONS,*	
ASSEMBLIES	T. *EDUCATION* (see also F)
Political, academic, business,	Libraries in universities during
professional; international sports	examination periods
competitions	
	U. *PEOPLE IN PRIVATE*
	DWELLINGS
R. *WORK HAVING DEADLINES*	Watching television, studying,
Farming at harvest time (tomatoes,	merrymaking, arguing, working
fruit), food canning centers	

and space phenomena, Santa Claus announcements, political campaign statements, winning lottery numbers, hair transplant information, and schedules for museums, athletic centers, community programs, cinemas, and the performing arts.

Computer information networks offer incessantly available retail services. They are on-line twenty-four hours a day, seven days a week, and provide rosters of merchants' catalogs and information about goods to subscribers of a computer-linked information service. The users can order catalogs or make credit card purchases directly.

Terminals located on the outside walls of banks can function as mechanical tellers and are available for deposits, withdrawals, and information about one's bank account.

C. A number of travel agencies operate incessantly. Other travel agents subscribe to clearinghouses of information and bookings that are accessible around the clock. One California chain (at more than three hundred locations) provides its own twenty-four-hour services to all branches. A major snowstorm at any hour will have many travelers trying to make last-minute changes in their schedules. Otherwise, the calls are usually requests for changes in reservations or for getting a hotel room or a rental car when there is a problem of overbooking or an oversight in the records at the desk.[6]

Data services linkable via telephone and computer are available, including stock price quotations, library searches, and information about public transportation.

A single office incessantly serves an entire nation or continent in a vitally important function that is needed relatively infrequently, such as emergency medical information about poisons.

Dealing with one of our most ancient concerns, an all-night confessional is operated in a church in New York City.

D. One of the earliest forms of incessant operations was introduced centuries ago on ships that gave up the safety of mooring near shore at night. Out on the ocean, the duties for officers and crew are still scheduled as a series of four- or six-hour "watches" on naval, cargo, and passenger ships. Railroads run at all hours. In addition to freight carriers, some passenger trains with sleeping compartments start out from one city in the evening and deliver their travelers to a distant place the next morning. For individual contracts, a private household moving company is on call twenty-four hours.

F. Educational endeavors after dark are recent innovations. Las Vegas has a full-fledged nighttime high school called Urban High, which uses the same facilities that the city's Valley High School uses in the daytime.[7] Other educational endeavors include a college that holds classes after midnight in Dobbs Ferry, New York; a twenty-four-hour junior college in Texas City, Texas; Colorado College in Colorado Springs; and corporations that employ teachers to provide instruction (including language lessons for immigrants) on all three work shifts.

H. The automobile repossession team, which does much of its work at night, is a version of auto towing.

I. Private vault companies offer twenty-four-hour access every day of the year so that, for example, a safe-deposit box holder can take out jewels to wear to a gala and then return them for safekeeping that same night.

J. Young law associates as well as clerks work overnight organizing research and preparing briefs and documents in some New

York offices. The firms provide food, sleeping rooms for those needing them temporarily, and taxi fare home. One firm pays for a new shirt at a nearby clothier if an associate who has worked all night decides to continue on the job the next day.

K. Brokerage houses keep their back offices busy catching up on registering transactions, securities, bills, and payments, in addition to having traders buy and sell gold and foreign currency after midnight. They accept orders for execution on the Tokyo, Hong Kong, Singapore, and London exchanges, as well as negotiating next-day orders and answering queries of clients for quotes in local markets.

L. Although on a much smaller scale than most of the ventures in this category, the manufacture of personalized goods to order for rapid delivery, such as custom-made garments by tailors in Hong Kong, also takes place year round.

M. Incessant sharing of the same space dons a distinctive form on oil production platforms at sea, which have four men taking turns at each job, two on duty in tandem twelve-hour shifts and two on leave, every two weeks. Extraction work goes on around the clock. Also, crew members are taken to and from the platforms by helicopter for their weeks off. Because space is scarce, each job is allocated one bed in a hotel-like room, which is the scene of shift sleep. When a worker leaves his bunk for his twelve-hour stint, it is filled again by another coming off duty.

Several entries in Table A–1 are tagged "on call." On-call services are potential activities. They are on reserve rather than self-initiated. Usually their employees are not at a work site but sleeping at home and can be aroused and summoned. Except for equipment repair technicians who have contracts with specific firms, most on-call categories are available to the public. Often an answering service acts as intermediary and signals the personnel into action. Small garages will do emergency auto towing on call via an answering service, whereas large garages maintain drivers on duty (H). A U.S. national organization of volunteers called REACT offers help to motorists by having members of its on-call teams monitor BB channel 9, the radio communications distress band, and respond accordingly. Taxicabs often operate via a central dispatcher (D). In Delhi, drivers doze on wood-framed rope cots at the taxi stations while awaiting telephone calls to summon them to fares. Although many on-call ventures provide urgent assistance, there are also nonemergency forms. You may hand in a written manuscript to a "night owl typing service" in late evening and pick up the completed copy next morning (K). In London you can deal with a dealer of rare books through an answering service at any time of night (E). Some immigration lawyers are on call twenty-four hours a day, seven days a week (J).

It is useful to separate year-round endeavors (Part I) from sporadic ones (Part II), because the types use time in different ways. Year-round organizations develop distinctive forms, confront puzzles in trying to staff themselves, and introduce new methods of managing personnel to assure continual functioning. Because night work pries its participants out of the community's main daily round, regular shift workers have different experiences from people who are occasionally caught up in incessance. It is one thing to join in Philadelphia's Mummers' parade (P) and stay up for thirty-six hours once a year, and quite another to be a shift worker. The marcher struts for a whiff of adventure and perhaps pays for it with a hangover. Night jobholders settle into a special way of life, asking family schedules and the physiological functions of their bodies to adjust to their novel timetables.

While year-round endeavors in Table A–1, Part I establish the main forms of incessance, other activities take place seasonally or lack a routine altogether. The events described in Part II are varied and frequent and fill the interstices of after-dark life. Some of them, such as the hectic scenes in packing and shipping departments of retail stores in the weeks before Christmas (R), and the week of Mardi Gras in New Orleans every February (P), are scheduled annually. Fundraising (N) also has periodic timing, as in the form of "telethons" to collect money for health research (e.g., muscular dystrophy). But there are also singular instances. For example, a Massachusetts community once broadcast a musical performance around the clock to raise money for victims of a particularly severe winter storm and has not done so since.

O. Recreation is a main way in which large portions of the population who are not habitual nighttimers join in late-hours activities. Although play and tourism themselves go on continually, and many indoor tennis courts have 365-day, twenty-four-hour schedules, this is a periodic activity rather than year-round, because most of the particular forms are seasonal. Outdoor ice skating rinks are illuminated and used all night during the winter. Golf courses are used day and night during balmy seasons, and golf ranges bathed by floodlights can be rented for hitting practice. There is some natural-light assistance to this recreation periodically. Every June, during the brief summer season when the sun does not set below the horizon above the Arctic Circle, a midnight golf tournament is played in Yellowknife, Alaska. Students play volley ball at midnight in Uppsala, Sweden, and more than a million tourists travel to Lapland to hike, pan for gold, or just look at the midnight sun. More frequently, one Caribbean resort advertises, "We go non-stop . . . we go through the night. . . . Forget about sleep." A popular sightseeing custom is a nighttime visit to a public monument such as the Lincoln Memorial in Washington, Nelson's Column in London, the Arc de Triomphe in Paris, and the Mamayev Memorial in Volgograd (formerly Stalingrad). In more organized fashion, the Society for Commercial Archaeology sponsors a night tour of traditional diners from Boston to Providence. In Baltimore a tour of historic houses is offered at 2 A.M. The Friends of Central Park in New York sponsor midnight bicycle rides, billed as Insomniacs' Tours, in the five boroughs and in other East Coast cities.

P. Local residents call the annual overnight film festival in Cambridge, Massachusetts, an "eyeball orgy," and parents and their children bring blankets and pillows along with food and watch endless cartoons or films of movie idols. While that event has been scheduled for several years in a row, a single "All Night Bard" offering was made by the Boston Shakespeare Company as part of its spring festival one year. An All-Night Jazz Concert has been an annual event for eleven years.

Q. At conventions people seize the moments of being away from home to stay up far into the night, enjoying old friends and new.

R. At peak season, harvesting machines with floodlights move several abreast across the fields. Many shops and factories turn to multiple shift work in their busy seasons, or else extend their hours to complete a special order by a particular deadline. In offices that usually see activity only during the daytime, lights are ablaze all night as the submission date for a report or proposal nears.[8]

About once a week, window decorators called display artists work at night to change the exhibits in department stores. The clamor for tickets to a popular musical show prompted the theater's box office to remain open around the clock to fill its customers' orders. Every year a chain of stores selling discount merchandise switches to staying open twenty-four hours for one month, until Christmas Eve.

S. The intense activity of technicians at terrestrial launch, descent, and monitoring posts during an aerospace mission happens sporadically, and in laboratories as well, when research calls for frequent measurements or for continual attention to animals.

U. People in the privacy of their homes contribute a large, diffuse aggregate of wakefulness. Watching television and working, either on tasks and papers left over from daytime responsibilities or increasingly on microcomputers, are the most widespread invaders of household time otherwise used for sleep.

This roster lists categories of activities that are incessant in various parts of the world. They suggest how fully people have expanded their use of the entire day. The public conception of night work is associated with great factories and mills because of their conspicuous position in modern times and their scale of operations, but the scope of affairs is much broader than the well-known after-dark businesses of entertainment and factory work. Almost all types of activity now go on in all twenty-four hours. At the end of the twentieth century, in some locales, the nighttime seems less of a frontier and more like a full-fledged colony extending the main community. The variety of what people do is homogenized over the hours, even though unequal numbers of people participate around the clock.

NUMBERS OF PEOPLE

A full-time census includes a tally of the people involved in each activity in Table A–1, supplementing the account of what is going on with its numerical aspect. Adding quantities gives more definiteness to the description and suggests the relative significance of the activities and their roles in the community.

To some extent the categories themselves indicate the concentrations of people. For, in the matter of geographic distribution, the incessant scene is industrially dense and service-diffuse. Workers gather differently in different enterprises. Manufacturing (L), extracting (M), and commercial production (K) bring larger numbers of people together than do information posts (C), retailers (E), or utilities (H). Manufacturing plants typically mobilize large concentrations of workers. Even on the night shift, many gather at one site in a mill or factory. On the other hand, each service enterprise, such as a gasoline station, café, or retail store, employs a small group of people. The myriad small service organizations active around the clock are scattered widely. Data processing offices in insurance and finance companies assemble an intermediate number of workers at one site at night. Institutions housing people, like hotels, hospitals, prisons, and military bases, have only skeleton staffs on duty then.

Table A–2 gives the number of all wage-and-salary workers by time of day in 1980. The data are based on excellent research, the

TABLE A–2

Wage and Salary Workers (Nonfarm; U.S. Total 78,142,000) on the Job at Each Hour Around the Clock in May 1980

Hour	(Thousands)	% of Total[a]
0700	21,909	28.0
0800	49,441	63.3
0900	60,793	77.8
1000	63,229	80.9
1100	64,155	82.1
1200	64,866	83.0
1300	64,811	82.9
1400	64,796	82.9
1500	65,395	83.7
1600	61,019	78.1
1700	46,133	59.0
1800	21,947	28.1
1900	13,845	17.7
2000	11,660	14.9
2100	10,444	13.4
2200	8,904	11.4
2300	8,360	10.7
2400	6,775	8.7
0100	4,492	5.7
0200	3,993	5.1
0300	3,700	4.7
0400	3,687	4.7
0500	4,140	5.3
0600	6,916	8.9

[a]Percent (% of 78,142,000) on job the hour given (rounded).
SOURCE: Current Population Survey, U.S. Bureau of Labor Statistics.

Current Population Survey (CPS), which is carried out regularly by the U.S. Bureau of Labor Statistics. The relevant portion of the information became the basis for the full estimate of nighttime activity. Several of the other quantities reported in Table A–3 are derived from those numbers.

Table A–3 shows the number of people up and about in the United States from midnight through early morning in May 1980 by categories of activity. It presents the distribution according to three main groupings: (I) at work, (II) otherwise outside, and (III) in the home. Some categories from Table A–1 are grouped together, because the source of the numerical data used a different classification. The two sets cannot be aligned exactly.

Twenty-nine million persons are up and about in the first hour after midnight. Hour after hour their number falls until 3 A.M. to 4 A.M., when activity is at its lowest ebb. Still, 10.6 million people are awake in that quietest interval. One large group that is omitted from the figures for people awake in the home are those persons in wake-sleep transition. In the late evening they are mostly the daytime group getting ready to sleep; in the morning they are mostly the daytime group waking up and preparing for the day. An estimate could be made from information of proportions of sleepers in large cities, for such data exist.[9] This group is excluded, however, because it would be misleading in the context of attention to wakeful people.

I. People at Work

a. *Nonfarm wage and salary workers on their principal jobs.* This group of gainfully employed persons makes up the main portion of the work force at night, as well as at all hours.

b. *Multiple jobholders on their second jobs.* "Moonlighter" is another name for a person who holds more than one job.

c. *Personnel on military bases, vessels, encampments, and head- quarters* stay awake for guard duty, radar and information monitoring, maintenance, and meal service. Maintenance includes keeping heating units operating. Many bases serve midnight meals as well as early breakfasts, and personnel do cleanup as well as food preparation throughout the night.

d. *Workers on call* who are activated at night are usually ones who work during the daytime and respond to emergency calls at any hour. An oil-burner serviceman, for example, may be called to a home at 4 A.M. by someone whose heating system stopped functioning. Other occupational groups that are typically roused include dentists, electricians, physicians, and plumbers, all of whom customarily work during the day.

Most persons in categories *e*, *f*, and *g* are not closely synchronized with other people's schedules. They can vary their time of work more. Because of that and for other reasons, larger percentages of these groups carry out their jobs after dark or before dawn.

e. *Farmers and farm workers* are early-phased in their work and are often up and about in the predawn hours, because they must put in long days of effort in certain seasons, to harvest and to load trucks with produce and dairy products to be transported to wholesale markets before the main work day begins, and to benefit from the cooler mornings.

f. *Unpaid family workers* may have separate jobs as well. They help out in family businesses when not at their own work, more likely after dark.

g. *Free-lancers* are not employed by others and often are employed irregularly. They and some self-employed persons not included in the CPS make up small numbers. Many of them tend to be late-phased when they work.

II. OTHERWISE OUTSIDE THE HOME

h. *Clientele of public enterprises.* After midnight people continue to be patrons of establishments, including customers of restaurants, shoppers in retail stores, and passengers on transportation systems. The clientele usually outnumber the employees in such enterprises. For every attendant on duty at an auto service station, scores of drivers stop to buy fuel. Each cook and waitress in an all-night restaurant serves several patrons. A bus driver or airplane crew is outnumbered by the passengers. Customers trickle through supermarkets and other stores that have only a few clerks on the job. Many employed persons on their way to work, or after leaving, become clientele elsewhere.

i. *People in private transit* are those traveling in their own cars

TABLE A–3
Number of Persons (Thousands) Active at Night (U.S., May 1980)[a]

Hours:	2300–2400	2400–100	100–200	200–300	300–400	400–500	500–600	600–700
I. AT WORK								
a. Wage workers	8360	6775	4492	3993	3700	3687	4140	6916
b. Moonlighters	120	97	64	58	53	53	59	100
c. Military	214	74	114	102	94	94	106	176
d. On call	8	7	4	4	4	4	4	7
e. Farmers	200	200	148	185	252	512	1178	2051
f. Unpaid family	8	7	4	4	4	4	4	7
g. Free-lancers	33	27	13	8	7	4	4	7
	8943	7187	4839	4354	4114	4358	5495	9264

II. OTHERWISE OUTSIDE

h. Clientele	23766	15594	6836	5426	4654	4638	5831	16269
i. In transit	8914	5564	3411	1934	1700	1919	2839	7800
j. Gleaners	50	10	5	2	1	—	—	—
k. Night people	110	8	7	6	5	4	2	1
	32740	21176	10259	7368	6360	6561	8672	24070

III. IN HOME[b]

l. Shift worker in household	88	119	123	40	53	161	775	1451
m. Social party	206	83	55	49	23	23	—	—
n. Work at home	726	294	195	173	80	80	179	301
o. Miscellaneous	867	198	75	26	16	13	48	88
	1887	694	448	288	172	277	1002	1840

| TOTALS | 43570 | 29057 | 15546 | 12010 | 10646 | 11196 | 15169 | 35174 |

[a]See text for explanation of categories, and appendix B for calculations and estimation procedures.
[b]Does not include people in transition between wakeful activity and sleep; numbers may be smaller than expected because of steps to avoid double counting in overlapping categories.

153

and not working. They may be commuting or driving for pleasure or on long trips such as vacations. This category augments h, for passengers on public transport systems are also in transit (and they are counted in h). In late evening people are coming from theaters and sports stadiums and shopping centers. Travel for shopping or recreation is heaviest from 11 P.M. to midnight and declines rapidly thereafter.

j. *Gleaners* are people at the fringe of subsistence who survive by foraging at night. In areas where refunds are given for returning glass and metal containers, people make the rounds of apartment houses and pick deposit bottles out of trash bins. Others look for resalable paper. In the United States homeless persons as well as other poor people do it. Tattered men and "shopping bag ladies" probe among the debris outside restaurants and markets for leftovers and half-rotted food. In the rapidly growing cities of developing nations children also scavenge and rake garbage after dark.[10]

k. *"Night people"* are part of a diffuse collectivity who stay out late and call themselves "night people." It includes those who intensely value their freedom in quiet spaces.

III. In the Home

l. *Other members of shift workers' households* are up and about because of the workers' comings and goings.

There is no usable information to estimate numbers for the following categories, *m*, *n*, and *o*. The chance that some of them may also be found in categories already mentioned compounds the uncertainty. In each instance, therefore, the estimate is conservative; the persons should be counted, but they should not be counted more than once.

m. *Sociable gatherings.* Parties that last far into the night and early morning usually occur on weekends, but in a nation whose population exceeds two hundred million we may assume that at every hour each night of the week somewhere there are some people merrymaking, people who are not referred to in any other category on this list.

n. *People working in their own homes.* Students pore over books till late, especially before an exam; executives bring home briefcases of papers from the office and work after the rest of the family has gone to sleep; writers struggle with their manuscripts; and computer devotees sit at their machines far into the night. Considering the frequency of impending work deadlines and school exams and the increasing number of personal computers in homes, these individuals make up a substantial number.

o. *Miscellaneous.* A diffuse group stays up to read, write letters, watch television,[11] or commune with the dark and quiet for personal pleasure. Insomniacs and such others as the elderly who sleep very few hours add to the group. People waken early for similar reasons.

The number of people active at home may seem low, because those who are in transition between sleep and wakefulness are not counted. That is why 5 A.M. shows only one million up and about in the home, and there are 20 million more people awake at 6 A.M. The very numerous group in sleep–wake transition is excluded, because it would distort the picture of the scale of wakeful activity.

The categories plus numbers prepare us to notice revisions in the proportions of types of nighttime activity. About one-third of all shift workers are employed in goods production.[12] A larger group, with diverse occupations subsumed, is employed in service industries. Reflecting a general trend, the percentage of shift work in manufacturing in the United States has leveled off.[13] Manufacturing activity used to be a larger portion of work in the United States. But the nation has experienced a slowdown in that area and distinct retrenchment in several industrial sectors, whereas the service sectors—also typically relying on shift work (in transportation, public utilities, retail trade, recreation, hot lines, and broadcasting)—have shown notable gains. If an industrial society is a manufacturing society, then the United States is no longer primarily that. It has grown significantly in white-collar and service sectors and is now a postindustrial society.[14]

Similarly, in the United Kingdom the rate of growth of after-dark work has been more rapid in the nonmanufacturing sector. In the 1970s the former's 3.2 percent rise (from 13.9 to 16.1) was surpassed by a 3.6 percent rise in the latter.[15] Throughout the world in advanced industrialized countries in the past thirty years the proportion of activity in blue-collar manufacturing activity stayed the same or declined slightly, whereas those in the service sector doubled.[16] Data for production of goods are often more readily available because of its past predominant place, but the trend for that sector alone is not indicative of all economic activity at night.[17]

These are some ways that the numerical data may help us deal with relevant questions. How much of the after-dark activity represents an absolute enlargement of all human activity and how much is a redistribution of people and their ventures? What are the relationships among those affairs? Is the participation of people in various activities stable at different hours? Are the proportions among the types changing? If so, in what way? Since this time census is the first try of a possible series, most answers to these questions await repeated censuses in the future.

APPENDIX B

Research Notes

One of the aims of this essay is to describe the scope and amount of nighttime wakefulness; the other is to evaluate the hypothesis that it is a frontier. This double goal required both broad collection of facts and specific procedures to test theoretical predictions. Both types of research were carried out together. The idea of expanding wakeful activity as a frontier is a general hypothesis that can be evaluated in many ways. It ought to withstand assorted tests before being accepted as valid, and in a variety of trials there will be enough chances for buffeting it with inconsistencies among the findings. This section does not repeat interpretations and descriptions that have been presented in the main text. It augments that information with details about methods used in several of the quantitative studies that involved probability sampling.

A main source of systematic information was a set of 166 two-hour field visits made in Boston in 1974, over the twenty-four hours, all days of the week, during summer, and fall, and winter, in combinations selected by a random sampling procedure.

Three teams of male and female researchers, with pairings reshuffled systematically across times of day and across sites, carried out the various observations and experiments, including the tallies of people on the street (Figure 3–2) and the experiments on helpfulness and friendliness reported in chapter 5 (including Figure 5–1). The field visits were planned for each of the four seasons, but the research assistants tired of them physically. The first trials were done in June. Balmy weather prevailed, and the researchers were enthusiastic. After the research period we held a party, with a magic show, and one researcher baked a rectangular sheet cake with a silhouette of the Boston skyline, using chocolate icing for the buildings, white icing for the sky, and yellow icing for the sun's rays coming up above buildings at dawn. In September it rained. Several assistants caught cold. With college classes under way again (they were graduate and undergraduate students), the physiological upsets from being up erratically every few nights were more punishing. In December the weather was severe. Many December visits took place in bitter cold or in snow. More researchers fell sick. End-of-semester exams had begun, and their concerns were focused elsewhere. The effort around the clock became grueling. One researcher said she would not go out for the next round, and a second spoke grimly and reluctantly about having to do so again. It would have been too costly to recruit and train a new crew, with possible risks of stylistic differences in the data collection, and we abandoned the spring 1975 sample.

The 166 field visits (56 in early June, 56 in early September, and 54 in early December), each two hours long, were distributed among three sites: a transportation hub, a residential street, and a shopping street. There were sixty-two, forty-two, and sixty-two visits respectively to those sites. The transportation hub is a major intersection and a terminal for public buses and trains, with a larger proportion of transients on the street than at either of the other two locations. The residential street is 1 mile away. There are no shops on it. The street is one-third of a mile from the nearest public transit station. The shopping street is a mile farther in a straight line from the hub through the residential street. It is a local market area for a clearly defined neighborhood.

The times of field visits were randomly selected from two-hour intervals around the clock. There were eleven such intervals in this sampling frame for two reasons: Certain times of day are clearly associated with certain kinds of activities, especially 0730–0929 as morning rush hours and 1615–1814 as evening rush hours (expressed according to the twenty-four-hour clock). Given the two rush hour spans, placed as they are in the daily cycle, and given the need for two-hour visits in order to accomplish the experiments and other studies in the research program, it was impossible to fit the remaining hours of the day neatly into two-hour intervals throughout the period. On the other hand, to force twelve two-hour intervals into the period would cut across the rush hours and other familiar time intervals. So eleven strata were established, and the remaining minutes scattered among them were left unsampled as follows: morning rush hour, 0730–0929; daytime, 0930–1129, 1130–1329 (1330–1344 omitted), 1345–1544 (1545–1614 omitted); evening rush hour, 1615–1814; evening, 1815–2014, 2015–2214, 2215–0014; and night, 0015–0214 (0215–0244 omitted), 0245–0444 (0445–0514 omitted), 0515–0714 (0715–0729 omitted). Thus the longest two phases (day and night) lose the unsampled minutes, forty-five minutes from the daytime and seventy-five minutes from night. By removing those amounts from the sample, the day, evening, and night phases are each six hours long, and each rush hour interval is two hours long. The numbers of visits for those phases of the day were: morning rush hour 13, daytime 47, evening rush hour 11, evening 48, and night 47.

For reporting pedestrians on the streets (Figure 3–2) the tallies for each time stratum were averaged (divided by the number of minutes in that stratum) to equalize the sampling fractions across strata. There were 456 five-minute tallies of people passing one way at eight checkpoints. During those counts the ages of passersby were also estimated. The accuracy and reliability of age estimates had been checked among the researchers beforehand. In that pretest, a comparison of the estimates made by the observers and the answers to age queries made of those 696 passersby yielded a correlation (within two years) of .96 for the six observers, with .93 the lowest coefficient for an observer.

No single measurement can provide enough evidence for the predicted pattern of helpfulness and friendliness. Accordingly, four tests were conducted, each having different social conditions. The selection of subjects for all the tests followed sampling procedures within the same intervals around the clock, and those time intervals can be used as bases for comparison. The four studies differ in several ways. The lost key test and the supermarket observations were unobtrusive; people did not know anyone was paying special attention to them. The directions and interview tests were explicit personal requests but were mild in demand.

The ratings for degree of helpfulness or friendliness in each of the tests were established in advance by a set of consultants, six consultants for tests 1, 2, and 4, and ten for test 3 (the lost key test). After each trial the two field researchers came to an agreement about the rating.

Tests 1 (asking directions) and 2 (requesting an interview) both called for the researcher couple (a male and a female) to follow a random selection procedure for periodic sampling of passersby. The selection procedure was adjusted to street population density. Density was gauged using the tally of people passing that contributed the data given in Figure 3–2. This count, disclosing the abundance of the street population at that hour, was used to set the sampling rate: If the number passing in five minutes was greater than twenty-five, once the test was to start the fourth person passing from that direction would be chosen. If the count was from five to twenty-five, the third person passing would be chosen; if three or four, then the second person would be chosen; and if two or fewer passed during the five-minute tally, then the first person passing from either direction would be selected. For the tests, persons walking together in a group were counted as one person; if a group was to be sampled, the passerby nearest the researchers was approached. A maximum of three requests for directions (test 1) and eight requests for interviews (test 2) was to be made during each visit. Sometimes the attempts were fewer—especially at night—if almost no one passed during the segment of the field visit in which the experiments were scheduled. The sampling was carried out silently by one researcher, who by nudging or an equally subtle signal told the other whom to approach. This minimized selection bias, for the researcher who was to carry out the test could not hesitate or overlook an unappealing passerby.

When asking for directions (test 1) strangers come face to face briefly. The situation imposes almost no cost or burden on a passerby, for the answer takes little time and effort, and one does not have to become personal in replying. The passerby is anonymous and has no formal obligation to cooperate. Nor does a person who chooses to be unhelpful expect a reprimand. The location sought was a well-known one about a mile and a half away. In asking, the couple turned toward the passerby and the male said, "Excuse me, I wonder if you could tell us how to get to _____[place])?" It is unlikely that anyone was aware of being studied. Asking for directions on a street is a common event, a direct, explicit, and mild appeal for help. The researchers were dressed in everyday fashion, acted politely, and spoke clearly.

Angry stares and gestures or stiff nonrecognition earned no points in our scoring scheme. Simply giving directions or admitting nicely that one did not know were scored one point each. Two points were given if the stranger expanded the scope of the encounter. Examples of these are given in chapter 5. The consultants decided that a penalty was not warranted if the person appeared to lack the information and admitted it politely. A check showed it made no difference whether polite refusals were included or omitted from the analysis. There were thirty instances of polite refusals, dispersed over the time of day, and their inclusion yielded the same ANOVA results as their exclusion. Of 363 persons approached, 11 (3 percent) refused in an unpleasant way, 331 (91.2 percent) gave only directions or declined politely, and 21 (5.8 percent) enlarged the encounter.

A gale blew through town during one night of research activity in December. Broad sheets of rain slanted to the ground, forming enormous pools of water and flooding the streets. At 4:30 A.M. two conscientious research assistants struggled along the avenue to collect data according to schedule and clung to lampposts to prevent being blown away. Only one man, loping along and leaping puddles, passed during that entire two-hour period. It happened to be at the moment in the schedule calling for the Directions Test, so the male researcher shouted the query. The man yelled "Follow me!" over his shoulder and beckoned as he sprinted on. The researcher took off in pursuit and chased him huffing and puffing into a subway station one street further. The stranger was waiting there, panting and dripping wet, and there, protected from the storm, he courteously provided the directions asked for. According to our criteria his response earned one point.

Concerning a request for a brief interview (test 2), both researchers took turns asking for them. A meeting of this sort is less common than the preceding, but it is not unfamiliar in a land of frequent polls. There is no emergency, no problem to be solved. This appeal differs from the other experiments in the personalism of its demand. The passerby is made self-conscious by the definition of the event because he will have to answer questions. The situation also calls for allocating a block of time in response to an explicit appeal, for the interview takes several minutes. He is asked to provide time, cooperation, and confidential information to someone unknown.

In test 2 the passersby are aware of being targets of study, but they are likely to think that the interview's content is the focus rather than whether they consent or refuse. It does not readily come to their minds that consenting or refusing would be information itself. The decision to cooperate can be taken as evidence of a willingness to help, though people who might otherwise aid someone in distress may refuse in this case because they dislike participating in surveys.

One interview on the residential street took place about midnight with a drunken man who happened to be chosen in the random sampling procedure. Inadvertently it turned into an instance of daytimer–nighttimer conflict brought on by our research project, for he was boisterous outside an apartment house. A third-floor window opened and a voice called out, "Quiet down there!" This excited the drunkard. He shouted insults toward the window and the person withdrew. Moments later, with the incident forgotten and the noisy interview drawing to its close, a large amount of water cascaded from the window and squarely hit the interviewer, not the drunken man.[1]

No points were given for a bad-tempered refusal, such as an abrupt "Not from me [do you get an interview]!" or one of the reactions listed as unpleasant in test 1. A polite refusal—such as the plausible reason, "I'm sorry, I have an appointment," or an equivalent delivered courteously—earned one point. And two points were scored for each person consenting to the interview. Of 1,129 attempts, 175 (15.5 percent) refused nastily, 258 (22.9 percent) refused nicely, and 696 (61.6 percent) consented.

Another test (test 3) checked if there is a difference, among the hours of the day, in people returning keys that they find in the street. The lost key experiment was the only one in which people were not in each other's presence. It is a test of remote helpfulness. Losing a key in the street is a plausible event, and the finder would be unaware of being a subject of study. Noticing that the key has a tag attached, one would believe that an appropriate action could reunite it with its owner.[2] Meanwhile the other person is not present. The finder imagines a faceless stranger and does not have to deal personally with someone in order to return it.

Each key was placed on the street in a lighted place but away from doorways, so that the finder would not think that another person could be asked to do something about getting the key back to its owner. The tags listed an address in a city (Northampton) 90 miles west of Boston, along with the request, "Please return." (Earlier, our pilot study had revealed no difference in return rates for tags saying "Please return" or "If found, drop in any mail box," so the phrase "Please return" was used on the tags.) In the United States, if an address-tagged key is dropped in a mailbox it is delivered and the recipient must pay the postage due. Two colleagues who lived in Northampton let their surnames and addresses be used on the key tags and acted as recipients for all the keys returned.

The keys were marked so that each was unique because of a system of coding that involved special notches on the back of the key and different letters of the alphabet as the first initials on the tag. The keys had the ridges and contours of real keys. All were cut for a lock in possession of the hardware store proprietor who prepared the keys to be used in the experiment. But they did not fit any lock in the home at the address. There was no sign that anyone tried to use a key for nefarious purposes. Even if the finder had larceny on his mind, he would have had to travel 90 miles to the town, not knowing what kind of lock to look for. The tag case was weak plastic, attached to the key by a 19-mm.-diameter tension ring that one would have to pry up and rotate to slide free, offering fuss and danger to one's fingernails. It was unlikely that the finder would judge the key tag case valuable for personal use.

Several keys were placed at different locations on the street at the beginning of each two-hour field visit. Two hours after depositing them, the researchers made the rounds again, retrieved all keys that had not been carried away, and made a record for each one that was gone. By collecting the ones left on the street at the end of the visit, they could record the time that each of the others had been carried away. Therefore, when a key was received in the mail, its unique identification told at just what time of day it had been picked up.

The test focuses only on those individuals who picked up a key and carried it away. Keys not received within twenty-one days after the trials were not counted in the study, on the assumption that different conditions had developed by then to affect the finder's conduct. Three weeks were allowed because mail for which the post office levies postage due moves slower than regular mail.

Of 326 keys carried away 220 (67.5 percent) were returned. The scoring scale reflects increased investments of time and of oneself to help an anonymous key owner. No points were earned for 106 keys (32.5 percent) taken but not returned. If the key was dropped unwrapped in the mailbox, it scored one point; 154 (47.2 percent) were sent back in this manner. The 38 keys (11.7 percent) that were returned wrapped in a stamped envelope netted two points each. Three point were given for each of 25 wrapped and stamped keys (7.7 percent) that came back with a personal note enclosed. A rating of four points each applied to three individuals who made personal contact by telephone along with mailing back the keys.

The fourth test was an observational study in three large supermarkets that stay open twenty-four hours a day. This setting brings people who are mostly strangers face to face in a mundane situation, one that is highly structured, brief, and standardized. The researcher couples noted the degree of sociability between customers and clerks at the checkout counters. The couples' work was unobtrusive, and neither checkout clerks nor other customers were aware of their quest, because they posed as customers, apparently conferring over a shopping list while preparing to get into line and occasionally gazing around. They had rehearsed in earlier trials to observational reliability averaging .92 between individuals in each pair.

The couples followed a random sampling procedure to visit the three supermarkets at various hours. The sample was similar to the sample for the street experiments (tests 1, 2, and 3). The same time intervals were listed in the sampling frame, and thirty visits were selected randomly (three in the morning rush hour, seven in the daytime, four in the evening rush hour, seven in the evening, and nine at night). In each visit the couple followed a systematically varied circuit among the three stores, for a total of ninety fifteen-minute observation periods. The quota for nighttime visits was higher because fewer customers would be observed on each occasion then.

Only single customers were studied, because two people going through the checkout procedure together may be attentive to one another, which would inhibit interaction with the checkout clerk.

Sociability was defined as showing warmth (such as smiling) and expanding the scope of interaction (such as chatting about a topic other than the transaction). Interaction between customer and clerk showed a high degree of mutuality. When one was impassive the other was too, and when one was sociable the other responded in kind. Therefore the scoring scheme was based only on customers rather than a computation that would have included the behavior of both parties. Two points were scored if a customer both smiled and chatted, one point if either happened alone, and no points were given if neither smiling nor chatting took place.

To what extent do people break through the confines of their roles at the supermarket checkout counter to offer even the mildest sociability to one another? Not much. Of the 752 customers, 562 (74.7 percent) did not smile nor talk about something other than the transaction. Smiling by itself occurred 98 times (13 percent), chatting by itself 26 times (2.5 percent), and 66 (8.8 percent) both chatted and smiled.

In Figure 5–1 the average score per time interval was computed separately for each test and then those values converted to standard scores (z-scores) to allow direct comparison of the five intervals around the overall average score (a standard score of zero) for the test. Averaging the scores within time intervals equalized the basis for comparing different numbers of people tested over different lengths of time. Table B–1 contains the data on which Figure 5–1 is based. The differences between nighttime and the next highest are not large in some cases, but if all periods are compared the results are statistically significant.

Information about the age, sex, and race of each subject was available for the three face-to-face tests (it could not be noted in the key test). On the whole, females were slightly more sociable than males. Older white females were most sociable in the daytime period, but only a handful of them were even present at night. Although there were more males out in the evening and at night, all the other combinations of female or male, black or white, and young or old displayed the highest rates of sociability in the nighttime.

An entirely separate program of inquiry yielded the information presented at the end of chapter 2, the data about numbers and characteristics of shift workers (Table 4–1) and the time census (Appendix A). The work began with establishing the categories for Table A–1, the first stage of the time census. The classification was developed from a number of sources.

Although most of the information pertains to the United States, at least 20 percent of it is based on personal observations abroad. Focused inquiries and information surveys over years of travel were made in London, Paris, Rome, Istanbul, Venice, Stockholm, Mexico City, San Francisco, New York, Boston, Athens, Zurich, Ge-

TABLE B-1
Findings of Four Tests of Helpfulness and Friendliness During Phases of the Twenty-Four Hour Cycle (in Boston)

	Morning rush hour 0730–0929	Daytime 0930–1614	Evening rush hour 1615–1814	Evening 1815–0015	Night 0015–0729	Totals $\overline{X}$	Analysis of Variance and Significance
ASK DIRECTIONS							
Nasty refusal =0	0	7	0	4	0	11	
Directs =1	30	105	25	115	56	331	
Expands =2	2	3	2	4	10	21	
No. of trials	32	115	27	123	66	363	$F = 4.917$
Mean score	1.06	.97	1.07	1.00	1.15	1.03	$p < .001$
ASK FOR INTERVIEW							
Nasty refusal =0	18	57	15	59	26	175	
Polite refusal =1	41	86	14	65	50	256	
Consents =2	34	223	52	239	150	698	
No. of trials	93	366	81	363	226	1129	$F = 4.531$
Mean score	1.17	1.45	1.46	1.50	1.55	1.46	$p < .002$

Time of Day

FIND LOST KEY

Not returned	=0	12	33	6	23	32	106	
Return unwrap	=1	10	54	15	47	28	154	
Return wrap	=2	4	19	3	10	2	38	
Return, letter	=3	3	7	2	12	1	25	
Return, phoned	=4	0	0	0	2	1	3	
No. of trials		29	113	26	94	64	326	$F = 3.972$
Mean score		.93	1.00	1.04	1.18	.61	.97	$p < .01$

SUPERMARKET SOCIABILITY

None	=0	57	146	122	149	88	562	
Smile or chat	=1	6	44	32	20	22	124	
Smile and chat	=2	5	22	7	10	22	66	
No. of trials		68	212	161	179	132	752	$F = 5.250$
Mean score		.24	.42	.29	.22	.50	.34	$p < .001$

neva, Montreal, Toronto, Lagos, Cairo, Tel Aviv, Jerusalem, Tokyo, and Osaka, as well as in other places. It included staying up and touring at night and observing and talking with persons encountered. Knowledgeable informants, such as taxicab dispatchers and drivers and public telephone operators, were interviewed. Nighttime jobs held years ago were another source of personal information. Those were augmented by reviewing research articles, historical records, newspaper and magazine and broadcasters' reports, advertisements in telephone directories offering twenty-four-hour service, and lists of "night owl" activities offered as newspaper supplements. Each entry in Table A–1 represents at least one instance that was confirmed by two sources: most of the entries represent many confirmations.

Quantitative information about the number of people active at night (Table A–3) and about shift workers (Tables 4–1 and A–2) are derived mainly from the United States Current Population Survey.

The Current Population Survey (CPS) is conducted in May of every year by the U.S. Bureau of Labor Statistics, Division of Labor Force Studies. The Survey regularly samples 47,000 or more households throughout the country and then calculates estimates for the total population. This is a very large sample. Its size can be appreciated by realizing that national attitude surveys and election polls achieve estimates with 3 percent error on sample sizes of less than 2,000 persons. Substantial care is used by the CPS in weighting and estimation procedures, and the error of estimate is small. Data from "Tables 12–16: The beginning and ending hours last week of wage and salary workers by various characteristics based on May, 1980 CPS (000)" were used to establish the information presented in Tables 4–1 and A–2. That unpublished information, existing on computer printouts for internal use at the agency, were made available at the bureau's office in Washington, D.C. The week studied is the Sunday through Saturday period in May that contains the twelfth day of the month; the actual survey is conducted in the following week, containing the nineteenth day of the month. Two questions in the Survey ask for the usual beginning and ending times of the principal job of each person in the household in the preceding week. (Information from other surveys was not incorporated, because the orientations and premises in other studies are more toward how individuals budget their time rather than for the activity in any hour.)

The procedures for the time census are presented in detail so that it may be a guide where it is workable and a target for improvement where it is faulty. The time census is plotted only for the nighttime portion of the daily round, but the example and the outlines of the estimation procedure may apply (with different weightings) to the other seventeen hours of the day for which the base information appears in Table A–2).

The purpose of the CPS survey, whose information is used to plot Table A–2 and category *a* in Table A–3, is different from achieving a twenty-four-hour census. The Survey does not aim to compute the total number of people working in each of the twenty-four hours. Thus, though needed in a time census, through no fault of its own the Survey omits some categories in assembling the statistics given in raw form in Tables 12–16. Those tables refer to wage and salary workers. Excluded from the tallies are more than 2.6 million farmers and farm workers, more than 2 million members of the armed forces, free-lancers, some self-employed persons, and unpaid family members who work less than fifteen hours a week. People in these groups often work in the hours before and after the main community cycle. Moreover, the Survey focused only on "sole or principal" jobs. Because persons interviewed were queried only about the hours they worked on their principal jobs, and because multiple job holders—often called moonlighters—are likely to have their second jobs evenings or nights, the Survey understated the total number of off-hours workers. Also, the CPS data underestimated the overall proportions of people working evening and night shifts, because the allocations to shifts followed a rule that if a tie occurred in the number of hours worked on two different shifts, day and evening, evening and night, or day and its preceding night, that person's stint was assigned to the first of the two shifts mentioned in these pairs. This results in overestimating the day shift numbers relative to evening or night, and overestimating evening shift numbers relative to night. In all these instances the night shift figures are the most understated.

By tallying the numbers of workers reported in Tables 12–16, counting each individual for each hour that the person worked, the sum for each hour of the day is established. The result appears in Table A–2. For example, if someone worked from 9 A.M. till noon, that person is tallied in each of the three hours, 9 to 10 A.M., 10 to 11 A.M., and 11 A.M. to noon. Modest adjustments are made for underreporting, because some persons responding to CPS interviews mentioned beginning work times but did not report ending times. That fraction is listed per hour in the CPS tables and was used to correct the number for the first hour of work (one cannot assume those persons worked more than one hour). Example: The fraction of those beginning work 4 A.M. to 5 A.M. and not reporting an ending time = .013 × 232,000 (total reporting beginning work in that hour) = 3,016. In the CPS tables, a zero is entered in cells having fewer than 500 persons; this occurs more often for evenings and nights, because fewer people work then. Amounts were added to compensate for that underrepresentation (e.g., 2,000 for the quietest hour 3 to 4 A.M., and smaller amounts to compensate other nighttime hours, such as 1,000 for midnight to 1 A.M.).[3]

Because information was not available in the same form, categories in Table A–3 do not match those in Table A–1. The groupings in Table A–3 reflect the knowledge available permitting direct estimates, weighted adjustments where a calculable assumption could be made, and derivative estimates based on further assumptions. The rank order of categories for the numbers reflect the degree of accuracy of knowledge, first among the three broad classes (we know most about work and least about events inside the household), and then within the classes (sounder assumptions can be made about households of shift workers than about households in general). The last estimates listed are the most uncertain. Also, the risk of counting persons more than once (persons already included in preceding categories) is greatest for these final categories.

The data in Table A–3 are like a moving average because the United States exists in four time zones, and this activity is distributed across them. Yet activity levels are not lower accordingly, because the hours of adjacent time zones contribute their affairs to each time span.

The categories and the computations of the census are explained in the paragraphs that follow, along with a calculation provided for an hour at night as an example. Overall, the quietest hour is 3 to 4 A.M., and this interval is usually used for the example. The method is to resort to proportions from CPS data, along with other information as a guide, to estimate the amounts for other categories in Table A–3. The procedure is a systematic extrapolation as used in scientific counts based on samples. All estimates are conservative, especially in latter categories, so as not to count the same persons more than once. If any of the categories mentioned later overlap with one already introduced, the estimate for the latter category is reduced in order to avoid double counting.

I. AT WORK

a. *Nonfarm wage and salary workers on their principal jobs.* The data for this category come directly from Table A–2.

b. *Multiple jobholders on their second jobs.* The portion of those in the work force holding more than one job have the times of their second jobs entered in this part of the tally for the time census. The multiple job-holding rate has been estimated at 4.6 percent of the work force,[4] but it is well known that many people do not report additional jobs in order to avoid paying income taxes. According to a report in 1975, "men between the ages of 25 and 54 have the highest percentage of moonlighting (between 6 and 7 percent)."[5] A recent study found, in its sample of couples, that 6.8 percent of all husbands and 2.6 percent of all wives had second jobs.[6] The rate for the time census was set at 6 percent; .06 × 78,142,000 (the total work force in category *a*, see Table A–2) = 4,688,520. About one-third of those second jobs (1,562,840) are performed after dark, and the remainder on weekends or during the usual daytime hours. To compute the percentage of the nighttime group all the percentages in category *a* from 1800 to 0700 hours are added, the sum (139.3) is set equal to 100 percent, its proportions calculated for each of the hours in that time span, and then 1,562,840 is multiplied by the proportion for each hour. Example: for 3 to 4 A.M., (4.7 ÷ 139.3 = 3.4%), .034 × 1,562,840 = 53,137.

c. *Personnel on military bases, vessels, encampments, and head-quarters.* According to the Bureau of Labor Statistics, there were more than two million persons in military service in 1980. Using the proportion in category *a* (see Table A–2), example for 3 to 4 A.M.: .047 × 2,000,000 = 94,000.

d. *Workers on call.* The Survey gave no specific instructions to deal with this group; it was left to the respondent to interpret and decide how to answer the question on times of day worked. Those who went out on call would not think to identify their occasional nighttime hours of work, especially if they had already labored during the daytime and reported those earlier times in answering the

Survey's questions. That can be assumed to be a small number; a factor of one one-thousandth of the number in category *a* is used throughout. Example: for 3 to 4 A.M., .001 × 3,700,000 = 3,700.

Using the data for category *a*, the proportional distribution of persons at work is taken and enlarged slightly to estimate numbers of people in each of the groups in categories *e*, *f*, and *g*:

e. *Farmers and farm workers.* There were 2,600,000 farmers and farm workers in 1980. Weighting fractions were established to deduct from the first hours of the night, and to add increasingly larger fractions as daybreak nears because farming begins early in the day. Example: for 3–4 A.M. add 5 percent to the proportion for category *a*; that is, .047 + .05 = .097 × 2,600,000 = 252,200.

f. *Unpaid family workers.* Persons who worked in family businesses without receiving pay are omitted from the CPS (although those who performed one hour or more of work for pay or profit are included). They can be assumed to be a small number and for each nighttime hour one one-thousandth of the tally in category *a* is added. Example: for 3 to 4 A.M., .001 × 3,700,000 = 3,700.

g. *Free-lancers.* A small factor of the number reported in category *a* is applied, from .004 at 11 P.M. to .001 at 6 to 7 A.M. Example: for 3 A.M., .002 × 3,700,000 = 7,400.

II. OTHERWISE OUTSIDE THE HOME

h. *Clientele of public enterprises.* The number of customers in service settings is calculated as a factor of the number of employees on the scene. Of workers on the job at night said to be service workers,[7] not every such employee has a job serving customers. This is adjusted for by assuming that on the average each worker in categories *a* and *b* serves only two customers during the quietest hour of the night. Then a weighting is introduced proportionate to the increase in service workers in each other hour to estimate the number of customers served then. Example: for 3 to 4 A.M., 3,753,000 × .62 = 2,327,800 (workers) × 2 (customers per worker) = 4,654,600. The ratio of service workers at midnight to 1 A.M. is 1.83 of the 3 to 4 A.M. figure (the ratios of tallies in categories *a* and *b*, Table A–2), so between midnight and 1 A.M. each worker served 3.66 customers, resulting in an estimated (6,872,000 × .62 × 3.66 =) 15,594,155 clientele of public enterprises at that hour.

i. *People in private transit.* CPS data are used to compute part of this estimate according to persons coming to or leaving work at a given hour. Some workers would use public transport, but in the nighttime many would be traveling by private car. At night 40 percent of those going to and from work were estimated to use their own transport in the hour just before or after the shift. This factor is small to avoid double counting, since some of those commuters already have been included in h, clientele of public enterprises. For recreational transit a factor of 15 percent of the clientele in public enterprises (category h) is introduced in the preceding hour plus 15 percent of such clientele in the following hour, for the hours till 4 A.M. For 11 P.M. to midnight, its own estimate of clientele in public places was multiplied by 1.5 for estimating the preceding hour in order to compute this value. From 4 to 7 A.M. clientele in public enterprises were assumed to be mostly people going to work, and the 4 to 5 A.M. estimate for nonwork transit was retained for the next two hours as well. Example: for 3 to 4 A.M., those ending work at 3 A.M. (244,328 from CPS tables) + those beginning work at 4 A.M. (232,000) = 476,328 × .4 = 190,531; and for nonwork transit, clientele in public enterprises 2 to 3 A.M. (5,426,000) + similar clientele 4 to 5 A.M. (4,638,000) = 10,064,000 × .15 = 1,509,600. Then 190,531 + 1,509,600 = 1,700,131.

j. *Gleaners.* Gleaners are few compared to most of the groups identified in this list, and their actual numbers are difficult to gauge. The estimate made is approximately two of every hundred thousand awake at midnight, thus 10,000 nationwide in the first hour after midnight, and 1,250 for 3 to 4 A.M.

k. *"Night people."* It is hard to estimate the number in this category, because many "night people" are on their own. Considering persons active (not sleeping outside), the estimate is 5,000 for 3 to 4 A.M., and this number, for those outside their homes, is assumed to rise about 1,000 higher for each preceding hour and drop 1,000 lower for each following one.

III. IN THE HOME

1. *Other members of shift workers' households.* The information is drawn directly from the CPS tables reporting the number of people beginning and ending work each hour. people likely to be up

and about in their own dwellings include those who ended work two hours earlier and people who will be at work two hours later. That is a borderline status to sleep–awake transition. An hour is allowed on each flank for travel time, and it is estimated that, on the average, one in twenty household members would be awake every night prompted expressly by the arrival or impending departure of the worker. That low ratio is meant to accommodate the portion of shift workers who do not share a household with others, and also to accommodate the likelihood that even in households where others are present they are not up every night. Example: for 3 to 4 A.M., others in households of workers ending work at 2 A.M. (407,334) plus those beginning work at 5 A.M. (662,000) = 1,069,334 × .05 = 53,467 likely to be up and about in their dwellings. A similar figure should be calculated for members of farmers' households and those of moonlighters, but the data on which to base the calculation are not available, and amounts were not added for them. Accordingly this category's estimate is conservative.

m. *Sociable gatherings.* At the quietest hour (3 to 4 A.M.) it is estimated that ten in every hundred thousand are still celebrating (226,545,805 [U.S. 1980 population] ÷ 100,000 = 2265 × 10 = 22,650). The same ratios (not the actual numbers) used in category *h* are employed for the other hours of night for these estimates, except that it is doubled for the hour before midnight.

n. *People working in their own homes.* To avoid multiple counting here—because these individuals may appear in other categories—the estimate is 80,000 for the quietest hour of night (3 to 4 A.M.); it is again weighted for the other hours using the ratios mentioned in category *m*.

o. *Miscellaneous.* Many in this category may have been counted in other categories above and should not be counted again here. Therefore this estimate is modest. Categories *l*, *m*, and *n* are summed, and a fraction of the sum for each hour of the night is taken as follows: .85, .40, .20, .10, .10, .05, .05, .05. Example: for 3 to 4 A.M., 53,000 + 23,000 + 80,000 = 156,000 × .10 = 15,600.

The small survey described in chapter 9 to note the effects of the 1973–74 fuel crisis on business hours was carried out in March 1974. In the Boston area 139 establishments were surveyed to learn their open hours before the crisis and whether a change in schedule had been made in response to it. As noted in the time census appendix, there is no comprehensive knowledge about the scope and amount of extended-day activity. Straightforward sampling in the city of Boston and the adjacent suburbs of Brookline, Cambridge, and Somerville was unfeasible. Several rosters of late-night establishments that were compiled in the course of studying nighttime activity, other lists published as Night Owl Guides in local newspapers, and energetic firsthand inquiries were the basis of this sample. Because such information had been collected for several years, it was assumed that at least 85 percent of the organizations open to the public after midnight were caught in the sampling net. Those extended-day organizations were then matched with others of the same type (in the same neighborhoods) whose hours were shorter. Even among restaurants, most of the cutbacks affected ones that usually stayed open less than the maximum each day. Only one of the sixty-five twenty-four-hour restaurants in the sample reduced its hours.[8]

Ecology, the study of the relationships between living things and their environments, does not have a systematic set of research principles. This book, written in the spirit of that approach, tried to fulfill a principle of ecological analysis: Look in all directions.

NOTES

An abbreviated reference is given if the publication is listed in the bibliography; if not, the reference is complete the first time it is cited and abbreviated thereafter.

CHAPTER 1. A CHANGING TIMETABLE

1. Except for bacteria and blue-green algae. Charles F. Ehret and John J. Wille, "The photobiology of circadian rhythms in protozoa and other eukaryotic microorganisms," in P. Halldal (ed.), *Photobiology of Microorganisms* (New York: Wiley Interscience, 1970) p. 371.

2. The free-running rhythm of the body (that is, the body's activity cycle when light does not vary) is 24.8 hours on the average. Gay Gaer Luce, *Biological Rhythms in Psychiatry and Medicine.* This apparently resulted from the earth's having rotated more slowly early in its existence, when that pace was instilled in living things.

3. Ignatius Donnelly, *Caesar's Column* (1890) (Cambridge, Mass.: Harvard University Press, 1960), p. 8. In this book Donnelly also foretold the inventions of radio and television. Amos Hawley summarized the ancient pattern and the contemporary trend. The human being "is primarily a diurnal animal. . . . It is the variation of light and darkness and the concomitant alternation of waking and sleeping that supply the fundamental rhythm of community life . . . the night phase marks a temporary suspension of most functions and a relaxation of routine and timing in those that are carried on." Then he

176

pointed out that after-dark activity was expanding in a way that the night phase was becoming like the daytime phase. Hawley, *Human Ecology*, pp. 293, 296, 302, 305. His analysis is among the most systematic we have of space and time arrangements in society.

4. At the end of the eighteenth century Joseph-Louis Lagrange recognized that time should be regarded as a fourth dimension of space. The idea gained a more formal place when Hermann Minkowski and Albert Einstein incorporated the four-dimensional space-time principle in their physics a century later. Contemporary scientists view length and motion as the two basic components of physical existence, but it is possible to think of length and time as basic, and of motion as derivative.

5. Given in defining the word "occupy," *American Heritage Dictionary* (Boston: Houghton Mifflin, 1976).

6. C. Northcote Parkinson, *Parkinson's Law* (1957) (Harmondsworth, Middlesex, England: Penguin Books, 1965), p. 11.

7. Time-shared realty business is carried on in both Europe and the United States. Together all the title-holders own the property for the fifty-two week span, year after year. One sales brochure proclaims: "We look upon interval ownership as the 'fourth tier' in the use of real estate . . . the clock and the calendar now make real estate ownership a function of time." Promotional literature from Sanibel Beach Club II, Sanibel Island, Florida, 1979. See also "Timesharing: New way to buy vacation home," *Kiplinger Magazine*, January 1978.

8. Philip Converse describes this approach and some of its limitations in "Time budgets," in David Sills (ed.), *International Encyclopedia of the Social Sciences* (New York: Macmillan, Free Press, 1968) 16:42–47.

9. Jean Bradford, "Getting the most out of odd moments," *Reader's Digest*, June 1971, p. 82, quoted by Barry Schwartz in "Waiting, exchange and power," p. 841.

10. Wilbert Moore introduced the phrase "temporal order" in *Man, Time, and Society*, p. v.

11. Eviatar Zerubavel, calling the daily structure of events "temporal coordination," describes it according to four categories: sequences, durations, phase locations, and rates of recurrence. Zerubavel, *Hidden Rhythms*, ch. 1.

12. Charles Elton provided an early statement of this in *Animal Ecology*, pp. 83–90.

13. Georg Simmel, "The metropolis and mental life" pp. 411–12.

CHAPTER 2. THE COLONIZATION OF NIGHT

1. Peking man (sinanthropus) was thought to be the first to have controlled fire; see Omer C. Stewart, "Fire as the first great force employed by man," in *Man's Role in Changing the Face of the Earth* (Chicago: University of Chicago Press, 1956) pp. 115–33. In October 1984 the Soviet news agency Tass re-

ported the discovery of a site in Siberia where people used fire 1.5 million years ago.

2. Lorus J. Milne and Margery J. Milne, *World of Night*, p. 2.

3. In the Gospels light is said to be either God or Jesus. "There was a man sent. . . . He was not that Light, but *was sent* to bear witness of that Light." Jesus entreated the people around him, "While ye have light believe in the light, that ye may be the children of light." John 8:12, 1:6,8, and 12:36; St. Augustine, *City of God*, Book 11, ch. 9.

4. Lawrence Wright, *Clockwork Man*, p. 39.

5. Zerubavel, *Hidden Rhythms*, pp. 32–41; G. J. Whitrow, *The Nature of Time*, p. 19.

6. Janice N. Hedges and Edward S. Sekscenski, "Workers on late shifts in a changing economy," pp. 14–22.

7. Terry Reynolds, "Medieval roots of the Industrial Revolution," *Scientific American* 251 (July 1984):128. A foundry in New England a century later was maintained twenty-four hours a day. E. Neal Hartley, *Ironworks on the Saugus* (Norman: University of Oklahoma Press, 1957), pp. 173–74.

8. Ruben C. Bellan, *The Evolving City* (New York: Pitman, 1971) pp. 45, 62 n. 8, 67–68.

9. Alan William, *The Police of Paris: 1718 to 1789* (Baton Rouge: Louisiana State University Press, 1979), pp. 223–25. In many societies the police developed from the paid night watchman. Vilhelm Aubert and Harrison White, "Sleep: A sociological interpretation—II," p. 2.

10. From the Middlesex Sessions Records (Sessions Books and Orders of Court), October 1745, quoted by M. Dorothy George in *London Life in the Eighteenth Century*. A piece of cotton twist formed the wick, oil such as fish oil was the fuel used, and lamplighters were employed to make the rounds trimming and lighting them. (New York: Capricorn edition, 1965), p. 101, ch. 2, p. 102.

11. Murdock accomplished this in 1792. He mentioned his experiments to Watt, declaring that coal-gas was superior to oils and tallow, and suggested several times that a patent should be taken out for its use in illumination. But Watt and Boulton were so harassed by lawsuits surrounding patents for their steam engine at the time that they were unwilling to act on this new enterprise, and nothing was done to protect the invention. Samuel Smiles, *Lives of Boulton and Watt*, pp. 422, 426–27.

12. *Ibid.*, p. 429.

13. Arthur M. Schlesinger, Jr., *Rise of the City: 1878–1895* (New York: Macmillan, 1933), p. 105; Lewis A. Erenberg, *Steppin' Out*, pp. 60 ff.; Jesse L. Lasky, *I Blow My Own Horn* (New York: Doubleday, 1957), p. 84.

14. *New York Times*, August 14, 1973, p. 16. Another airline advertised: "The cost of living goes up every day, but the cost of leaving goes down every night."

15. "Sunday work is key issue as miners prepare to strike," *New York Times*, March 22, 1981, p. 24.

16. "More night people, more night life," *Wall Street Journal*, January 4, 1967, p. 1. This rationale spreads beyond industry and commerce. Citizens concerned with the high cost of municipal buildings argue that the same school or courthouse should be used on a two- or three-shift basis instead of remaining empty twelve to sixteen hours a day. In Las Vegas, where a school is run at night in the same buildings used by a completely separate school during the daytime, the school superintendent believed that the double shifts quieted disgruntled taxpayers and helped pass bond issues for new buildings. "Round-the-clock learning," *Newsweek*, January 4, 1971, p. 32. Also "Courthouses seen as family classrooms," *Boston Globe*, January 30, 1973, p. 1.

17. Charles Perrow, *Normal Accidents*, pp. 181, 188, 189, 197.

18. The Fair Labor Standards Act of 1938 stipulated payment of 150 percent of regular wages ("time and a half") for workdays or workweeks beyond prescribed standards. The industries that turned to the forty-hour week and multiple shifts, that is to shorter labor hours within long plant hours, were those that had been relying on long hours for labor and therefore faced a large potential expense because of the new wage-hour legislation. Murray F. Foss, "Long-run changes in the workweek of fixed capital," p. 60. Hedges and Sekscenski also treat this issue in "Workers on late shifts." Since the expense of shift work bonuses offsets some of the economies in operating around the clock, the variation in the size of these premiums will bear on how much they discourage multiple shifting. In Great Britain in the early 1970s the usual shift work premium was in the range of 17–25 percent. In Colombia it was legislated to be 50 percent. India had considered a mandatory 10 percent. Gordon Winston, "The theory of capital utilization and idleness," pp. 1306, 1313. High shift pay premiums as ordered in Colombia could have generated a labor cost that diminished the pull toward night work. Different schedules and methods of payment for labor are possible, and the choice of shift pattern affects the net economic advantages. Charles M. O'Connor calculated the ratio of savings of fixed overhead costs from adding a second and third shift in "Late-shift employment in manufacturing industries," *Monthly Labor Review* 93 (1970):37–42; Frank Fishwick reviewed the options in several multiple shifting plans, using case examples of firms in different industries, in *The Introduction and Extension of Shiftworking*, cases 2, 5, and 7.

19. British firms intentionally left their plants idle for this reason. Robin Marris, *Economics of Capital Utilization* (Cambridge: Cambridge University Press, 1964); Winston calls this "optimal idleness of capital" in "Theory of capital utilization," pp. 1305, 1301. See also Gordon C. Winston, "Capacity: An integrated micro and macro analysis," *American Economic Review* 67 (1977):418–22; Foss, "Long-run changes"; Murray F. Foss, "The utilization of capital equipment: Postwar compared to prewar," *Survey of Current Business* 43 (June 1963):8–16; and M. F. Foss, *Changes in the Workweek of Fixed Capital*.

20. International Labour Organisation, *Management of Working Time in Industrialized Countries*, p. 9; Richard L. Meier, "Notes on the creation of an efficient metropolis: Tokyo," in G. Bell and J. Tyrwhitt (eds.), *Human Iden-*

tity and the Urban Environment (Baltimore: Penguin Books, 1967), p. 576; "1,000 concerns asked to alter hours," *New York Times*, July 31, 1972; "Transit difficulties grow in many nations," *New York Times*, January 26, 1975, p. 53.

21. Lewis Mumford, *The City in History* (New York: Harcourt Brace, 1961), p. 218.

22. "Cairo is abuzz over new rule curbing noise," *New York Times*, November 30, 1980, p. 19.

23. Robert Sidney Smith, *Mill on the Dan*, p. 20.

24. Municipal courts in upstate New York also hear civil cases then. The sheriff of San Francisco exhorted its judges to hold night sessions because of increasingly crowded dockets. "The cities: New sheriff in town," *Newsweek*, March 20, 1972, p. 63. See also "For first time, Jerseyans get a night civil court," *New York Times*, January 18, 1981, p. 42.

25. A printed leaflet titled "TOUR" (acronym for time of use rates) by Boston Edison Company for May 1978 was explicit: "[T]he rates are designed to encourage customers to shift electric use to low demand times. By doing so, the need for additional costly transmission and generating facilities can be slowed." Peak periods are defined as 11 A.M. to 5 P.M. on summer weekdays (June through October), and shoulder periods are 9 to 11 A.M. and 5 to 10 P.M. on those days, as well as 9 A.M. to 10 P.M. on winter weekdays.

26. "Late shift to save energy irks employees," *New York Times*, January 21, 1977, p. A-12.

27. Michael Hugo-Brunt, "Hong Kong housing," p. 483.

28. Roderick D. McKenzie, "The ecological approach to the study of the human community," p. 74.

29. Richard J. S. Gutman and Elliott Kaufman, *American Diner* (New York: Harper/Colophon, 1981).

30. This process was termed "functional magnetism" by Charles Colby and the appropriately descriptive "deviation-amplifying mutual causal processes" by Magoroh Maruyama. Charles C. Colby, "Centrifugal and centripetal forces in urban geography" (1933), reprinted in Harold M. Mayer and Clyde F. Kohn (eds.), *Readings in Urban Geography* (Chicago: University of Chicago Press, 1959) p. 295; Magoroh Maruyama, "The second cybernetics: Deviation-amplifying mutual causal processes," *American Scientist* 51 (1963):164–79, reprinted in Walter Buckley (ed.), *Modern Systems Research for the Behavioral Scientist* (Chicago: Aldine, 1968) pp. 304–13.

31. "Round-the-clock learning," *Newsweek;* also "Crowds in rest of Atlantic City are sparse, but casino is packed," *New York Times*, May 28, 1978, p. 22.

32. U.S. Federal Communications Commission "Broadcast services," p. 18.

33. General information about such activity is provided in appendixes in Alexander Szalai (ed.), *The Use of Time*. The growth in shift work is an estimate made by the AFL-CIO, cited in David Margolick, "The lonely world of night work," p. 114. See also J. Carpentier and P. Cazamian, *Night Work*, p. vi, and Appendix A, note 17.

34. Michael Young and Peter Willmott, *The Symmetrical Family*, p. 175; and Derek L. Bosworth and Peter J. Dawkins, *Work Patterns*, pp. 90–91.

35. In 1973, 2 percent more than in 1961. Mary Shapcott and Philip Steadman, "Rhythms of urban activity," in Carlstein, Parkes, and Thrift (eds.), *Timing Space and Spacing Time*, II:58.

36. *Campaign* (London) January 31, 1986, p. 1.

37. "A help line aids Russians under stress," *New York Times*, August 22, 1982, p. 11.

38. Richard L. Meier, "A stable urban ecosystem," *Science* 192 (June 4, 1976):965. See also Y. M. Yeung, "Periodic Markets: Comments on spatial-temporal relationships," *Professional Geographer* 26 (1974):148.

39. Edward N. Luttwak, "Seeing China Plain," *Commentary*, December 1976, p. 29, quoted in Paul Hollander, *Political Pilgrims* (New York: Oxford, 1981) p. 376.

40. See the "Time Census," Figure A–3, and "Research Notes," Appendix B, for details of the sample and estimates.

Chapter 3. Frontier Comparisons

1. To choose a case for comparison I reviewed materials on the American West, the Australian Outback, the eastward emigrations to Siberia from Russia across the Urals, and present-day ventures in the Amazon interior. A number of scholarly volumes are available concerning other frontiers, but not in the abundance, accompanied by firsthand documents, in which they are at hand for the U.S. West. The development of the Amazon basin and its rimlands would have been an ideal comparison since it is contemporary. But that is also the reason for the current documentary incompleteness, fragmentary reports, and temporary inaccessibility of Portuguese and Spanish materials to universities in English-speaking countries. The parallels between land and time frontiers outlined in this chapter may some day be tested against the history of the development of the Amazon region.

2. William H. Goetzmann, *Exploration and Empire*, p. xi.

3. Frederick Jackson Turner, *America's Great Frontiers and Sections*, p. 59; *idem*, *The Frontier in American History*, pp. 12, 19–20.

4. Ray Allen Billington, *Westward Expansion*, pp. 4–5.

5. Goetzmann, *Exploration*, p. xii.

6. Accounts before and during the nineteenth century can be found in the histories by Goetzmann, *ibid.*, and Katharine Coman, *Economic Beginnings of the Far West*.

7. Mary C. Rabbitt, "John Wesley Powell: Pioneer statesman of federal science," *The Colorado River Region and John Wesley Powell*, Geological Survey Professional Paper #669 (Washington, D.C.: U.S. Government Printing Office, 1969), p. 3.

8. Churches founded outposts in the virgin territories even earlier. "The only flourishing enterprises in California [in the mid-to-late 1700s, the era of Spanish dominion] were the missions." Coman, *Economic Beginnings*, 1:145.

9. Bernard DeVoto, *Across the Wide Missouri* (Boston: Houghton Mifflin, 1964), pp. 300–301.

10. Coman, *Economic Beginnings*, 2:63.

11. Earl Pomeroy, "Toward a reorientation of Western history," p. 387.

12. M. Kabaj, "Searching for an optimum shift-work pattern," p. 86.

13. Joanna L. Stratton, *Pioneer Women*, p. 138; Robert E. Riegel, *America Moves West*, p. 624; Edwin L. Godkin, "The frontier and the national character" (1896), in M. Ridge and R. A. Billington, (eds.), *America's Frontier Story*, p. 13; Everett Dick, *Sod-House Frontier*, pp. 7, 232.

14. Appendix B provides details of the tallies for Figure 3–2.

15. Dick, *Sod-House Frontier*, pp. 7, 232, 18.

16. Similar findings are reported in Stuart F. Chapin, Jr. and Pearson H. Stewart, "Population densities around the clock."

17. Billington, *Westward Expansion*, p. 4.

18. Roy M. Robbins, *Our Landed Heritage* (Princeton, N.J.: Princeton University Press, 1942), p. 148.

19. John S. C. Abbot, *Christopher Carson, Familiarly Known as Kit Carson* (New York, 1873), pp. 183–84.

20. Daniel Glaser, *Social Deviance* (Chicago: Markham, 1971), p. 25.

21. Turner, *Frontier in American History*, pp. 37, 259; *idem*, *The Significance of Sections in American History*, p. 25.

22. Philip Durham and Everett L. Jones, *The Negro Cowboy* (New York: Dodd, Mead, 1965).

23. Cecil Woodham-Smith, *The Great Hunger* (New York: Harper & Row, 1962).

24. Rodman Wilson Paul, *Mining Frontiers of the Far West*, p. 144; Roger D. McGrath, *Gunfighters, Highwaymen, and Vigilantes*, p. 253.

25. Walter P. Webb, *The Great Frontier* (Boston: Houghton Mifflin, 1952). Noting how people responded to the prospect of the frontier, Turner was led to propose that the West was a safety valve for the congestion and unemployment in Eastern cities, that it drew off some of the people who might otherwise contribute to social unrest and riots in urban areas, because the discontented and jobless moved from one region to the other. Turner, *Frontier in American History*, p. 259.

At first his idea persuaded historians, for they had neglected the role of the West in their chronicles, and his creative essay transformed their study of United States history. Then scholars challenged both aspects of his safety valve notion, that unemployed workers from the East Coast had migrated and that it prevented strife in the East by serving as an outlet for the discontented unemployed. They found little evidence that city laborers made their way west and succeeded as farmers. The urban jobless did not have the money needed to travel or to buy stock and tools and build farmsteads. Nor did they have the skills to feed and shelter themselves until a crop could be made. See Carter Goodrich and Sol Davidson, "The wage earner in the westward movement," p. 114. Instead, most of those who homesteaded across the Mississippi were experienced farmers; many of them had been successful and were now seeking a still better life. Moreover, it could not be shown that urban turmoil was forestalled; during the period of western expansion, economic recessions in Eastern cities fomented disturbances and conflict there.

More recently Turner's idea has been reinterpreted favorably in a larger sense. Leave aside the exact text of his claim, say the economists and historians, and do not limit the boundaries of the safety valve to Eastern cities alone and to the urban jobless alone. Not only prosperous farmers came west. By attracting farmers from less fertile regions, the bountiful Western territory upheld wages in the cities, for those farmers might otherwise have ended up as wage workers in factories. Instead they went to the West and did not exacerbate the unemployment in the big cities. Goodrich and Davidson, "Wage earner," p. 115; Norman J. Simler, "The safety-valve doctrine re-evaluated," *American History* 32 (1958):250–57.

Also, the objectors to the safety valve idea may have overlooked the difference between the dynamics of migration and the conditions of successful adaptation. We know that people turned back because of their bafflement in coping with the frontier's rigors and demands. "When eastern workers did attempt to take up land, they appear very frequently to have failed and returned home discouraged." Goodrich and Davidson, "Wage earner," p. 115. The fact that many people went west despite their unpreparedness for the rigors suggests that the process of a safety valve was operating. Those who could not adapt retraced their way, or lay beneath makeshift headstones along the trails.

For more on this debate see Richard Hofstadter, *The Progressive Historians* (New York: Knopf, 1969), pp. 154–55, 474–75; George R. Taylor (ed.), *The Turner Thesis*; Eric McKitrick and Stanley Elkins, "A meaning for Turner's frontier," *Political Science Quarterly* 69 (September 1954):321–53.

26. Henry Nash Smith, *Virgin Land*, p. 239.

27. Told by Richard Carruthers, who was raised as a slave, in George P. Rawick, *From Sundown to Sunup*, pp. 33–37.

28. Billington, *Westward Expansion*, pp. 96, 746.

29. Hawley, *Human Ecology*, p. 306.

30. Smith, *Virgin Land*, pp. 51–52; Frederick Law Olmsted, *A Journey Through Texas* (New York: 1859), p. xix (note); Harmon Zeigler *Interest Groups in American Society* (Englewood Cliffs, N.J.: Prentice-Hall, 1964), p. 164.

31. Turner, *Frontier in American History*, p. 251.

32. Seth K. Humphrey, *Following the Prairie Frontier*, p. 128. Walter P. Webb wrote that "the Plains—mysterious, desolate, barren, grief-stricken—oppressed the women, drove them to the verge of insanity in many cases." *The Great Plains* (Boston: Ginn, 1931), p. 248. Their depression and distress is mentioned in Cathy Luchetti and Carol Olwell, *Women of the West*, pp. 28–29.

33. William Hogarth, Plate IV of the series "The Four Times of the Day" (1738), in *Engravings by Hogarth* (New York: Dover, 1973), plate 45.

34. Harold Grey, "Orphan Annie," comic strip syndicated by New York News, Inc., December 27 and 28, 1974.

35. See Howard Becker, *Outsiders: Studies in the Sociology of Deviance* (New York: Free Press, 1963), pp. 79, 97, 98.

36. Marcia Millman, *The Unkindest Cut*, pp. 168, 170–73.

37. Howard Robboy, "At work with the night worker," p. 509.

38. *Ibid.*, reported by Noel Byrne.

39. John D. Hicks, *The Federal Union* (Boston: Houghton Mifflin, 1948), p. 508.

40. Recollection of Miriam Davis Colt in Luchetti and Olwell, *Women of the West*, p. 84.

41. Smith, *Virgin Land*, pp. 175, 180.

42. Arthur M. Schlesinger, Jr., "Introduction," in Stratton, *Pioneer Women*, p. 12.

43. *Encyclopaedia Britannica*, 15th ed. (Chicago: Wm. Benton, 1974), V:104.

44. See diary of Keturah Penton Belknap in Luchetti and Olwell, *Women of the West*, pp. 139, 144; James Truslow Adams, "Our lawless heritage," *Atlantic Monthly* 142 (December 1928): 732–40.

45. From Rob Armstrong, "Nightsounds," broadcast by CBS Radio Network, May 30, 1981.

46. McGrath, *Gunfighters, Vigilantes*, p. 167.

47. Goetzmann, *Exploration*, p. 169; Coman, *Economic Beginnings*, 2:85; Keturah Belknap's diary in Luchetti and Olwell, *Women of the West*, pp. 143, 144.

48. Francis Parkman, *The Oregon Trail* (1849) (New York: New American Library, 1964), p. 8.

49. Ray Allen Billington, *The American Frontiersman* (London: Oxford University Press, 1954), p. 8; Joseph Doddridge, "Life in the old west" (1912), in Ridge and Billington, *America's Frontier Story*, p. 103; Richard M. Brown, *Strain of Violence*, p. 125. Vigilante groups in the West sought to serve where the constituted authorities failed, and thus they took the law into their own hands. They seemed to serve well acting as policemen but exceeded the law when acting as courts. See J. W. Smurr, "Afterthoughts on the vigilantes," *Montana, The Magazine of Western History* VIII (April 1958):8–20; Thomas J. Dimsdale, *The Vigilantes of Montana* (1859) (Norman: University of Oklahoma Press, 1953); McGrath, *Gunfighters, Vigilantes*, pp. 242–45.

50. Timothy Flint, "Frontier society in the Mississippi Valley" (1826), in Ridge and Billington, *America's Frontier Story*, p. 401; McGrath, *Gunfighters, Vigilantes*, p. 247; W. Turrentine Jackson, "Pioneer life on the plains and in the mines," in R. A. Billington (ed.), *People of the Plains and Mountains* (Westport, Conn.: Greenwood Press, 1973), pp. 97–98.

51. Hollon concludes that there was "a natural tendency to exaggerate the truth and emphasize the exception . . . not a single shoot-out took place on main

street at Dodge City or any of the other Kansas cow towns in the manner of the face-to-face encounter presented thousands of times on television." W. Eugene Hollon, "Frontier violence: Another look," in Billington, *People of Plains and Mountains*, pp. 97–98. His conclusion is based on Robert Dykstra's *The Cattle Towns* (New York: Knopf, 1968), whose statistics were compiled from local newspapers of the 1870–80 era.

52. J. B. Frantz and J. E. Choate, *The American Cowboy: Myth and Reality* (Norman: University of Oklahoma Press, 1955), p. 83; Billington, *Westward Expansion*, p. 63; Hollon, "Violence: Another look," p. 96; McGrath, *Gunfighters, Vigilantes*, pp. 268–69, 248–51, 253–55.

53. "Like all previous mining frontiers, the Black Hills attracted a mixture of the restless, the ambitious, the curious, and the outlaws from all parts of the country. In Deadwood . . . the resemblance was understandable enough because so many of the people who were now in the Black Hills had once been in the Boise Basin or Helena, and were leading essentially the same life that they had known." Paul, *Mining Frontiers*, p. 178.

54. "The night is the safe time for robbers, as the light for just men," wrote Euripedes. Aubert and White, "Sleep: A sociological interpretation—II," p. 2.

55. During the oil embargo of 1973–74 black market deliveries of fuel to gasoline stations took place from 3 A.M. to 4 A.M. From *NBC Nightly News* (television), November 30, 1973; "Drug trafficking on rise in South," *Boston Globe*, June 12, 1983, p. 2. During the insurrection in Nicaragua in 1978, secret arms shipments from abroad were delivered to the National Guard during the nighttime. "Both sides prepare for bloodletting in Nicaragua," *New York Times*, November 19, 1978, sec. 4, p. 1.

56. Hans von Hentig, *The Criminal and His Victim; New York Times*, September 4, 1977, pp. 1, 26.

57. Riegel, *America Moves West*, p. 627; Billington, *Westward Expansion*, p. 480. Concerning nighttime, in Boston the shortage of officers on duty at night was reported in "Boston police today," *Boston Globe*, April 4, 1977, p. 1. Some officers on duty make themselves unavailable then by sleeping in their cars, a long-time habit in New York City, where it is called "cooping." " 'Cooping': An old custom under fire," *New York Times*, December 15, 1968, sec. 4, p. 6E.

58. The group conducts its patrols unarmed and relies on its presence to intimidate potential troublemakers. For the most part its members have maintained self-discipline (there have been only a few reports of overzealous detentions) and have made most passengers feel safer. Julie Michaels, "The underground angels," *Boston Globe Magazine*, May 24, 1981, pp. 8–9 ff; "Effectiveness of Guardian Angels called uncertain," *New York Times*, August 7, 1981, p. 18.

59. For many examples, see Luchetti and Olwell, *Women of the West*.

60. William Darby, "Primitivism in the lower Mississippi valley" (1818), in Ridge and Billington, *America's Frontier Story*, p. 400; Frantz and Choate, *American Cowboy*, p. 64; Billington, *Westward Expansion*, p. 96; Riegel, *America Moves West*, p. 81; Dick, *Sod-House Frontier*, p. 512; Stratton, *Pioneer Women*, pp. 129 ff.

61. Flint, "Frontier society," pp. 402–3; W. Eugene Hollon, *Frontier Violence*, p. 212.

62. Quoted in Hollon, *Frontier Violence*, pp. 211–12.

63. Thomas Wright, *The Great Unwashed* (1868) (London: Frank Cass, 1970), pp. 195–96.

64. Smith, *Virgin Land*, pp. 234–35, 8, 238. The second quotation is drawn from the first session of the 36th Congress, *Congressional Globe*, April 10, 1860. Policies for the Western lands did not work out as expected. Advocates of the Homestead Act who proposed to settle farmers on the public domain assumed an indefinitely large quantity of fertile land on the frontier. The quantity of land, of course, was finite. Also, the Homestead Act did not lead to ownership by great numbers of individuals, who then tilled their own property. The General Land Office quickly became corrupt and inefficient, allowing speculators and monopolists to buy up much of the land and then rent it out.

65. The nation's natural resources were not protected until a half-century later by conservation legislation and the introduction of the National Park System. William Goetzmann observed that only in a late stage come "sober, second thoughts as to the proper nature, purpose, and future direction of" frontier settlement and use. Goetzmann, *Exploration*, p. xiv.

66. The policy is discussed by a number of writers: Kabaj, "Shift work and employment expansion: Towards an optimum pattern," p. 245; R. T. Betancourt and Christopher K. Clague, "An economic analysis of capital utilization," *Southern Economic Journal* 42 (July 1975):69–78; Daniel Schydlowsky, "Latin American trade policy in the 1970s: A prospective appraisal," Report 150, *Economic Development Reports*, Center for International Affairs, Harvard University, 1970; Daniel Schydlowsky and Juan Wicht, *Anatomy of an Economic Fiasco: Peru 1968–78* (Lima: Centro de Investigacion de la Universidad del Pacifico, 1979). Nations that undertake multiple shifting as a means of creating more jobs and putting their unemployed masses to work would also offer chances for members of minority groups and other disadvantaged persons to establish a foothold in the work force, for shift work disproportionately engages some underemployed sections of the population. However, those job openings are also available to people already employed. An increase in opportunities is likely to attract some workers from other labor force sectors who seize shift work openings without giving up the jobs they already have, which would detract from its unemployment-reducing promise.

67. Daniel Schydlowsky, "Capital utilization, growth, employment, balance of payments and price stabilization."

68. Carpentier and Cazamian, *Night Work*, pp. 7, 3.

69. Kabaj, "Searching for shift-work pattern," pp. 86–87; *idem*, "Shift work and employment expansion"; *idem*, "Shift work: Towards optimum pattern."

70. Bosworth and Dawkins, *Work Patterns*, p. 226.

71. George B. Dantzig and Thomas L. Saaty, *Compact City*, pp. 190–93.

72. Richard L. Meier, "A stable urban ecosystem," (ch. 2, note 38), p. 965.

73. V. D. Patrushev, "Aggregate time-balances and their meaning for socio-economic planning," in Szalai, *Use of Time*, p. 429.

74. Turner, *Significance of Sections*, pp. 25–30; *idem, Frontier in American History*, p. 207; *idem*, America's Great Frontiers, p. 54.

75. Robbins, *Our Landed Heritage*, (note 18 above), p. 271.

76. "Prostitutes speak of pride, but they are still victims," *Boston Globe*, June 25, 1976, pp. 1, 10.

77. Christiaan Huygens, *Traité de la Lumière* (Leyden, 1690), p. 4. In the original French the passage "by spherical surfaces and waves: for I call them waves from their resemblance" is written "par des surfaces & des ondes sphériques: car je les appelle ondes à la ressemblances." "Onde" comes from the Latin *unda,* meaning "running water." Huygens also discussed light as being small bodies that "float" about in the air ("de petit corps que nagent"), p. 11.

78. Riegel, *America Moves West*, p. 1.

79. Turner, *Frontier in American History*, p. 38.

CHAPTER 4. WHO IS ACTIVE AT NIGHT?

1. "Migration" means both a relatively permanent movement to a new region and a cyclic move with periodic returns to former locales. Both apply to night-timers, for they adopt a different routine and yet they often cycle between that schedule and daytime involvements.

2. The ecologist McKenzie wrote that a "natural surplus of population is forced to emigrate. . . . Competition becomes keener within the community, and the weaker elements either are forced into a lower economic level or are compelled to withdraw from the community entirely." Roderick D. McKenzie, "The ecological approach," pp. 64, 71.

3. Stouffer proposed that in spatial migration the distance traveled is in inverse ratio to the presence of intervening opportunities. Samuel Stouffer, "Intervening opportunities: A theory relating mobility and distance," *American Sociological Review* 5 (1940):845–67. This is not an explanation for people who have off-hours occupations such as in the performing arts and some professional sports.

4. S. M. Lipset and M. A. Trow, *Union Democracy* (Glencoe, Ill: Free Press, 1956), p. 135.

5. Hedges and Sekscenski, "Workers on late shifts," pp. 18–19.

6. While 16 percent of black males and 30 percent of black females work in service jobs, among whites these groups are 8 and 18 percent, respectively. *Ibid.*, p. 20. For semiskilled manual workers and laborers, the 1982 figures from the U.S. Bureau of Labor Statistics are, for white males, 15 percent semiskilled workers and 6 percent laborers, for black males 20 and 11 percent in the same categories; for white females 9 and 1 percent semiskilled workers and laborers, for black females 15 and 1 percent in the same categories. Re-

ported in Curt Tausky, *Work and Society* (Itasca, Ill.: F. E. Peacock, 1984), Table 3–4, p. 61. Although "black" in the table refers to "blacks and other nonwhites," about 90 percent are black workers.

7. National Industrial Conference Board, *Night Work in Industry*, p. 19.

8. John Fryer, "Where have all the drivers gone?" *Times* (London) June 10, 1973.

9. Marc Maurice, *Shift Work*, p. 118; Alice Kessler-Harris, *Out of Work*, pp. 192–93.

10. Bosworth and Dawkins, *Work Patterns*, pp. 172, 97, 190.

11. Mark C. Stafford and Omer R. Galle, "Victimization rates, exposure to risk, and fear of crime," *Criminology* 22 (May 1984):173–85. The indicator of exposure to risk was the number of hours spent away from home minus the hours of employment.

12. "125,000 New Yorkers work the whole night through," *New York Times Magazine*, April 5, 1964, p. 55; "Women who clean offices through the night: A lonely life," *New York Times*, November 21, 1973, p. 38; *Time Out* magazine (London), 1976.

13. "Studying the woes of night work," *New York Times*, April 5, 1978, p. 17; "Women who clean offices," *New York Times*.

14. See Appendix B for details of the Survey and how it is used here. For technical reasons the actual numbers of workers on evening and especially on night shifts are understated.

15. The distributions by marital status are likely to reiterate those by age and need not be checked separately. That is, the largest portion of "never married" would be in the youngest group, and the largest portion of separated, divorced, and widowed persons would be older workers.

16. William F. Hornby and Melvyn Jones, *An Introduction to Population Geography* (Cambridge, U.K.: Cambridge University Press, 1980), p. 125.

17. From a television documentary about night workers, broadcast on *The Today Show*, NBC, April 16, 1981.

18. David Margolick, "Lonely world of night work," p. 113.

19. Howard Robboy, "They work by night," p. 251.

20. S. Cotgrove, J. Dunham and C. Vamplew, *The Nylon Spinners* (London: Allen & Unwin, 1971).

21. Jane C. Hood, "When changing shifts means changing jobs."

22. Maurice, *Shift Work*, pp. 66–69. Farmers also moonlight to improve their income. Foss, "Long-run changes," p. 62.

23. Paul E. Mott, Floyd C. Mann, Quin McLoughlin and Donald P. Warwick, *Shift Work*, p. 24.

24. Howard Robboy, "False labeling and the breakdown of temporal social control," paper presented at the meeting of the Society for the Study of Social Problems, San Antonio, August 1984; *idem*, "They work by night," p. 253.

25. In the United States in 1981, in more than one-third of dual-earner couples with children, in which both spouses worked full time, one of the partners (usually the husband) did shift work. The spouses worked different shifts with no overlap in hours away from home in about one-tenth of the couples. Har-

riet B. Presser and Virginia S. Cain, "Shift work among dual-earner couples with children."

26. Except for this instance of females who work evenings, the patterns are the same for full-timers and part-timers separately. The power of the minority group selection, whether because of racial discrimination, social class disadvantage, or single parenthood, is revealed for female licensed practical nurses and aides in a large hospital. Table 4–2 shows that a larger proportion of black women worked evenings and nights.

TABLE 4–2

Work Shifts for Female Licensed Practical Nurses and Aides in a Large Metropolitan Hospital

	Blacks	*Whites*	*Total*
Day or rotate	15	102	117
	(25.9%)	(53.3%)	
Evening or night	43	76	119
	(74.1%)	(42.7%)	
	58	178	236

SOURCE: Based on 24 percent random samples taken every four months for three years (i.e., nine selections) beginning November 1963. Data from research supported by grant MH-1305 from the National Institute of Mental Health. Chi Square (1df) = 17.30; for one-tailed test $p < .001$, Somer's $d.yx = .23$.

27. The greater one's mobility, the less one is disposed to stay and struggle. See Ralf Dahrendorf, *Class and Class Conflict in Industrial Society* (Stanford, Calif.: Stanford University Press, 1959), p. 220; Albert O. Hirschmann, *Exit, Voice, and Loyalty* (Cambridge, Mass.: Harvard University Press, 1970).

28. Bill Harris, *New York at Night*, p. 74.

29. Lipset and Trow, *Union Democracy* (note 4 above), p. 138.

30. Robboy, "They work by night," p. 271.

31. Marcia Millman tells of hospital night workers: They "were distinguished by odd manners, bizarre physical appearances, and noticeable idiosyncracies." *Unkindest Cut*, pp. 168, 171.

32. Erenberg, *Steppin' Out*.

33. "Broadway," *Atlantic Monthly* 125 (June 1920):854–56.

34. Harris, *New York at Night*, p. 49.

35. Other functions, for example the secretion of the human growth hormone, also show twenty-four-hour cycles but peak during the night or at different hours. Jürgen Aschoff, "Circadian rhythms in man"; Luce, *Biological Rhythms;* Rütger A. Wever, *The Circadian System of Man;* the journal *Chronobiologia*.

36. It is the suprachiasmatic nucleus, also called the retinohypothalamic tract, and is located in the anterior hypothalamus region of the brain, where it sits on a pathway from the retina.

37. See Martin Zatz and Michael J. Brownstein, "Injection of alpha-bungarotoxin

near the suprachiasmatic nucleus"; W. J. Rietveld, "The role of the supra-chiasmatic nucleus afferents in the central regulation of circadian rhythms," *Progress in Clinical and Biological Research* 59 (1981):205–11. Some evidence suggests that the length of daylight or the ratio of light and dark spans, rather than the intensity of illumination, is the dominant cue to which the body responds. Karsch *et al.*, "Neuroendocrine basis of seasonal reproduction"; Whitrow, *The Nature of Time*, p. 49.

38. Luce, *Biological Rhythms*, p. 140. See chapter 1, note 2.

39. J. L. Cloudsley-Thompson, "Time sense of animals," p. 310. I have been told that lions in East Africa, habitually diurnal creatures, have in the early 1980s taken to hunting at night in order to avoid being shot by humans.

40. John B. Calhoun, "Population density and social pathology," *Scientific American* 206 (February 1962):142.

41. The study, carried out in the 1930s, is cited in Young and Willmott, *Symmetrical Family*, p. 148.

42. John Horton, "Time and cool people," p. 3.

43. Gwynneth de la Mare and J. Walker, "Factors influencing the choice of shift rotation," p. 1.

44. Fishwick, *Introduction of Shiftworking*, p. 15. His report is drawn from A. Aaronsen, *Shift Work and Health* (Oslo: Scandinavian Books, 1964).

CHAPTER 5. ADVERSITY AND GOOD WILL

1. Dick, *Sod-House Frontier*, p. 510. Ray Allen Billington, "Frontier Democracy," in Taylor (ed.), *The Turner Thesis*, p. 166.

2. Konrad Lorenz, *On Aggression* (New York: Harcourt Brace Jovanovich, 1963), p. 143.

3. Emile Durkheim, *The Division of Labor in Society*, pp. 58–59.

4. Stanley Schachter, *The Psychology of Affiliation* (Stanford, Calif.: Stanford University Press, 1959).

5. The University Heights public housing project in The Bronx, New York, over-looks both the Harlem River railroad tracks and the Major Deegan Express-way and is situated under a flight route to Newark Airport.

6. Barry Schwartz, "Notes on the sociology of sleep."

7. "Government weakens airport noise standards," *Science* 207 (March 1980):1189; "Fly-by-night days ending," *New York Times*, September 6, 1981, sec. 4, p. 6E.

8. "County loses on night-flight ban," *New York Times*, August 28, 1983, sec. 4, p. 6E; "Sued over curfew at airport, Westchester set to negotiate," *New York Times*, December 13, 1981, p. 48. The opposing organizations were the National Business Aircraft Association, Panorama Flight Service Inc., and the Aircraft Owners and Pilots Association.

9. "U.S. sues to keep L.I. airport open at night," *New York Times*, September 19, 1982, p. 46.

10. "Dukakis decides to go against Logan curfew," *Boston Globe*, August 12, 1976, pp. 1, 20; "Logan anti-noise plan offered," *Boston Globe*, August 13, 1976, p. 35.

11. Brian Burnes, "East of midnight the frontier lives," *Kansas City Star, Weekly Magazine*, September 9, 1979, pp. 8–10 ff.

12. "City may give disco dancers a break," *Houston Chronicle*, January 5, 1979, pp. 1, 12.

13. Georg Simmel, *Conflict* (1908), trans. Kurt Wolff (Glencoe, Ill.: Free Press, 1955), pp. 91–92, 99, 103.

14. William Graham Sumner, *Folkways* (1906) (New York: Mentor, 1960), p. 27.

15. For the United States, see U.S. Office of Management and Budget, *Social Indicators: 1973* (Washington, D.C.: U.S. Government Printing Office, 1974), pp. 58–59, 73. Also "The streets of Cambridge . . . the shadow of fear," *Boston Globe*, March 8, 1978, p. 3.

16. Michael Young, "Never go out after dark," p. 99.

17. "Rising crime rates have been used effectively . . . in promotional literature for increased outdoor lighting. The argument used is that the crime rate will drop where illumination is increased, and some statistical studies are put forward in support of this idea. (Joint Committees of the Institute of Traffic Engineers and the Illuminating Engineering Society. *Illumination Engineering*. New York v. 59, n. 585, 1966.) . . . Such studies have been confined to a few small areas [yet] most people now believe that outdoor lighting buys them security. It is possible that any demonstrated reduction of the crime rate in a brightly lit area may be negated as criminals simply move to a softer target area." Kurt W. Riegel, "Light pollution," pp. 1289–90.

Occasionally subway crime in New York City prompts the mayor to introduce a program of posting more police officers on trains during the nighttime. Decoy police officers have been active after dark in parks and near the twenty-four-hour mechanical tellers of banks. "Police officer kills an assailant on Upper East Side," *New York Times*, February 19, 1978, p. 41.

18. Gregory P. Stone, "City shoppers and urban identification: Observations on the social psychology of city life," *American Journal of Sociology* 60 (July 1954):37.

19. Stanley Milgram, "Experience of living in cities," p. 1464.

20. Jane Jacobs, *The Death and Life of Great American Cities* (1961) (Harmondsworth, England: Penguin Books, 1974).

21. This general influence was described in Georg Simmel, "Metropolis and mental life."

22. John Darley and C. Daniel Batson, "From Jerusalem to Jericho."

23. This belief may have been supported by the address on the tag, in a small city 90 miles away, which might prompt the thought that someone visited Boston in the daytime and lost the key before returning home for the night.

24. Durkheim characterized these bases of cohesion as mechanical and organic solidarity, respectively. Emile Durkheim, *Division of Labor.*

CHAPTER 6. INCESSANT ORGANIZATIONS

1. Aubert and White observed that the night contains a time-reservoir which allows completion of unfulfilled tasks. "Sleep: A sociological interpretation—II," p. 11.
2. "Holland Tunnel tube to close some nights," *New York Times*, June 24, 1984, p. 23. This practice is often overlooked in plans for evacuating an area in an emergency, for example, within a given radius of a nuclear power plant. Roadways, entrance and exit ramps, and bridges, presumed to be clearer of traffic and to have more throughput capacity at night, are at times actually closed during the night for maintenance work.
3. Max Weber, "Bureaucracy," sections 1, 2, 6.
4. Moore, *Man, Time, and Society,* p. 95.
5. "Full text report on Palace intruder," *Times* (London), July 22, 1982, pp. 1, 4; "Whitelaw details list of Palace mistakes," *Times* (London), July 15, 1982, p. 1.
6. Abramson, Wald, Grenvik, Robinson, and Snyder, "Adverse occurrences in intensive care units."
7. By a fortunate coincidence, the live victims of the Manchester (England) air disaster of August 22, 1985, arrived at the nearby hospital just at shift change-over, and both the night and the morning staffs were on hand to provide the needed medical aid.
8. Eviatar Zerubavel, *Patterns of Time in Hospital Life,* p. 55.
9. Durkheim, *Division of Labor,* p. 39.
10. "The disaster in Bhopal," *New York Times*, January 30, 1985, pp. A1, A6.
11. Karl Mannheim, "The problem of generations," p. 296.
12. Perrow, *Normal Accidents.*
13. "Disaster in Bhopal," *New York Times.*
14. Georg Simmel noted that a person who is anonymous and impersonal can be best fitted into someone else's place to ensure the continuity of a group. Simmel, "The persistence of social groups," p. 672.
15. Sir James Frazer, *The Golden Bough* (1890) (New York: Macmillan, 1922), ch. 18.
16. Barry Schwartz, "Notes on the sociology of sleep," p. 489.
17. Barry Schwartz notes that "the privacy of the upper ranks is insured structurally; it is necessary to proceed through the lieutenant stratum if the top level is to be reached." Schwartz, "The social psychology of privacy," p. 743.
18. He gave instructions to turn on the flare tower to burn off the escaping gas, but the tower had not been fixed after the last time it had broken down; experts (later) thought it would have made no difference at that stage. "Disaster in Bhopal," *New York Times.*

19. Jane C. Hood and Nancy Milazzo, "Shiftwork, stress, and wellbeing."

20. Lola Jean Kozak, "Night people: A study of the social experiences of night workers," p. 59.

21. The main sources of information are U.S. Congress, Senate, *Attack upon Pearl Harbor by Japanese Armed Forces;* U.S. Congress, Senate, *Hearings Before the Joint Committee on the Investigation of the Pearl Harbor Attack;* and Gordon W. Prange, *At Dawn We Slept.*

22. U.S. Senate, *Hearings,* pp. 564, 566–67.

23. Prange, *At Dawn,* p. 587; Roberta Wohlstetter, *Pearl Harbor: Warning and Decision* (Stanford, Calif.: Stanford University Press, 1961), p. 309.

24. Prange, *At Dawn,* p. 736. A different interpretation is offered by John Toland in *Infamy: Pearl Harbor and Its Aftermath* (New York: Doubleday, 1982). His main argument is that General Marshall and President Roosevelt deliberately delayed responding to clear reports of the impending Japanese assault because such an attack would sweep aside any hesitation in the American public about finally entering the war on the Allies' side, and that the two had confidence that Pearl Harbor's competent naval forces could repulse the attack without incurring serious loss. The author deals selectively with facts, hearsay, and speculation that support his viewpoint and glosses over evidence to the contrary. He cites instances of forewarnings of a strike against Pearl Harbor as if those were the only intelligence reports received. Such information did not stand alone for all to see and readily comprehend. Instead it was delivered through espionage and diplomatic channels and was mixed among communiqués forecasting attacks on other targets. Intelligence officers were faced with sifting through and evaluating a welter of conflicting information.

    That kind of challenge occurs repeatedly. There had been many terrorist threats and warnings about bombs in vehicles before the successful suicidal truck-bombing of the U.S. Marine headquarters in Beirut on October 23, 1983. With one or two such messages arriving daily, it became difficult to sort out what was accurate in that jumble of information.

25. Wohlstetter, *Pearl Harbor,* p. 310.

26. Prange, *At Dawn,* pp. 406, 724; U.S. Senate, *Hearings,* p. 504.

27. Prange, *At Dawn,* pp. 406, 495; U.S. Senate, *Attack upon Pearl Harbor,* pp. 11–12; U.S. Senate, *Hearings,* pp. 553, 569, 520; Richard B. Morris and Graham W. Irwin (eds.), *Harper Encyclopedia of the Modern World* (New York: Harper & Row, 1970), p. 502.

28. Prange, *At Dawn,* p. 736.

29. U.S. Senate, *Hearings,* p. 567; Prange, *At Dawn,* p. 457.

30. Prange, *At Dawn,* p. 486.

31. Concerning his whereabouts on the night of Saturday, December 6, during the court-martial of the Pearl Harbor commanders in 1944 General Marshall testified, "I don't know where I was. I never thought of it until this instant." *Ibid.,* p. 629.

32. U.S. Senate, *Hearings,* p. 560.

33. "To the shores of Tripoli," *Newsweek*, August 31, 1981, pp. 14–18; "U.S. Navy F-14s down two Libyan jet fighters," *Facts On File*, August 21, 1981; pp. 589–90.

34. Prange, *At Dawn*, pp. 699–700, 706–7.

35. On April 6, 1985, Sudanese armed forces staged a coup and ousted the president, suspended the constitution, and declared a state of emergency throughout their land. The President of the United States was again vacationing in California, and although word of this seizure of power reached his National Security Adviser there at 2:30 A.M., he chose not to wake the President, having decided that there was "no imminent threat" to Americans in the Sudan. *Los Angeles Times*, April 6, 1985. On another occasion, in the morning of Thursday, June 20, 1985, the President was awakened to be informed that Americans had been shot to death in an outdoor café in San Salvador.

36. There is a "reluctance of the [chemical] industry to review accidents in a public, accessible form . . . efforts [to get information about U.S. chemical plant accidents] with companies and trade and technical associations were generally met with the statement that, 'We do not want to wash our dirty linen in public.' " Perrow, *Normal Accidents*, pp. 102–3.

37. John Kemeny, *Report of the President's Commission on the Accident at Three Mile Island*, p. 29; Daniel F. Ford, *Three Mile Island: Thirty Minutes to Meltdown* (New York: Viking, 1982) pp. 98–99, 163. If any of several simple, correct interventions had been made, the danger would have been averted. The risk of radioactive contamination arose after many officials knew about the malfunctioning reactor and continued to worsen in the next two hours because of confused signals from equipment and mistakes in response to them.

38. An exception, for a much longer period, would be ships at sea, which have had experience with shifts, called watches.

39. Reported in the *Wall Street Journal*, February 21, 1982, p. 13; quoted in Ford, *Three Mile Island*, p. 13. Charles Perrow documents how plants have failed to learn from the accident at Three Mile Island in taking steps to alter the indicated risks and pitfalls. Perrow, *Normal Accidents*, pp. 12, 45, 48, 54.

40. James D. Thompson, *Organizations in Action* (New York: McGraw-Hill, 1967), p. 150.

CHAPTER 7. SHIFT WORKERS

1. This point is made by a number of observers. Hawley noted that shift work brought "isolation from a large part of collective life. . . . Night work confused the individual's family life and excluded him from many neighborhood and community affairs. Hawley, *Human Ecology*, p. 10. See also *Working Environment [Arbetsmiljo]* (Stockholm, 1980), p. 11.

2. "Sanitation men here aggrieved by abuse and changing hours," *New York Times*, September 9, 1970, pp. 1, 29.

3. Fred Cottrell, "Of Time and the Railroader."

4. *Boston Globe*, November 1, 1981, p. 49.

5. A. Aanonsen, "Medical problems of shift-work," in *Industrial Medicine and Surgery* (Chicago: Industrial Medicine Publishing Co., September 1959), pp. 422–27; Maurice, *Shift Work*, p. 41.

6. Murray Melbin, "Organization practice and individual behavior."

7. A wife whose husband worked till midnight said, "It always takes a couple of hours to calm him down. We never get to bed before four." Barbara Garson, *All the Livelong Day* (Garden City, N.Y.: Doubleday, 1975), p. 93.

8. There are some equally clear-cut elevations in secretions of other hormones. For a roster of sleep attributes see John Orem and Judith Keeling, *Physiology in Sleep*, pp. 315–35.

9. Czeisler *et al.*, "Human sleep."

10. L. J. Monroe, "Psychological and physiological differences between good and poor sleepers."

11. Czeisler *et al.*, "Human sleep."

12. Tasto, Colligan, Skjei, and Polly, *Health Consequences of Shift Work*, pp. 6–8. Some shift workers report they have less appetite; they eat irregularly and suffer from digestive and stomach disorders. But these difficulties are not universal among them. Although many problems are mentioned here, the evidence for permanent harm is inconclusive. However, if the persons most affected quit their jobs soon, it may explain the lack of consistent evidence for permanent harm of shift work. Similar problems are reported in England. J. M. Harrington, *Shift Work and Health* (London: Health and Safety Executive, Her Majesty's Stationery Office, 1978). In another English study of 951 workers, the researchers found that the night men slept a half-hour less than the other groups. De la Mare and Walker, "Choice of shift rotation," p. 10.

    Health risks of night work are greater for older persons. For further discussion see O. Ostberg, "Interindividual differences in circadian fatigue patterns"; Carpentier and Cazamian, *Night Work*, pp. 27–28.

13. For an overview, see Jürgen Aschoff (ed.), *Handbook of Behavioural Neurobiology*, pp. 81–93.

14. Luce, *Biological Rhythms*, p. 52. Individuals vary in the speed with which they are capable of adjusting to phase shifts.

15. C. G. Hauty and T. Adams, "Phase shifts of the human circadian system and performance deficit during the periods of transition . . . —I. East-West flight" (Oklahoma City: Federal Aviation Agency, Civil Aeromedical Research Institute, AM 65–28, December 1965). And by the same authors, "Phase shifts— . . . II. West–East flight" (AM 65–29, December 1965).

16. Richard J. Wurtman, "The effects of light on the human body," p. 75.

17. W. P. Colquhoun, M. J. F. Blake, and R. S. Edwards, "Experimental studies of shift work," p. 876; Tasto *et al.*, *Health Consequences*. If the worker is returned to the former customary day–night schedule soon, the body adapts quicker. It is easy to adjust to being "back home" after being away for only a little while. Mann and Hoffman report that workers could tolerate a weekly rotational pattern more than a monthly rotation schedule. Floyd C. Mann

and R. L. Hoffman, "Case history in two power plants" (1956), excerpted in Charles R. Walker, and A. G. Walker (eds.), *Modern Technology and Civilization* (New York: McGraw-Hill, 1962), p. 174. The French also believe that for most persons rapid rotations are better than prolonged spells on the shifts. "When workers on fast shift rotation [every two or three days] are compared with workers on weekly shift rotation, it is found that there are fewer cases of ill effects on health among the former." Carpentier and Cazamian, *Night Work*, p. 59. The authors, however, mention other studies that show frequent rotations cause adjustment difficulties.

18. People can adapt to the new timing faster if their activity is in phase with their environment. This is usually the case for travelers who cross several time zones by jet airplane and then follow a routine in the daytime of their destination. But when the environment stays locked in its rhythm and only the shift worker changes, there is less external support and the body takes weeks to adapt altogether. Phase shifts back to regular daytime patterns are easier. The body settles down faster.

19. International Labour Organisation, *Management of Working Time*, p. 26. Performance, mood, and memory peak in the daytime and are worst in the middle of the night. Frank A. Brown, Jr., "Periodicity, biological," p. 74. In this matter, as in most, there are differences affected by personal factors. See Maurice, *Shift Work*, p. 38.

20. J. N., "Engine cleaner," in M. A. Pollock (ed.), *Working Days*, p. 19.

21. "Auditor raids at 3 state hospitals find 22 night employees asleep," *New York Times*, June 26, 1977, p. 14.

22. National Industrial Conference Board, *Night Work in Industry*, p. 33; Ben B. Morgan, Jr., Bill R. Brown, and Earl A. Allusi, "Effects on sustained performance of 48 hours of continuous work and sleep loss," *Human Factors* 16 (1974):413.

23. B. Bjerner, A. Holm, and A. Swenson, "Diurnal variation in mental performance," *British Journal of Industrial Medicine*, April 1955, pp. 103–10. A diagram showing the number of errors made per hour in reading gas meters, from J. Hardy, *Physiological Problems in Space Exploration* (Springfield, Ill.: Charles C. Thomas, 1964), is reprinted in Brown, "Periodicity," p. 74.

24. R. Browne, "The day and night performance of switchboard operators."

25. Robert S. Smith, *Mill on the Dan*, p. 220.

26. Fishwick, *Introduction of Shiftworking*, p. 24.

27. Hentig, *Criminal and His Victim;* Fishwick and Harling, *Shiftworking in the Motor Industry.*

28. Maurice, *Shift Work*, p. 40.

29. *Nova* TV program, "What time is your body?" WGBH, Boston, January 1975. Concerning the risk of inferior performance resulting from sleep disturbance and sleep deprivation among flight crews, researchers believe it attributable to trying to sleep during inappropriate phases of the circadian cycle. Czeisler *et al.*, "Human sleep."

30. Perrow, *Normal Accidents*, pp. 67, 9, 246, 249.

31. Kemeny, *Report of the Accident at Three Mile Island*, p. 81.

32. *Ibid.*, pp. 94, 96.

33. *Ibid.*, p. 91.

34. These matters are ignored in the Kemeny Report, nor are the key terms "circadian rhythms," "performance deficits," and "schedules of work" mentioned in its glossary. On the other hand, terms like "general emergency," and "safety-related" are mentioned. The matter of the operators' physiological rhythms was raised in the inquiry but was dismissed at the outset. After the accident, in rewriting the requirements for working conditions, document "#0694 TMI-2 Related Requirements" of the Nuclear Regulatory Agency mentioned the problem of working hours; and document NUREG #0737 declared that overtime should not be excessive and forbade the operators to work more than sixteen hours in a row.

35. From a half-hour special report by Bill Buzenberg on National Public Radio, August 24, 1985. The Pemex company has kept information about the disaster confidential and has not cooperated with queries from other oil and gas companies. The American Petroleum Institute pieced together several unauthorized reports into a scenario of what probably happened; so did the Swedish Fire Protection Association. An expert engineer, B. F. Olsen of Tempe, Arizona, also produced a knowledgeable report.

36. United Press International, in *Boston Globe*, September 1, 1985, p. 10; *New York Times*, September 1, 1985, p. 3.

37. This interpretation was being made informally about this time and was reported in a number of newspapers. See *Boston Globe*, May 27, 1986, pp. 1, 8.

38. Howard Robboy, "They work by night," pp. 196, 197, 200–2.

39. Dean Baker, "The use and health consequences of shift work," citing research of R. Caillot of France. Sleeping difficulties may be greater in developing countries, for it is more likely that people share sleeping quarters, the number of children per family is higher, and the household consists of fewer rooms. In Pakistan seven times as many off-hours workers as daytime workers reported that they had problems sleeping in their homes. Gordon C. Winston, *The Timing of Economic Activities*, ch. 10. A worker in an industrialized country, Winston observes, comes home from the night shift to an air-conditioned bedroom with window shades and screens that bar daylight and insects and a door and windows that muffle noises from the active household and neighborhood. In contrast the night worker in a poor country returns home and tries to sleep in his house without adequate shielding from light, sounds, heat, and bugs.

40. Hood and Milazzo, "Shiftwork, stress, and wellbeing."

41. Kozak, "Night People," p. 43.

42. Robboy, "They work by night," p. 178.

43. Michael Grumly, *After Midnight*, pp. 154–55.

44. Cottrell, "Of time and the railroader," p. 196.

45. Mott *et al.*, *Shift Work*, p. 298. As control over one's schedule increases, there is less interference with family life and more time to spend with one's children. Graham L. Staines and Joseph H. Pleck, *The Impact of Work Schedules on the Family*, pp. 78–85, 124.

46. Finch, *Married to the Job*, pp. 26–27, 30, citing M. Cain, *Society and the Policeman's Role* (London: Routledge & Kegan Paul, 1973), pp. 7, 137, and unpublished data from research by Cain.

47. Young and Willmott, *Symmetrical Family*, pp. 106–7.

48. Mott *et al.*, *Shift Work*, pp. 19, 95, 111–12; Robboy, "They work by night"; and Maurice, *Shift Work*, p. 50.

49. "Lark–Owl marriages," *New York Times*, January 24, 1982, p. 21Y.

50. Robboy, "They work by night," pp. 136, 217, 277.

51. Mott *et al.*, *Shift Work*, pp. 154–55, 168–69.

52. Kozak, "Night people," p. 46; "The night shift," *Boston Globe*, July 18, 1976, p. 38.

53. "Creatures of the night," *News* (Bernardsville, New Jersey), August 20, 1981.

54. See Millman, *The Unkindest Cut*, pp. 170–73.

55. "It has been found that there is more cohesion within teams of workers during the night than by day." Carpentier and Cazamian, *Night Work*, p. 52.

56. Claude Fischer, *To Dwell Among Friends* (Chicago: University of Chicago Press, 1982), pp. 97, 105–6.

57. Zerubavel, *Patterns of Time*, pp. 82–83.

58. Marianne Frankenhaeuser, "Coping with job stress—A psychobiological approach," in Bertil Gardell and Gunn Johannson (eds.), *Working Life: A Social Science Contribution to Work Reform* (New York: Wiley, 1981), p. 226.

59. See Grumly, *After Midnight*, p. 42; *New York Times*, January 23, 1972, sec. 3, pp. 1, 5; Fishwick, *Introduction of Shiftworking*, p. 12; "Night work: Another life style," *Boston Globe*, November 24, 1974, pp. A-8, A-12; "The night shift," *Boston Globe*, July 18, 1976, pp. 37–38.

60. De la Mare and Walker, "Choice of shift rotation," p. 2.

61. Ronald H. Bohr and Arnold B. Swertloff, "Work shift, occupational status, and the perception of job prestige" *Journal of Applied Psychology* 53 (1969):227–29.

62. A. Marsh, *Women and Shiftwork* (London: Office of Population, Censuses, and Surveys, Social Survey Division; printed by Her Majesty's Stationery Office, 1979), p. 83, cited in Finch, *Married to the Job*, p. 25.

63. One exception is a song by Frank Loesser in the theatrical musical, *Guys and Dolls* (1950), in which the singer declares that the "dark time" is his "time of day."

Chapter 8. Coinciding Trends

1. Karl Marx, *Capital*, ch. 10, sec. 4, including notes.

2. Bosworth and Dawkins, *Work Patterns*, pp. 41–43.

3. Kessler-Harris, *Out to Work*, pp. 363, 191.

4. Louis D. Brandeis and Josephine Goldmark, *The Case Against Night Work for Women*.

5. Marx, *Capital*, ch. 10, sec. 4 and n. 6.

6. David Brody, *Steelworkers in America* (1960) (New York: Harper & Row, 1969), p. 35.

7. Kessler-Harris, *Out to Work*, pp. 194, 211.

8. *Ibid.*, 194–95.

9. Carpentier and Cazamian, *Night Work*, p. 4; Baker, "Use and consequences of shift work," p. 418; "Night work opposed in Japan," *New York Times*, February 23, 1978.

10. David Margolick makes this point, referring to Mexican farmhands. Margolick, "Lonely world of night work," p. 114.

11. Maurice, *Shift Work*, pp. 53, 106, 61, 71.

12. Daniel Bell wrote that "the rising number of divorces may indicate not the disruption of the family but a freer, more individualistic basis of choice and the emergence of the 'companionship' marriage." Daniel Bell, *The End of Ideology* (New York: Free Press, 1962), p. 37. See also Harold L. Wilensky, "Family life cycle, work, and the quality of life," in Bertil Gardell and Gunn Johannson (eds.), *Working Life: A Social Science Contribution to Work Reform* (New York: Wiley, 1981), p. 239.

13. A summary and interpretation of such research is offered in Alison Clarke-Stewart and Greta G. Fein, "Early childhood programs," in Paul H. Mussen, *Handbook of Child Psychology*, vol. II: *Infancy and Developmental Psychobiology*, ed., by M. M. Haith and J. J. Campus (New York: Wiley, 1983), pp. 917–99.

14. William H. Whyte, Jr., *The Organization Man* (New York: Simon & Schuster, 1956), pp. 275–76.

15. John Kasarda and Morris Janowitz, "Community attachment in mass society," *American Sociological Review* 39 (June 1974):328–29.

16. Lyn Lofland, *A World of Strangers* (New York: Basic Books, 1973), p. 178. City dwellers establish personal, close, and intimate social ties. Wendell Bell and Marion Boat, "Urban neighborhoods and informal social relations," *American Journal of Sociology* 62 (January 1957):391–98. The urbanite is integrated in a broad network of family and friends and enjoys their emotional support. Fischer, *Among Friends* (ch. 7, note 56), pp. 258–62.

17. Richard J. Wurtman, "Effects of light on man," p. 479. Another study found a strong correlation between the amount of melatonin in the body and those persons' reports of sleepiness. Akerstedt, Gillberg, and Wetterberg, "The circadian covariation of fatigue and urinary melatonin."

18. Harris R. Lieberman *et al.*, "Effects of melatonin on human mood and performance." The authors cite three earlier reports pertaining to the relationship.

19. The wavelength of light that appears to make the pineal gland suppress its melatonin production is about 509 nanometers. That falls in the blue-green

section of the sun's light spectrum. It is also produced by most artificial fluorescent lights, somewhat less by incandescent lamps. Its effect occurs in many
species.

When an animal is exposed to light for prolonged periods, its pineal gland
decreases in weight and size. "One means by which light exposure may induce
an increase in ovary growth and in the incidence of estrus is by inhibiting the
synthesis of melatonin, a hormone which inhibits both these functions." R. J.
Wurtman, Julius Axelrod, and Lawrence S. Phillips, "Melatonin synthesis in
the pineal gland: Control of light," *Science* 142 (November 1963):1073. See
also Lewy *et al.*, "Light suppresses melatonin secretion in humans." It happens under consistent, long-term exposure or very bright light. If adults are
exposed to ordinary light for only brief periods (e.g., one hour at a time) the
melatonin level in the blood is not reduced. Vaughan *et al.*, "Melatonin, pituitary function, and stress in humans," p. 361; Vaughan, Bell, and de la
Pena, "Nocturnal plasma melatonin in humans." See also R. W. Pelham, G.
M. Vaughan, K. L. Sandock, and M. K. Vaughan, "Twenty-four hour cycle
of a melatonin-like substance in the plasma of human males," *Journal of Clinical Endocrinology and Metabolism* 37 (1973):341–44; George M. Vaughan,
John P. Allen, William Tussis, Theresa M. Siler-Khodr, Augustin de la Pena,
and Jeffery W. Sackman, "Overnight plasma profiles of melatonin and certain
adenohypopophyseal hormones in man," *Journal of Clinical Endocrinology
and Metabolism* 47 (1978):566–70. The influence of light on the pineal's hormone production continues if a person's sleep–waking (and dark–light) cycle
is shifted; the melatonin rhythm switches to the new cycle in about a week.
G. M. Vaughan, R. W. Pelham, S. F. Pang, L. L. Laughlin, and M. K.
Vaughan, "Influence of altered light and sleep cycles on plasma melatonin
and urine 5-HIAA in young men," *Endocrinology* 94 (Supp., 1974):A311.

20. See Lewy *et al.*, "Light suppresses melatonin"; Vaughan *et al.*, "Melatonin,
pituitary function, and stress"; Karsch *et al.*, "Neuroendocrine basis," pp.
212, 217–19; and Fred W. Turek, Jennifer Swann, and David J. Earnest,
"Role of the circadian system in reproductive phenomena," *Recent Progress
in Hormone Research* 40 (1984):143–83, esp. 162–63.

21. This pattern of earlier puberty is the subject of some controversy, and the
following summary includes an explanation for it with suggestions for rec-
onciling disagreements over interpreting some of the evidence.

The age of sexual maturation is clearer for girls, because menarche, their
first menstruation, is a signal whose date is easy to note. Other signs that
appear earlier in pubertal development, such as the growth of pubic hair and
swelling of breasts, happen more gradually. Menarche (and seminal emis-
sions, its equivalent in boys) begins about two years after the onset of puberty.
Menarche indicates the phase in which reproductive organs become capable
of functioning. Herant Katchadourian, *The Biology of Adolescence* (San
Francisco: W. H. Freeman, 1977), pp. 60–62. It is a clearly identifiable event
that lends itself as a marker for the timing of sexual development. Adolescent
boys' first seminal discharges could be used as evidence, but boys are often
surprised and embarrassed by their "wet dreams" and rarely tell their parents

about them. Jeffrey S. Victor, *Human Sexuality* (Englewood Cliffs, N.J.: Prentice-Hall, 1980), p. 209. Most girls, on the other hand, report the onset of menstruation to their mothers. Sometimes the information is recorded in physician's records. Data about menarche in girls have become the prime basis for establishing the timing of puberty.

Reports long ago mention diverse ages for menarche's occurrence, often after fourteen, and they point not only to wide variation but also to the challenge of interpreting the unsystematic pre-nineteenth-century information. Galen, a distinguished Greek physician in antiquity, noted: "Some begin puberty . . . at once on the completion of the fourteenth year but some begin a year or more after that." A Byzantine physician noted that menstruation begins about the age of fourteen in most women, "but in a few as early as 12 or 13 and in quite a number after 14." James M. Tanner, *A History of the Study of Human Growth*, p. 11. The best evidence that the mean age of menarche was over fourteen in earlier times is given by certain laws. In classical times Roman law fixed the legal beginning of puberty for boys at age fourteen and for girls at age twelve, thus marking the time at which instruction of children would end and setting the legal age of permission to marry. *Ibid.*, p. 12. That is fairly easy to interpret, for the legal ages of permission are not the average ages for that event but the *earliest* ages acceptable in a given society. Laws of permission (as for consuming alcoholic drinks in public, voting, leaving school, driving a car, and so on) are designated beginnings and try to include the entire population in their purview. Roman lawmakers, therefore, marked the lower end of the wide range in which children were known to become capable of reproduction.

Some researchers refer to the Roman law to support a viewpoint denying a long-term downtrend in menarcheal age. They also note that in the sixteenth century the Council of Trent set the earliest legal age for marriage at fourteen for boys and twelve for girls, and call attention to statutes in medieval Arabic law that sometimes identified twelve as the onset of menstruation. Leona Zacharias and Richard J. Wurtman, "Age of menarche," *New England Journal of Medicine* 280 (April 1969):873; Vern L. Bullough, "Age at menarche: A misunderstanding," *Science* 213 (July 1981):365–66. However, they interpret these as the average timing of menarche in those eras. Because of the meaning of legally designated ages, and since the timing of menarche shows wide variation, it is plausible that the years cited by the Romans, by the Council of Trent, and in Islamic law were far below the mean. Since laws are supposed to encompass entire populations, the average menarcheal age was probably several years older.

Systematically assembling data from many sources for recent centuries, James M. Tanner reported that the average age at menarche had been getting earlier by some three to four months per decade in Western Europe over the period 1830–1960. James M. Tanner, *Growth at Adolescence*, 2d ed. (Oxford: Blackwell, 1962), p. 154; Phyllis B. Eveleth and J. M. Tanner, *Worldwide Variation in Human Growth*, pp. 261, 217–18, 260, 269, 213–14 (Table 15); Carol J. Diers, "Historical trends in the age at menarche and menopause," *Psychological Reports* 34 (1974):931–37. The trend refers mainly to the industrialized countries of Europe, including England, Sweden, Norway, Finland, Denmark, Netherlands, Germany, and Russia. Tanner, *Growth at Adolescence*, p. 152; *idem*, "Earlier maturation in man"; *idem*, "Menarcheal age," *Science* 214 (November 1981):604. Once the trend was noticed, researchers began keeping better records by interviewing mothers and their daughters. They found that the daughters were coming to menarche at an earlier age. See Harley N. Gould and Mary R. Gould, "Age of first menstruation in mothers and daughters," *Journal of the American Medical Association* 98 (April 1932):1349–52; Paul Popenoe, "Inheritance of age of onset of menstruation," *Eugenical News* 13 (1928):101. One of the most systematic reports is based on the discovery of medical records from Oslo hospitals that had been preserved in the cellar of the Women's Clinic in that city. Drawing careful, matched samples for 113 years in a row, the researchers found a clear downtrend in menarcheal age. It fell from above 15.6 years for women born around 1850 to 13.3 years for women born after 1940. J. E. Brudevoll, K. Liestøl, and L. Walløe, "Menarcheal age in Oslo during the last 140 years," *Annals of Human Biology* 6 (1979):407–16. In Japan, too, average age of menarche for a large number of girls was 14.8 nationwide about 1890, whereas it is 12.8 in the 1980s. Tanner, *History of Human Growth*, p. 298. In the United States the average has shown a consistent decline as well. In the 1870s and 1890s a mean of 14.2 or 14.3 was reported, whereas in the 1970s for similar females it was 12.8 years. *Ibid.* Another summary of six different studies in the United States showed the following trend: 1934, 13.5 years; 1937, 13.1; 1940, 13.1; 1948, 12.9; 1953, 12.8; 1969, 12.8; and 1976, 12.8. Table 7 in Leona Zacharias, William M. Rand, and Richard J. Wurtman, "A prospective study of sexual development and growth in American girls." The researchers did not find a statistically significant difference in their own study of mothers and daughters. Most such investigations rely on recall by the mothers of their menarcheal age. In one follow-up study of women whose age of menarche had been recorded earlier, it was shown that when asked about it over a decade later they consistently erred by about six months downward. The actual mean was 12.8 years, but their average remembered age was 12.3. Since such recall was mistaken on the younger side, the above-mentioned difference between mothers and daughters may have been wider than that found by relying on the mothers' memories. Norman Livson and David McNeill, "The accuracy of recalled age of menarche," *Human Biology* 34 (September 1962):218–21.

Thus, although variation in the event is large, the overall evidence for a decline in average age is remarkably consistent, and there are no contradictory findings. See note 23.

22. Rose E. Frisch and Roger Revelle, "Height and weight at menarche and a hypothesis of critical body weights and adolescent events," *Science* 169 (July 1970):397–99. The role of body weight is supported by a finding that menarche came earlier in stouter girls. Zacharias, Rand, and Wurtman, "A prospective study," p. 330.

23. Eveleth and Tanner, *Worldwide Variation in Growth*, p. 244. Some of Tanner's data for the nineteenth century distinguishes between working-class and middle-class girls and reveals that the middle-class youngsters had earlier menarche, which points to the higher standard of living as an explanation.

Tanner, *History of Human Growth*, pp. 286–98. Also, there is a difference in menarcheal age between city and countryside in industrial nations. Urban girls reached puberty at a younger age than did rural girls in the same nations—Finland, Poland, Rumania, India (in Madras State), and Africa (among the Bantu). Eveleth and Tanner, *Worldwide Variation in Growth*, fig. 197, pp. 259, 256.

Where the downtrend in age of puberty has been challenged by mentioning instances of its occurrence at older ages among some groups, those groups happen to be peoples who have poorer diets and lower body weights, like those in the less developed regions or tropical zones, such as among the Melanesians of New Guinea or the Bantu. Vern L. Bullough writes "The Bantu, some of the Maya, and some residents of New Guinea exceed 15 years. One isolated New Guinea group averages over 17, according to one observer." Bullough, "Age at menarche." During the years that the average menarcheal age for U.S. girls was about 12.8, it was 14.3 years for girls in Nigeria, Central India, Burma, Assam, and among Eskimos in Alaska. Zacharias and Wurtman, "Age at menarche," p. 869; Zacharias, Rand, and Wurtman, "A prospective study," p. 333. The lack of wealth among those groups is accompanied by poorer nutrition and lower body weight. They are also groups whose daylight periods have been extended by artificial illumination only recently, if at all.

24. N. A. Jafarey, M. Yunus Khan, and S. N. Jafarey, "The role of artificial lighting in decreasing the age of menarche."

25. Plants grow more as the photoperiod lengthens, and their flowering is affected by the relative spans of daytime and night. As daylight length contracts, plants slow down in growth and become dormant. W. W. Garner and H. A. Allard, "Effect of the relative length of day and night and other factors of the environment on growth and reproduction in plants," *Journal of Agricultural Research* 18 (1920):553. The effects of natural and artificial light are not exactly the same, and the impact varies according to the spectral lengths of the light.

26. H. Allen Tucker and Robert K. Ringer, "Controlled photoperiodic environments for food animals," *Science* 216 (June 1982):1383, 1382, 1385.

27. When female rats are kept under prolonged illumination, their ovaries grow larger and they come into heat sooner. The breeding season in ferrets, too, is hastened by continuous exposure to light. Wurtman, "Effects of light on human body," p. 77; Richard J. Wurtman, Willard Roth, Mark D. Altschule, and Judith J. Wurtman, "Interaction of the pineal and exposure to continuous light on organ weights of female rats," *Acta Endocrinologica* 36 (1961):617, 618; and Richard J. Wurtman, Julius Axelrod, and Elizabeth W. Chu, "The relation between melatonin, a pineal substance, and the effects of light on the rat gonad," *Annals of the New York Academy of Sciences*, 117 (September 1964):228–30.

28. Jafarey, Khan, and Jafarey, "Role of artificial lighting."

29. See the review of what is known in Lawrence Tamarkin, Curtis J. Baird, and O. F. X. Almeida, "Melatonin: A coordinating signal for mammalian reproduction?" *Science* 227 (February 1985):714–20.

30. George M. Vaughan, George G. Meyer, and Russell J. Reiter, "Evidence for

a pineal-gonadal nexus in the human," esp. pp. 215–16; W. F. Ganong, "Endocrine system, human," *Encyclopaedia Britannica*, 15th ed., (Chicago: Wm. Benton, 1974)6:816.

31. Sexual maturation in healthy young boys goes forward as the concentration of melatonin diminishes, and fully matured boys have melatonin levels no different from those of mature adults. The production of the hormone itself decreases as one grows older. At the end of puberty its presence in the blood is about one-quarter what its earlier levels of concentration were. R. E. Silman, R. M. Leone, R. J. L. Hooper, and M. A. Preece, "Melatonin, the pineal gland, and human puberty."

32. This explanation does not attribute earlier puberty to the effects of light exclusively. Nutrition and body weight are important influences. Light's impact is probably milder than nutritional effects, so the pace of its influence may be masked or diffused by the tempo of nutritional improvement. But it allows a testable prediction. If children who are brought up in lengthened photoperiods show precocious development, it should be possible to study the dates when gas lighting and electric lighting were introduced in communities, and to check for the timing of declines in menarcheal age. When first introduced over a century ago, gas lighting was probably unevenly adopted. Not every household acquired it at the same time. However, there are still parts of the world where no form of lighting is yet available from a central power source. When that is introduced in those locations, it is more likely that a wholesale impact would occur, which would probably be revealed as a quantum jump down in the average age of puberty.

　　Several researchers have an impression that the descent in age of puberty is now tapering off in modern urban and suburban populations. Diers, "Historical trends," (note 21 above), p. 934; Zacharias, Rand, and Wurtman, "A prospective study"; and Tanner, "Menarcheal age." A slowdown in the rate of decreasing age does not in itself deny the explanation, for it may be the result of any combination of conditions: stabilized nutrition, an approach to a natural minimal menarcheal age, stabilized exposure to lighting. There may be a lower limit to sexual maturity in our species. (Biological lower limits may have slowed the drop in the more prosperous group. In the United Kingdom "There was . . . a drop in age at menarche in working class girls of about twenty-two months in the fifty years from 1910 to 1960; and in the middle-class girls during the same period a drop of about fourteen months [rates of 4.4 months per decade and 2.8 months per decade respectively]." Tanner, *History of Human Growth*, pp. 286–98, quotation on p. 293.) Or the slowdown could reflect stabilized light conditions, for the pace of increase in lighting exposure has slackened too. Growth in the intensity of artificial illumination may have moderated after fluorescent lights were introduced for home lighting about two decades ago. The decelerated trend would still be consistent with the hypothesis. John Hartung, "Light, puberty, and aggression," pp. 280, 282–83.

33. Laurance D. Steinberg and John P. Hill, "Patterns of family interaction as a function of age, the onset of puberty, and formal thinking," *Developmental Psychology* 14 (November 1978):683–84.

34. Our changes are occurring in the course of both biological and psychological maturation after individuals are born. The cultural and developmental alterations happen long before possible changes in gene frequencies in a population, and genetic change need not occur at all for the pattern to continue. A species that actively alters its environment is likely to change faster through life development and cultural evolution than through alterations in inherited traits.

CHAPTER 9. FUTURE TIMES

1. The judge who approved night court sessions in Elizabeth, New Jersey, said: "It's an experiment, really. . . . It's an attempt to meet the needs of a fair number of people for whom going to court in the daytime is a hardship. The poorer people—people with regular salaried jobs—find it most difficult. "For first time, Jerseyans get a night civil court," *New York Times*, January 18, 1981, p. 42.

2. In several ways it is the same as territorial behavior found in other species. See V. C. Wynne-Edwards, *Animal Dispersion in Relation to Social Behavior* (Edinburgh: Oliver & Boyd, 1962); *idem*, "Self-regulating systems in populations of animals," *Science* 147 (March 1965):1543–48.

3. Smith, *Mill on the Dan*, p. 220.

4. "Down go the thermostats," *Newsweek*, November 19, 1973, p. 110; "Italy forsakes her true love for day," *New York Times*, December 3, 1973, p. 49; "British TV shuts down at 10:30 to save energy," *New York Times*, December 18, 1973, p. 20; "Tokyo douses lights to conserve oil," *New York Times*, November 7, 1973, pp. 71, 74; "Madrid shuts down its nightlife earlier to save on energy," *New York Times*, January 26, 1975, p. 11; "Athens calls time on all-night revels," *New York Times*, October 28, 1979, sec. 10, p. 3; and *Boston Globe*, November 21, 1973, p. 8.

5. One year later gasoline was plentiful, but auto fuel prices were high. By then a number of the twenty-four-hour organizations we had surveyed the year before had cut back to a twenty-hour or an eighteen-hour day. Those places were offering nonessential services such as dining out or recreation. Why did enterprises that resisted the initial shortage cut back later? It is difficult to sort out influences, because many events, economic and otherwise, took place in the course of the year. The pricing mechanism may have shown its strength here indirectly. A steep cost of energy will inhibit enterprise at any hour of the day, and fuel-using activities such as travel will be particularly subdued. Higher gasoline prices deterred automobile use, incurring a slow-moving but cumulative change in people's recreational habits. Since recreation is a larger part of community pursuits after dark, such a decline would be more noticeable then. Some managers confirmed this impression. The proprietor of a coffee shop explained its retrenched hours by saying, "It was not the energy shortage, it was the customer shortage."

6. The energy required to collect that oil would be considerable, so that the net

amount extracted might be of only marginal benefit. The idea of net energy, the residual available after investing refined energy to extract and refine a natural energy source, is discussed by Rufus E. Miles, Jr., in *Awakening from the American Dream* (New York: Universe Books, 1976), p. 47.

7. Called Xiuxi (shoo-shee), the two-hour break was a long-honored custom as "the right to rest." Financial Times Service (London), December 8, 1984.

8. Alan Lakein, *How to Get Control of Your Time and Your Life*, p. 11.

9. R. Alec Mackenzie, *The Time Trap* (1972) (New York: McGraw-Hill, 1975), p. 1.

10. Peter Drucker, "How to be an effective executive," *Nation's Business* 49 (April 1961):34–48, *passim.*

11. Lois Pratt, "Business temporal norms and bereavement behavior," *American Sociological Review* 46 (June 1981):323.

12. Meyer Friedman and Diane Ulmer, *Treating Type A Behavior and Your Heart* (New York: Knopf, 1984).

13. Steffan Linder, *The Harried Leisure Class*, p. 48. Earlier Max Weber noted an attitude in Europe that the waste of time through excessive sleep was immoral. Weber, *The Protestant Ethic and the Spirit of Capitalism* (London: Allen & Unwin, 1930), pp. 157–58.

14. Lakein, *How to Control Your Time*, p. 59; J. Friedmann *et al.*, "Performance and mood during and after gradual sleep reduction," *Psychophysiology* 14 (1977):245–50.

15. Szalai, *Use of Time*, p. 582; television program "Live on 4," WBZ-TV, Boston, February 27, 1984, 5:30 P.M.

16. Barry Schwartz, "Notes on the sociology of sleep," p. 486. In a novel portraying a society that has banished sleep, its inhabitants were not prepared to be ever accessible socially or always engaged in some activity, and some of them found it oppressive. Diane Gillon and Meir Gillon, *The Unsleep* (New York: Ballantine, 1962).

17. Studies looking into possible physical and mental harm to humans deprived of sleep have found few direct adverse effects. Wilse B. Webb, *Sleep, the Gentle Tyrant*. There are several known states of resting other than slumber, including psychological inattention, daydreaming, and dozing. Meditation is an altered state of consciousness that is restful. With disciplined practice, transcendental meditation can become a technique to induce switching from beta brain waves to the alpha rhythms that are more common in sleep.

18. C. Idzikowski, "Sleep and memory," *British Journal of Psychology* 75 (1984):444; H. L. Williams, A. Lubin, and J. J. Goodnow, "Impaired performance with acute sleep loss," *Psychological Monographs*, vol. 73, no. 484 (1959). Some mammals carry out sleeplike processes while being somewhat active. Dolphins and porpoises, for example, perform "hanging behavior" in the water, swimming slowly in circles or in place. Other animals break up sleep and disperse it over the twenty-four-hour period. Scott S. Campbell and Irene Tobler, "Animal sleep: A review of sleep duration across phylogeny," *Neuroscience and Biobehavioral Reviews* 8 (1984):282, 244. The authors remark that sleep has come to be defined according to a singular reliable mea-

surement of it, and therefore we may be disregarding other information available. Pp. 269, 272. See comments by Ernst Hartmann about experiments in nature in *The Functions of Sleep*, and by Nathan Kleitman concerning dreams in *Sleep and Wakefulness*, p. 107.

19. 1 *Corinthians* 15:51.

20. "Regarding between-species differences in sleep time and longevity there turns out to be a *negative* correlation across mammalian species (for whom data are available) between longevity and sleep time (− .45 for either REM or NREM sleep). . . . Even if we control for metabolic rate (correlated + .64 with total sleeping time), the longer sleeping organism is not the longer living organism." David Cohen, *Sleep and Dreaming*, p. 53.

21. Gabriel Garcia Marquez, *One Hundred Years of Solitude* (1967) (New York: Harper & Row, 1970), p. 45.

Appendix A. A Time Census

1. Roderick D. McKenzie wrote: "Let us tentatively define human ecology as a study of the spatial and temporal relations of human beings," but his temporal element refers to the length of the "period of time within which a given ecological formation develops and culminates." McKenzie, "The ecological approach," p. 63. That is not the same formulation as for space.

2. Gerald Breese, *The Daytime Population of the Central Business District of Chicago*.

3. F. Stuart Chapin, Jr., focused on people's time budgets, the portions that are discretionary, as well as a conception of a metropolitan area as an array of space-time activity systems. Chapin, *Human Activity Patterns in the City*; F. Stuart Chapin, Jr., and Pearson H. Stewart, "Population densities around the clock."

4. Two compendiums of theory and data on the topic are Szalai, *Use of Time*, and Carlstein, Parkes, and Thrift (eds.), *Timing Space and Spacing Time*.

5. Grumly, *After Midnight*; John Bowers, *In the Land of NYX*; Anne Cauquelin, *La Ville, La Nuit*, pp. 22–28.

6. "24-hour-day travel agent is coming to the aid of business travelers," *Washington Post*, April 13, 1985.

7. "Round-the-clock learning," *Newsweek*, January 4, 1971, p. 32.

8. A thematic photograph of this appears on the cover of *Science*, 219 (February 18, 1983), referring to the work of preparing the U.S. President's budget proposals for Congress every January.

9. See Szalai, *Use of Time*, pp. 711–71.

10. See "Colombia is a nation in a state of urban crisis," *New York Times*, October 9, 1977, sec. 4, p. 3.

11. The numbers for this category are small because some of the people are already counted in preceding categories. For example, spouses while interacting

with their shift worker mates may watch television, cook, or be involved in other activities.

12. In the United States in 1978, 45 percent. Hedges and Sekscenski, "Workers on late shifts," p. 17.

13. *Ibid.*, p. 15.

14. Daniel Bell, *The Coming of Postindustrial Society* (New York: Basic Books, 1973), p. 133.

15. Bosworth and Dawkins, *Work Patterns*, p. 91.

16. U.S. Bureau of the Census, *Historical Statistics of the United States, Colonial Times to 1970* (Washington, D.C.: U.S. Government Printing Office, 1975); World Bank, *World Development Report 1984* (New York: Oxford University Press, 1984), table 21, pp. 258–59, referring to 1960–80 period.

17. The International Labour Office gathers information about work forces on shifts, but the percentages are not directly comparable because various countries categorize shift work differently and do not always refer to the same occupations and industrial sectors in their surveys. Sometimes the surveys refer only to manufacturing. Often only industrial workers are included, and others such as self-employed or farm workers are excluded. Here is some information on the incidence of shiftworking (all sectors) by country: Australia, 20–30 percent estimated in 1973; Denmark, 16 percent in 1970; France, 22 percent in 1974; Japan, 12 percent in 1977; Netherlands, 22 percent in 1959; Switzerland, 10 percent in 1973; United States, 24 percent (manufacturing only) in 1965; United Kingdom, 21 percent in 1968. International Labour Organisation, *Management of Working Time*, pp. 108, 20. Frank Fishwick reported the proportion of all industrial employees on some kind of shift work (not distinguishing full time or part time) as 18.3 percent in Great Britain in 1975, but 26 percent among adult manual workers in manufacturing. Continuing to refer to all industrial employees on some kind of shift work, Fishwick cited 19.5 percent in France, 20.2 percent in Germany, 22.3 percent in Italy, and 37 percent (of manufacturing employees) in Japan. Fishwick, *Introduction of Shiftworking*, p. 6.

APPENDIX B. RESEARCH NOTES

1. Anne Cauquelin mentions a similar incident in Paris. Cauquelin, *La Ville, La Nuit*, p. 78.

2. The idea for using a key in a helping experiment is described in Gordon B. Forbes, R. D. TeVault, and H. F. Gromoll, "Regional differences in willingness to help strangers: A field experiment with a new unobtrusive measure," *Social Science Research* 1 (1972):415–19.

3. Additional sources used to interpret the CPS data included: U.S. Department of Labor, Bureau of Labor Statistics, "Concepts and Methods Used in Labor Force Statistics Derived from the Current Population Survey," BLS Report No. 463, series P-23, no. 62, October 1976; pages 273–74 from a report entitled

"Employment and Earnings," concerning hours of work and related data, BLS, *circa* 1976; and U.S. Department of Labor, Bureau of Labor Statistics, "Long Workweeks and Premium Pay," Special Labor Force Report 188, *circa* 1976–77, published as a reprint from the *Monthly Labor Review*, April 1976, with supplementary tables and explanatory notes.

4. U.S. Department of Commerce, Bureau of the Census, *Statistical Abstract of the United States* (Washington, D.C.: Government Printing Office, yearly).

5. Kopp Michelotti, "Multiple jobholders in May 1975," *Monthly Labor Review* (November 1975), pp. 56–62. Harold Wilensky found that 6 percent of the male labor force moonlighted. "The Moonlighter," pub. 219 (Berkeley: University of California Institute of Industrial Relations, 1964), pp. 104–24.

6. Presser and Cain, "Shift work among dual-earner couples," p. 877. Their data also come from the 1980 Current Population Survey.

7. Of wage and salary workers in the U.S. in 1978, 62%. This is a dichotomy used with manufacturing, in Hedges and Sekscenski, "Workers on late shifts," pp. 15, 17.

8. More details of this study are provided in Murray Melbin, "The colonization of time," in Carlstein, Parkes, and Thrift, *Timing Space and Spacing Time*, *II:*100–113.

SELECTED BIBLIOGRAPHY

Abramson, Norman S.; Karen Silvasy Wald; Ake N. A. Grenvik; Deborah Robinson; and James V. Snyder, "Adverse occurrences in intensive care units," *JAMA* 244 (October 1980):1582–84.

Akerstedt, T.; M. Gillberg; and L. Wetterberg. "The circadian covariation of fatigue and urinary melatonin." *Biological Psychiatry* 17 (1982):547–54.

Aschoff, Jürgen. "Circadian rhythms in man." *Science* 148 (June 1965):1427–32.

———(ed). *Handbook of Behavioural Neurobiology.* New York: Plenum Press, 1981.

Aschoff, Jürgen; K. Hoffman; H. Pohl; and R. Wever. "Re-entrainment of circadian rhythms after phase-shifts of the zeitgeber," *Chronobiologia* 2 (1975):23–78.

Aubert, Vilhelm, and Harrison White. "Sleep: A sociological interpretation—I." *Acta Sociologica* 4, no. 2 (1960):46–54.

———. "Sleep: A sociological interpretation—II." *Acta Sociologica* 4, no. 3 (1960):1–16.

Baker, Dean. "The use and health consequences of shift work." *International Journal of Health Services* 10 (1980):405–20.

Billington, Ray Allen. *Westward Expansion.* New York: Macmillan, 1949.

Bosworth, Derek L., and Peter J. Dawkins. *Work Patterns: An Economic Analysis.* Aldershot, Hants. England: Gower, 1981.

Bowers, John. *In the Land of Nyx.* 1984. New York: Carroll & Graf, 1985.

Brandeis, Louis D., and Josephine Goldmark. *The Case Against Night Work for Women.* Rev. ed. New York: National Consumers' League, 1918.

Breese, Gerald. *The Daytime Population of the Central Business District of Chicago*. Chicago: University of Chicago Press, 1949.

Brown, Frank A., Jr. "Periodicity, biological." *Encyclopaedia Britannica*. 15th ed. vol. 14. Chicago: Wm. Benton, 1974, pp. 69–75.

Brown, Richard M. *Strain of Violence: Historical Studies of American Violence and Vigilantism*. New York: Oxford, 1975.

Browne, R. "The day and night performance of teleprinter switchboard operators." *Occupational Psychology* 23 (1949):121–26.

Carlstein, Tommy; Don Parkes; and Nigel Thrift (eds.). *Timing Space and Spacing Time*. 3 vols. London: Edward Arnold, 1978.

Carpentier, J., and P. Cazamian. *Night Work*. Geneva: International Labour Office, 1977.

Cauquelin, Anne. *La Ville, La Nuit*. Paris: Presses Universitaires de France, 1977.

Chapin, F. Stuart, Jr. *Human Activity Patterns in the City: Things People Do in Time and in Space*. New York: Wiley, 1974.

Chapin, F. Stuart, Jr., and Pearson H. Stewart. "Population densities around the clock" (1953). Reprinted in H. M. Mayer and C. F. Kohn (eds.), *Readings in Urban Geography*. Chicago: University of Chicago Press, 1959, pp. 180–82.

Cloudsley-Thompson, J. L. "Time sense of animals." In J. T. Fraser (ed.), *The Voices of Time*. New York: Braziller, 1966, pp. 296–311.

Cohen, David. *Sleep and Dreaming: Origins, Nature and Functions*. New York: Pergamon Press, 1979.

Colquhoun, W. P.; M. J. F. Blake; and R. S. Edwards. "Experimental studies of shift work—III. Stabilized 12-hour shift systems." *Ergonomics* 12 (1969):865–82.

Coman, Katharine. *Economic Beginnings of the Far West* (1912). 2 vols. New York: Macmillan, 1930.

Cottrell, Fred. "Of time and the railroader." *American Sociological Review* 4 (1939):190–98.

Czeisler, Charles A.; Elliot D. Weitzman; Martin C. Moore-Ede; Janet C. Zimmerman; and Richard S. Knauer. "Human sleep: Its duration and organization depend on its circadian phase." *Science* 210 (December 1980):1264–67.

Dantzig, George B., and Thomas L. Saaty. *Compact City*. San Francisco: W. H. Freeman, 1973.

Darley, John, and C. Daniel Batson. " 'From Jerusalem to Jericho': A study of situational and dispositional variables in helping behavior." *Journal of Personality and Social Psychology* 27 (1973):100–108.

De la Mare, Gwynneth, and J. Walker. "Factors influencing the choice of shift rotation." *Occupational Psychology* 42 (1968):1–21.

Dick, Everett. *The Sod-House Frontier 1854–1890* (1937). New York: Appleton-Century, 1954.

"The disaster in Bhopal," *New York Times*, January 30, 1985, pp. A1, A6.

Downie, J. H. *Some Social and Industrial Implications of Shiftwork.* London: Industrial Welfare Society, 1963.

Durkheim, Emile. *The Division of Labor in Society* (1893). Trans. W. D. Halls. New York: Free Press, 1984.

Elton, Charles. *Animal Ecology.* London: Sidgwick & Jackson, 1927.

Erenberg, Lewis A. *Steppin' Out: New York Nightlife and the Decline of Victorianism 1890–1930.* Westport, Conn.: Greenwood Press, 1981.

Eveleth, Phyllis B., and James M. Tanner. *Worldwide Variation in Human Growth.* Cambridge: Cambridge University Press, 1976.

Finch, Janet. *Married to the Job: Wives' Incorporation in Men's Work.* London: Allen & Unwin, 1983.

Fishwick, Frank. *The Introduction and Extension of Shiftworking.* London: National Economic Development Office, 1980.

Fishwick, Frank, and C. J. Harling. *Shiftworking in the Motor Industry.* London: National Economic Development Office, 1974.

Foss, Murray F. *Changes in the Workweek of Fixed Capital: U.S. manufacturing, 1929 to 1976.* Washington, D.C.: American Enterprise Institute, 1981.

———. "Long-run changes in the workweek of fixed capital." *American Economic Review* 71 (May 1981): 58–63.

Geotzmann, William H. *Exploration and Empire.* New York: Norton, 1966.

Goodrich, Carter, and Sol Davidson. "The wage earner in the westward movement." *Political Science Quarterly* 50 (1935):161–85; 51 (1936):61–116.

Grumly, Michael. *After Midnight.* New York: Scribner's, 1978.

Harris, Bill. *New York at Night.* New York: Stewart, Tabori & Chang, 1983.

Hartmann, Ernst. *The Functions of Sleep.* New Haven: Yale University Press, 1973.

Hartung, John. "Light, puberty, and aggression: A proximal mechanism hypothesis." *Human Ecology* 6 (1978):273–97.

Hawley, Amos. *Human Ecology.* New York: Ronald Press, 1950.

Hedges, Janice N., and Edward S. Sekscenski. "Workers on late shifts in a changing economy." *Monthly Labor Review* 102 (September 1979):14–22.

Hentig, Hans von. *The Criminal and His Victim.* New York: Archon Books, 1967.

Hollon, W. Eugene. "Frontier violence: another look." In R. A. Billington (ed.), *People of the Plains and Mountains.* Westport, Conn.: Greenwood Press, 1973, pp. 86–100.

———. *Frontier Violence.* New York: Oxford University Press, 1974.

Hood, Jane C. "When changing shifts means changing jobs: Quality of worklife for custodial workers on the day shift" Unpublished, 1985.

Hood, Jane C., and Nancy Milazzo. "Shiftwork, stress, and wellbeing." *Personnel Administrator* 29 (December 1984):95–97, 100–102, 104–5.

Horton, John. "Time and cool people." *Society* (formerly *Transaction*), April 1967, pp. 3–5.

Hugo-Brunt, Michael. "Hong Kong housing." In H. W. Eldredge (ed.), *Taming Megalopolis*. Garden City, N.Y.: Doubleday Anchor, 1967, 1:477–93.

Humphrey, Seth K. *Following the Prairie Frontier*. Minneapolis: University of Minnesota Press, 1931.

Huygens, Christiaan. *Traité de la Lumière*. Leyden, 1690.

International Labour Organisation. *Management of Working Time in Industrialised Countries*. Geneva: International Labour Office, 1978.

Jafarey, N. A.; M. Yunus, Khan; and S. N. Jafarey. "The role of artificial lighting in decreasing the age of menarche." *The Lancet*, August 1970, p. 471.

Kabaj, M. "Shift work and employment expansion." *International Labour Review* 91 (January 1965):47–62.

――――. "Shift work and employment expansion: Towards an optimum pattern." *International Labour Review* 98 (September 1968):245–74.

――――. "Searching for an optimum shift-work pattern." In International Labour Organisation, *Management of Working Time in Industrialised Countries*. Geneva: International Labour Office, 1978, pp. 76–89.

Karsch, Fred J.; Eric L. Bittman; Douglas L. Foster; Robert L. Goodman; Sandra J. Legan; and Jane E. Robinson. "Neuroendocrine basis of seasonal reproduction." *Recent Progress in Hormone Research* 40 (1984):185–232.

Kemeny, John (chairman). *Report of the President's Commission on the Accident at Three Mile Island*. Washington, D.C., October 1979.

Kessler-Harris, Alice. *Out to Work: A History of Wage-Earning Women in the United States*. New York: Oxford University Press, 1982.

Kleitman, Nathan. *Sleep and Wakefulness*. Chicago: University of Chicago Press, 1963.

Kozak, Lola Jean. "Night people: A study of the social experiences of night workers." *Summation* (Michigan State University, East Lansing) 4 (Spring/Fall, 1974):40–61.

Lakein, Alan. *How to Get Control of Your Time and Your Life*. New York: New American Library, Signet, 1973.

Lewy, Alfred J.; Thomas A. Wehr; Frederick K. Goodwin; David A. Newsome; and S. P. Markey. "Light suppresses melatonin secretion in humans." *Science* 210 (December 1980):1267–69.

Lieberman, Harris R.; Franz Waldhauser; Gail Garfield; Harry J. Lynch; and Richard J. Wurtman. "Effects of melatonin on human mood and performance." *Brain Research* 323 (1984):201–7.

Linder, Steffan B. *The Harried Leisure Class*. New York: Columbia University Press, 1970.

Luce, Gay Gaer. *Biological Rhythms in Psychiatry and Medicine*. Chevy Chase, Md.: U.S. Department of Health, Education, and Welfare (PHS Pub. 2088), 1970.

Luchetti, Cathy, and Carol Olwell. *Women of the West*. St. George, Utah: Antelope Island Press, 1982.

Mannheim, Karl. "The problem of generations." In Paul Kecskemeti (ed.), *Essays on the Sociology of Knowledge*. London: Routledge & Kegan Paul, 1952, pp. 276–319.

Margolick, David. "The lonely world of night work." *Fortune*, December 15, 1980, pp. 108–14.

Marx, Karl. *Capital*. (1867, 1890). New York: Modern Library, 1906.

Maurice, Marc. *Shift Work*. Geneva: International Labour Office, 1975.

McGrath, Roger D. *Gunfighters, Highwaymen, and Vigilantes*. Berkeley: University of California Press, 1984.

McKenzie, Roderick D. "The ecological approach to the study of the human community." In Robert E. Park, Ernest W. Burgess, and Roderick D. McKenzie, *The City* (1924). Chicago: University of Chicago Press, 1925, pp. 63–79.

Melbin, Murray. "Organization practice and individual behavior: Absenteeism among psychiatric aides." *American Sociological Review* 26 (February 1961):14–23.

Milgram, Stanley. "The experience of living in cities." *Science* 167 (March 1970):1461–68.

Millman, Marcia. *The Unkindest Cut: Life in the Backrooms of Medicine*. New York: Morrow, 1977.

Milne, Lorus J., and Margery J. Milne. *The World of Night*. New York: Harper & Row, 1956.

Monroe, L. J. "Psychological and physiological differences between good and poor sleepers." *Journal of Abnormal Psychology* 72 (1967):255–64.

Moore, Wilbert E. *Man, Time, and Society*. New York: Wiley, 1963.

Mott, Paul E.; Floyd C. Mann; Quin McLoughlin; and Donald P. Warwick. *Shift Work*. Ann Arbor: University of Michigan Press, 1965.

National Industrial Conference Board. *Night Work in Industry*. New York: National Industrial Conference Board, Inc., 1927.

Orem, John, and Judith Keeling. *Physiology in Sleep*. New York: Academic Press, 1980.

Ostberg, O. "Interindividual differences in circadian fatigue patterns in shift workers." *British Journal of Industrial Medicine* 30 (1974):341–51.

Paul, Rodman Wilson. *Mining Frontiers of the Far West: 1848–1880*. New York: Holt, Rinehart & Winston, 1963.

Perrow, Charles. *Normal Accidents*. New York: Basic Books, 1984.

Pollock, M. A. (ed.). *Working Days*. London: Jonathan Cape, 1926.

Pomeroy, Earl. "Toward a reorientation of Western history: Continuity and environment." *Mississippi Valley Historical Review* 41 (March 1955):579–60. Reprinted in Edward N. Saveth (ed.), *Understanding the American Past*. 2d ed. Boston: Little, Brown, 1965, pp. 377–99.

Prange, Gordon W. *At Dawn We Slept: The Untold Story of Pearl Harbor*. New York: McGraw-Hill, 1981.

Presser, Harriet B., and Virginia S. Cain. "Shift work among dual-earner couples with children." *Science* 219 (February 1983):876–79.

Rawick, George P. *From Sundown to Sunup: The Making of the Black Community.* Westport, Conn.: Greenwood, 1972.

Ridge, M., and R. A. Billington (eds.). *America's Frontier Story.* New York: Holt, 1969.

Riegel, Kurt W. "Light pollution." *Science* 179 (March 1973):1285–91.

Riegel, Robert E. *America Moves West.* New York: Holt, 1947.

Robboy, Howard. "They work by night: Temporal adaptations in a technological society." Ph.D. dissertation, Rutgers University, 1976.

———. "At work with the night worker." In H. Robboy and C. Clark (eds.), *Social Interaction.* 2d ed. New York: St. Martin's Press, 1983, pp. 506–19.

Schwartz, Barry. "The social psychology of privacy." *American Journal of Sociology* 73 (1968):741–52.

———. "Notes on the sociology of sleep." *Sociological Quarterly* 11 (Fall 1970):485–99.

———. "Waiting, exchange, and power." *American Journal of Sociology* 79 (January 1974):841–71.

Schydlowsky, Daniel. "Capital utilization, growth, employment, balance of payments and price stabilization." Discussion Paper #22, Center for Latin American Development Studies, Boston University, December 1976.

Silman, R. E.; R. M. Leone; R. J. L. Hooper; and M. A. Preece. "Melatonin, the pineal gland, and human puberty." *Nature*, November 15, 1979, pp. 301–3.

Simmel, Georg. "The persistence of social groups." *American Journal of Sociology* 3 (1897):672.

———. "The metropolis and mental life" (1902–3). In Kurt Wolff (ed.), *The Sociology of Georg Simmel.* Glencoe, Ill.: Free Press, 1950.

Smiles, Samuel. *Lives of Boulton and Watt.* London: John Murray, 1865.

Smith, Henry Nash. *Virgin Land* (1950). Cambridge, Mass.: Harvard University Press, Vintage ed., 1957.

Smith, Robert Sidney. *Mill on the Dan: A History of Dan River Mills, 1882–1950.* Durham, N.C.: Duke University Press, 1960.

Staines, Graham L., and Joseph H. Pleck. *The Impact of Work Schedules on the Family.* Ann Arbor: Institute for Social Research, University of Michigan, 1983.

Stratton, Joanna L. *Pioneer Women: Voices from the Kansas Frontier.* New York: Simon & Schuster, 1981.

Szalai, Alexander (ed.). *The Use of Time.* The Hague: Mouton, 1972.

Tanner, J. M. "Earlier maturation in man." *Scientific American* 218 (1968):21 ff.

———. *A History of the Study of Human Growth.* Cambridge: Cambridge University Press, 1981.

Tapp, W. N., and F. A. Holloway. "Phase shifting circadian rhythms produces retrograde amnesia." *Science* 211 (March 1981):1056–58.

Tasto, Donald L.; Michael J. Colligan; Eric W. Skjei; and Susan J. Polly. *Health Consequences of Shift Work*. Washington, D.C.: U.S. Government Printing Office (NIOSH pub. no. 78-154), March 1978.

Taylor, George R. (ed.). *The Turner Thesis: Concerning the Role of the Frontier in American History*. 3d ed. Lexington, Mass.: D. C. Heath, 1972.

Tepas, Donald. "Shiftworker sleep strategies." *Journal of Human Ergology* 11 (supp. 1982):325–36.

Tucker, H. Allen, and Robert K. Ringer. "Controlled photoperiodic environments for food animals." *Science* 216 (June 1982):1381–86.

Turner, Frederick Jackson. *The Frontier in American History* (1893). New York: Holt, 1920.

––––––. *The Significance of Sections in American History*. New York: Holt, 1932.

––––––. *America's Great Frontiers and Sections*. (1965) (unpublished essays edited by W. R. Jacobs). Lincoln: Nebraska University Press, 1969.

U.S. Congress, Senate. *Attack upon Pearl Harbor by Japanese Armed Forces*. Document 159 (microfiche serial set 10676), 1942.

U.S. Congress, Senate, *Hearings Before the Joint Committee on the Investigation of the Pearl Harbor Attack*. 79th Cong. Document 244 (microfiche serial set 11033), 1946.

U.S. Federal Communications Commission. "Broadcast services." (information bulletin, 39 pp.) Washington, D.C.: Jan 1977.

Vaughan, G. M.; R. Bell; and A. de la Pena. "Nocturnal plasma melatonin in humans: Episodic pattern and influence of light." *Neuroscience Letters* 14 (1979):81–84.

Vaughan, George M.; Stephen D. McDonald; Richard M. Jordan; John P. Allen; Rodney Bell; and Edwin A. Stevens. "Melatonin, pituitary function, and stress in humans." *Psychoneuroendocrinology* 4 (1979):351–62.

Vaughan, George M.; George C. Meyer; and Russell J. Reiter. "Evidence for a pineal-gonadal nexus in the human." *Progress in Reproductive Biology* 4 (1978):191–223.

Webb, Walter P. *The Great Plains*. Boston: Ginn & Co., 1931.

Webb, Wilse B. *Sleep, the Gentle Tyrant*. Englewood Cliffs, N.J.: Prentice-Hall, 1975.

Weber, Max. "Bureaucracy." In Hans Gerth, and C. Wright Mills (eds.), *From Max Weber: Essays in Sociology*. New York: Oxford University Press, 1946.

Wever, Rütger A. *The Circadian System of Man*. New York: Springer-Verlag, 1979.

Whitrow, G. J. *The Nature of Time* (1972). Harmondsworth, England: Penguin Books, 1975.

Winston, Gordon C. "The theory of capital utilization and idleness." *Journal of Economic Literature* 12 (1974):1301–20.

––––––. *The Timing of Economic Activities*. Cambridge: Cambridge University Press, 1982.

Wright, Lawrence. *Clockwork Man.* New York: Horizon Press, 1969.

Wurtman, Richard J. "Effects of light on man." *Annual Review of Physiology,* 1975, p. 479.

———. "The effects of light on the human body." *Scientific American* 233 (July 1975):69–77.

Young, Michael. "Never go out after dark." *New Society,* January 15, 1981, pp. 99–100.

Young, Michael, and Peter Willmott. *The Symmetrical Family* (1973). Harmondsworth, Middlesex, England: Penguin Books, 1975.

Zacharias, Leona; William M. Rand; and Richard J. Wurtman. "A prospective study of sexual development and growth in American girls: The statistics of menarche." *Obstetrical and Gynecological Survey* 31 (1976):325–37.

Zatz, Martin, and Michael J. Brownstein. "Injection of alpha-bungarotoxin near the suprachiasmatic nucleus blocks the effects of light on nocturnal pineal enzyme activity." *Brain Research* 213 (June 1981):438–42.

Zerubavel, Eviatar. *Patterns of Time in Hospital Life.* Chicago: University of Chicago Press, 1979.

———. *Hidden Rhythms.* Chicago: University of Chicago Press, 1981.

INDEX